Fort Publishing

PROUD KILMARNOCK: STORIES (

Frank Beattie was born in Kilmarnock in 1952 and educated at Bentinck Primary School, James Hamilton High School and Kilmarnock Academy. He joined the editorial staff of the *Kilmarnock Standard* in 1972, and had a keen interest in local history even before he joined the paper. Today his 'Memories' page is one of the *Standard's* most popular features. He is also the author of a number of books on Kilmarnock. Frank Beattie lives in the village of Waterside, near Fenwick, with his wife Lorna and three children Fraser, Grant and Rosie.

PROUD KILMARNOCK:
STORIES OF A TOWN

FRANK BEATTIE

FORT PUBLISHING LTD

First published in 2002 by Fort Publishing Ltd, Old Belmont House, 12
Robsland Avenue, Ayr, KA7 2RW.

Front cover illustration: 'Kilmarnock Cross' by David O. Hill,
courtesy of Museums, Arts and Theatre Service, East Ayrshire Council.

Graphics by Paul McLaughlin.

Typeset in 11pt Sabon by Senga Fairgrieve, 0131 658 1763

Printed by Bell & Bain, Glasgow

ISBN 0-9536576-8-X

A catalogue record for this book is available from the British Library.

For my wife, Lorna.

Till clay-cauld death sall blin my e'e,
Ye shall be my dearie

'Ca' the Yowes to Knowes'
Robert Burns.

CONTENTS

LIST OF ILLUSTRATIONS

All illustrations from the author's collection except where indicated.

ACKNOWLEDGEMENTS

I never need much of an excuse to delve into old books and records, particularly if there are 'new' old stories to be discovered. The same goes for speaking to people conducting their own research. They always have something new to find out about Kilmarnock's past – for the past is a very big place.

I have had great fun chasing up and writing the stories, and I am grateful for the substantial help of very many people. Ann Amor from Bolton for the chapter on J. & M. Craig; Bob Brill of California for Edgar Allan Poe; James Gracie from East Kilbride for Kirsty Wark; Francisco Haro, from Stewarton, for the air raid on Kilmarnock; Craig McAvoy, from Ayr, for Joe McGregor; James McCarroll, my publisher, for Kilmarnock Football Club; Margaret Hunter Weaver, of the USA, for John Kelso Hunter.

Many more people helped by willingly volunteering their knowledge and an acknowledgement is included in the bibliography at the end of the book. Finally, John Hall of Stewarton provided help with the military history and some of the other out of the way facts. John died while I was writing this book. He will be sadly missed by all those who love Ayrshire's history.

Frank Beattie
Kilmarnock, 2002

ONE

IN THE BEGINNING

IT WAS GLOBAL WARMING, no doubt about it; not that anyone called it that at the time, but the climate was changing and the ice sheets were being pushed back, leaving vast new tracts of land to be explored.

It was ten thousand years ago . . . the end of what we now call the Ice Age. As the ice receded, and the centuries rolled on, explorers, adventurers and nomads made their way north. At first they probably only came in the short warm summers, but as the climate continued slowly to improve, they stayed longer and eventually settled at the edge of the area of land we know today as Ayrshire. The first visitors came by boat and stayed on the coast, for inland was fraught with danger. They lived off the sea and from any animals they could hunt and kill, supplemented by whatever they could harvest from the forest. When they did venture inland it was again by boat, following the rivers. There were wild animals in the thick forests, and once trapped and killed, the animals provided food. The skins were used for clothing and to cover their shelters, bones were used as tools and weapons. But we can only imagine the harsh life that our ancestors had to contend with at that time in our Ayrshire, for few traces have been left.

Stones were also used for making tools. The earliest stone tools and arrowheads from Ayrshire are thought to be five or six thousand years old. Most remains have been found near the coast. But the coastal settlers relentlessly pushed inland. Stone axes were used to cut down trees. This provided space for homes, building materials and fuel. There are only a few scattered remains of early man in the Kilmarnock area. An ancient urn found in Titchfield Street in 1888 contained three flint arrowheads of a type that suggests they belonged to someone of considerable importance. There is evidence that an Iron Age fort was established near Fenwick. In 1999 a pot thought to be 3,500 to 4,000 years old was found at old Rowallan Castle and an ard, part of an ancient plough, was found not far from what is now Glencairn Square. The remains all suggest that people were living in the area, but there is nothing that gives us any hint that there was a village or a community at what is now Kilmarnock.

Whoever was living in southern Scotland in AD 80 was in for a major shock, with the arrival of Agricola and 20,000 Roman soldiers. England had been a relatively easy conquest, but the 'barbarians' of

Scotland, or Caledonia, as the Romans called the land, were fiercely independent and resisted the Roman invasion.

The Romans were never quite comfortable in the south of Scotland. The last Roman campaigns in Scotland were in the fourth century, and in AD 401 the Roman soldiers were withdrawn to deal with the Goths. They had been in southern Scotland since AD 80. It is not known what kind of network of roads the Romans built in Ayrshire, but they would certainly have remained in use long after their withdrawal.

There are few certainties about what the Romans left in this outpost of their vast empire. By the nineteenth century, historians tended to assign any ancient works to the Romans. There was a Roman fort at Loudoun Hill and a road from Dalmellington to Ayr. A well at Beansburn was known to be ancient and was often referred to as the Roman Well; and, close to the well, according to ancient tradition, there was a Roman encampment.

There was still no town or community at Kilmarnock. Just how Kilmarnock started is simply not known. The most plausible explanation is that a church was established near the river and the community grew around the church. While such a scenario is possible, probable even, it does not explain why that particular point was chosen for a church.

Indeed, in the fourth and fifth centuries there is still no evidence for anything approaching a community in Kilmarnock. The nearest evidence we have for what life was like then in this area comes from Buiston Crannog.

In 1990, Historic Buildings and Monuments (HBM) provided money for an archaeological investigation of the crannog at Buiston near Kilmaurs. It was dated to some time between the fourth and sixth centuries AD, significantly, perhaps, the time when the Romans left. Crannogs are lake or marshland settlements made by driving a circle of heavy wooden piles into the lakebed and filling the circle with stones and earth, to create an artificial island. The uprights supported a wooden floor and circular huts were built on the platforms. The structures were often surrounded by a palisade. Crannogs were generally secure places, with access only available by canoe, or sometimes a causeway. The HBM archaeologists at Buiston uncovered a dugout boat. It was the first boat to be found in an archaeological context in Scotland in modern times.

Buiston turned out to be a particularly fine example of a crannog. The other main one in Ayrshire was at Lochlea near Tarbolton. In 1839 two canoes were found at what later turned out to be the

Lochlea Crannog and one of them went to the Dick Institute where it is displayed from time to time.

Buiston, of course, is not at the heart of Kilmarnock. The ancient church may well have been. The choice of the location still gives rise to speculation. Would a church have been built in a remote and unpopulated area? Perhaps the church that was built by, or dedicated to, St Marnock was situated at some ancient crossroads, somewhere in the bleak, sparsely populated land between the coast and that long-abandoned Roman fort. Perhaps, but there is no firm evidence to support this theory. It is thought that it was attached to the Abbey at Kilwinning. Maybe the monks of such abbeys set up a network of churches, not so much for the general populace, but to provide shelter and a place of worship for themselves when they were on their travels.

The theory goes that, having been established, the church started to attract a few followers who built their homes near the church to which they were devoted. But there was no industry yet – no community. Kilmarnock must have remained as little more than a cluster of huts, probably for a few more hundred years.

However, well before the second millennium it had not just a church, but a name as well. Archibald McKay's *History of Kilmarnock* (1848) states that St Marnock founded his church here at the end of the sixth, or start of the seventh, century and that he is buried in the area. The name, it is said, comes from *kil*, the Celtic word meaning church or burial place, and Marnock.

Marnock is something of an enigmatic figure – despite being a relative of St Columba – and we must search for information about him under his older name of Mhearnog. Mhearnog's life was researched in the 1920s by David Barnett Warnock of Pennsylvania. The Warnocks are descended from a branch of the Mhearnog family. He wrote up his findings in 1930 and pointed out that Columba was one of St Patrick's most ardent followers. Columba was born on 7 December 521, probably in Gartan, Donegal. This was just a few years after St Patrick's death. Columba spent his early life among the Scots in Ireland and later became the apostle to the Picts in Scotland. He established the first Christian monastery in Scotland at Iona. Columba's parents were Feidlimid, a member of the ruling family in Ireland, and Eithne. His sister was Cuimne who married Decuil and their son was Mhearnog who was born about 550.

One of the sources quoted by Mr Warnock is *The Martyrology of Donegal*, a compilation of Irish saints put together in 1630. The manuscript was lost for two centuries but was eventually found in

15

1846 in a library in Brussels and was translated and published in 1864. Kilmarnock, it seems, owes its name at least to the nephew of Saint Columba.

Not everyone agrees that there is a saintly connection to the origin of the name of Kilmarnock. James R. Irving, in a feature in the *Kilmarnock Standard Annual* of 1965 raised an alternative possibility. While admitting that the theory he put forward was based on debatable evidence, he cautioned that we should never close our minds to possibilities other than the most popular theory. Breaking down the word into its constituent parts – Kil-mar-nock – Irving argued that the Kil was a burial ground rather than a place of worship. Mar-nock, he suggested, might relate to local geography rather than a saint. *Mor* in the ancient language of our ancestors meant big or great, and a knock was a hill. Put the three parts together and we have Kil-mor-nock, or the hill of the great grave. Which is the right theory will no doubt continue to be debated. Whatever the truth, Kilmarnock remained undeveloped for centuries after the time of Mhearnog.

The earliest mention of Kilmarnock in literature is in Barbour's *Life of Bruce*. Kilmarnock is noted as one of the places through which an English knight, Sir Philip de Mowbray, retreated after his defeat in 1306. The fourteenth and fifteenth centuries were noted for the construction of strong stone castles, and yet the little church by the river, the one dedicated to St Marnock, remained in its rural setting, surrounded by a few huts and, perhaps, farms or crofts.

Few documents have survived to provide any detailed information on Kilmarnock's early history. But, in 1547, a new parish priest came to Kilmarnock. Significantly, he was elected, or at least approved, by the townspeople. The document that relates this suggests that there were some 300 families living in the parish; a population of, perhaps, about 1,400. The Kilmarnock parish at that time included Fenwick. While Kilmarnock was still a rural community, there was thriving commerce for, in 1591, Kilmarnock was made a Burgh of Barony, which allowed the merchants a whole range of new rights and privileges.

The first significant account of early Kilmarnock comes from Timothy Pont, who visited the town early in the seventeenth century, probably in 1609. He described Kilmarnock as being a large village that was in excellent repair. He said the people held a weekly market. He mentioned the bridge which at that time was at the Sandbed, saying that it was a 'faire stone bridge', and he described the church as being 'pretty'.

A generation later, in 1657, another visitor arrived in Kilmarnock and recorded what he saw. He was Richard Franck, who apparently came to Scotland on a fishing tour, hence the particular attention he paid to the river. He had fought with the Parliamentarians in the civil war and, soon after his visit to Scotland, Cromwell died. Franck fled to America, fearing retribution. There he wrote his *Northern Memoirs* in 1658, although it wasn't published until nearly thirty years later, after he had returned to England.

In this remarkable volume he noted that Kilmarnock was an ancient corporation, crowded with mechanics and brewhouses. He described the streets as 'crazy, tottering ports'. The streets were dirty, except when heavy rain washed the muck into the river. The houses of the time he described as ugly and little better than huts. In fact, he took the view that there was not one good structure in Kilmarnock. The bridge that Pont had described as a 'faire stone bridge' was said by Franck to be 'wretchedly ancient'. The church did not rate a mention.

Franck also gave an idea of the trades of the town. He said that there was bonnet making and weaving but he highlighted the metal workers who, he argued, were the best in Scotland. Perhaps the skills of the men of those days were passed on to later generations who, in their turn, became the engineers responsible for establishing the great industries of the town in the nineteenth century.

TWO

WHEN KNIGHTS WERE BOLD

ANCIENT TALES OF KNIGHTS and castles have been passed down from generation to generation, gathering exciting new details as they are told and retold. The stories we are left with today are a mix of truth, legend and sheer speculation. It may now be impossible to separate fact from fiction in these old, fascinating stories.

The tales of the glorious days of gallant knights still make thrilling stories. They are deeply ingrained into our culture. Some of the best known stories concern King Arthur and the Knights of the Round Table. But the idea that this Arthur was the first king of all England does not stand up to even the most basic of inquiries because Arthur did not fight for the Angles, but against them.

And, because of the power of the legend, many local historians find it hard to grasp the fact that one of King Arthur's first major victories against the Angles was in a battle fought here in Ayrshire. In the middle years of the sixth century AD, before Scotland had been moulded into a nation, the people of the south-west of Scotland were fighting against the Angles and the Saxons who had invaded this part of the country. The local people naturally looked to their Celtic brothers in Wales for support, and so it came to pass that the resistance to the invasion was led by a certain Arthur, king of the Silures, from the south of Wales. The decisive battle was fought about the year AD 542 near the Glen Water, a small and rather insignificant stream which joins the River Irvine near Darvel. This was the first of at least twelve battles fought by Arthur against the incursions of the Angles and Saxons. Arthur had some progressive ideas and decided that his key advisers would be treated as equals. There was, accordingly, no one at the head of the table and to emphasise the point, he had a round table made. Soon his chief advisers were collectively known as the Knights of the Round Table, a name that would live on down through the centuries to a time when even the existence of a King Arthur would be questioned. Arthur was later slain by his nephew, Modred, and was buried at Glastonbury.

Another of the ancient leaders with an involvement in Ayrshire history was King Coilus, better known as King Cole, or Old King Cole. As every child in the country knows he was a merry old soul. According to the nursery rhyme:

Old King Cole was a merry old soul,
A merry old soul was he.
He called for his pipe and he called for his bowl
And he called for his fiddlers three.

Of course, his pipe was a musical pipe and not one for smoking tobacco, which was then unheard of in this part of the world. This rhyme, however, is the modern version. A much older version appears in Ayrshire literature in the eighteenth century and even then it is thought to have been a very old rhyme.

King Cole, or Coilus, is thought to have been a king of the Britons early in the eighth century. The land of Ayrshire was then being fought over, and Fergus, the leader of the Scots, is reputed to have defeated and killed Coilus who was then buried near Dalmellington. This merry old king, who may have taken his name from Kyle, shares his name with Coilsfield, Coylton and the water of Coyle.

Information on the early history of Ayrshire comes to us largely thanks to the families who owned and occupied the great castles, simply because they kept records. There were many castles in the vicinity of Kilmarnock in centuries gone by: the castle of the Wallaces at Riccarton and later at Craigie; the castles of Rowallan and Dundonald which have royal connections; and there were also the great castles of Caprington and Craufurdland, which are still in existence. Today, because it is open to the public, the castle most people associate with Kilmarnock is the Dean Castle.

Dean Castle acquired its name because the structure was built in a shallow area where the ground gently rises around it; a *den* in the old language. This mutated through the years to become Dean. The Dean Castle of today does not much resemble the ancient edifice that existed in the fourteenth century. Little is known for certain about its earliest occupants; still less about any fortification that may have existed on that site before the Dean was built.

The fourteenth-century stone keep, much of which survives today, may have been the property of the Lockarts or Lockharts, who had extensive property in Ayrshire and Lanarkshire. Some historians, such as John Macintosh, author of *Ayrshire Nights Entertainment*, say that at one time the Dean was briefly held by Lord Soulis, but firm evidence is difficult to come by. Lord Soulis remains something of an enigma in Kilmarnock history.

But, as for the Boyd family, their presence in Kilmarnock is well recorded. There was one knight, Sir Robert Boyd, who answered the call to defend Scotland against a fearsome invader. Sir Robert trekked to Largs in 1263 to repel an army of fierce Viking warriors. In fact, he distinguished himself during the battle at a place called Goldberry Hill, near Hunterston, and was rewarded by King Alexander III with the grant of land and power in Cunninghame. Ayrshire did not exist in those far off days and the hamlet of Kilmarnock was north of the River Irvine and therefore in Cunninghame. The family included the motto Goldberry in their coat of arms to commemorate their part in the battle of Largs. The town of Kilmarnock later used Goldberry and a coat of arms very similar to that of the Boyds. The Battle of Largs was a key turning point in Scottish history, as it marked the end of the Norse plans to dominate mainland Scotland.

Sir Robert's son, another Sir Robert Boyd, was also a champion of the noble cause of freedom. He joined another local hero – Sir William Wallace – in 1297, fighting with him at Loudoun Hill, at Ayr and in several other places. He later fought with Bruce at Bannockburn and helped secure independence for Scotland.

This Robert Boyd's reward was more land and power. An ancient document describes the lands ceded to his control as Kilmarnock, Bondington (Bonnyton), Herschaw (Hareshaw), Kilbride (West Kilbride), Ardneil and others. This Sir Robert continued to fight in battles, and he probably initiated the building of the stone keep at the Dean.

The location suggests that the castle was built to be concealed rather than to play a defensive role and yet some interesting defensive devices are built into the structure. Staircases are intentionally narrow to impede the advance of an attacker and at least one spiral stair turns upwards for a few steps before running into a stone wall. Imagine invaders rushing up there in the dark and the inevitable confusion that would ensue. As the years passed the Boyds grew in stature; so much so that, in the fifteenth century, they added the palace. The Boyds flirted with the royal family and nobility of Scotland, falling in and out of favour.

But the centuries rolled on. In 1735 a disaster overwhelmed the castle and much of it was seriously damaged by fire. The family moved its main residence from the castle to Kilmarnock House. Money was never available for the restoration of the castle and, in an attempt to secure his future, the last Lord Boyd of Kilmarnock backed the rebellion of 1745. It was a fatal mistake and he was arrested, found guilty of treason and executed in London. His lands

The Dean Castle today.

changed ownership but by the end of the eighteenth century the old castle at the Dean appeared to be beyond repair. It continued to be ravaged by nature for the next hundred years, but in the twentieth century Lord Howard de Walden began an extensive restoration project and, in 1975, gifted the property to the people of Kilmarnock.

Other local castles have equally colourful histories. Rowallan Castle is perhaps the best known. The earliest part of old Rowallan, for there are two, is thought to be of thirteenth-century origin. But this is only a small portion of the old castle, which was built on the site of an ancient fort. Various changes were made over the years. The most distinctive features of the old Rowallan Castle are two round turrets and a long and high stairway entrance. They were added in the middle of the sixteenth century. This work was the inspiration of John Mure, the then occupant, and his wife Marion. Their coats of arms were incorporated into the building along with various others that were important to the family at the time. It was at Rowallan that Elizabeth Mure was born. She married King Robert II.

The Wallace family held land at Riccarton and occupied Riccarton Castle. Nothing remains of that. They later occupied Craigie Castle, which is now a ruin. It is incredible that a castle so closely linked with Scotland's greatest hero has been allowed to fall into such a ruinous state. Little of the castle remains today, but it was once a building of considerable importance. In the days when it was one of the most magnificent castles in Ayrshire, Craigie Castle had about four acres of land, all surrounded by a moat served by a drawbridge.

It had been the property of a family called Lindsay or Lyndesay. The Wallaces of Riccarton acquired the castle through marriage and occupied it until the very start of the seventeenth century, when they moved to Newton-on-Ayr.

They never sold the old castle at Craigie, nor did they make use of it. They simply abandoned it, leaving it vulnerable to the ravages of weather. The family drew upon themselves the wrath of the local minister. They were not in the habit of regularly attending church and, worse, some members of the family even went out riding on the Sabbath. This annoyed the minister, a Mr Inglish, who made an explicit reference to this one Sunday when Sir Hugh Wallace was in the kirk. But Sir Hugh was outraged and threw a knife at the minister who only saved himself by a reflex duck. The curse that the minister then uttered against the Wallace family does not seem to have made much impact on them.

Something similar is said to have happened to the Mowat family at Busbie Castle near Kilmaurs. Like so many others, Busbie Castle appears to date from the middle of the fourteenth century. Curiously, the minister in this case is a Mr Welsh but his role was similar to the Mr Inglish just referred to. Mr Welsh came from Ayr but he decided to take on the family who lived at Busbie, for they were a foul lot.

Despite being asked, they refused to stop entertaining guests at Busbie on a Sunday; and worse, they played football and other games on the Sabbath. Such foul wickedness could not go unpunished, so Mr Welsh put a curse on the family. It is said that before the curse the family finances were sound, but immediately after it, there was trouble at every turn. Things went from bad to worse and soon the Mowat family were forced to sell their ancestral home.

THREE

THE DEVIL TO PAY

SO MANY TALES OF devils, witches, water pixies and so on are told in local folklore that it is not easy to decide which ones were first told as fiction and only for entertainment, and which ones were passed off as real. These were perhaps designed as a warning to an audience much less sophisticated than the readers and listeners of today. Most of the tales in this category are very old and were originally passed on from one generation to the next only by the spoken word. Later, much later, some of them were collected and eventually appeared in print.

One popular tale about a visit by the Devil concerns the laird of Rowallan Castle, and, of course, in those far off days it was the old Rowallan Castle that was inhabited by the lord of the manor. It is said that one of the steps leading up to the old building is cracked but local legend holds that it was not the weather nor age that cracked the step, but Auld Nick himself, an uninvited and unwelcome guest.

According to this tale, the laird was busy preparing to hold a party. But on the night planned for the happy event, a storm blew up. It was a storm of rare ferocity and none of the guests was able to get to the castle for the party. The laird was annoyed. He had hoped for an enjoyable and profitable evening playing cards with his guests. He roamed the empty rooms getting more and more bored with every passing minute. Eventually, he made what seems to have been a rather rash declaration. He said that he would play cards with anyone, even Auld Nick himself.

Just then, there was a thunderous hammering at the door of the castle. The laird's train of thought evaporated at the prospect of at least one of his guests having made it through the storm. The door was opened and the servant did not recognise the visitor but he was told: 'Your master is expecting me.'

And so the stranger was taken through the castle to where the master of the house was sitting, waiting patiently now, for his guests. As it happened, the laird did not recognise the visitor, but he was pleased to have someone to play cards with; at least he was pleased at first. Somehow the stranger just kept on winning. He won every game and the laird became more and more agitated, but soon he was suspicious, for who could win every hand but a cheat? After a while he challenged the stranger: 'You play like the very devil. Who are you?'

He grabbed the stranger's cloak and was horrified to find that he had indeed been playing cards with the Devil. But the Devil was startled at being discovered and made off through the castle at top speed. As he fled, his tail crashed into the stairs, causing the crack that can still be seen to this day.

*

A devil of a very different sort haunted the farm of Beanscroft near Fenwick. The farm is still there today on the Grassyards Roads. Unlike the tale of the Rowallan devil, the story of the Beanscroft devil is well documented and can be placed at the end of the eighteenth century. It was probably a fairly typical farm of the time with nothing peculiar about the place or its people, except that the farmer's son dabbled in the ungodly art of chemistry, but that was kindly tolerated by the good neighbours of the family.

But then strange things started to happen around Beanscroft. In the night there were thumpings and moans; creakings and groans. Efforts to trace the source of the noises came to nothing and as time went on the Devil, the spirit, or whatever it was, grew bolder and stronger.

The moans soon became screams; the shrieks became yells and it was always in the dead of night when everything else was quiet. And then the strange lights started to appear: flashing lights and steady lights; sometimes red, sometimes white and sometimes an unearthly blue. Cattle left tied up at night were found roaming free in the morning and yet they had not been untied and the ropes had not been cut with a knife. They appeared to have been melted.

The terrified farm servants soon left and word got round that the Devil himself was haunting Beanscroft. Eventually the farmer had had enough. He called in the Church to exorcise the devil, but he was disappointed to learn that the Church of Scotland is very practical and does not have a formula for exorcisms. Even so, the minister came from the little church at Fenwick and read a few lines from the Bible. The force behind the disturbance was not impressed. It stayed at Beanscroft and it continued to intensify its efforts. The family was divided about what to do: the old farmer was in favour of leaving the farm, while the eldest son bravely said that he would stay and manage it alone.

In Kilmarnock, as in Fenwick, the haunting was the talk of the town and one of the more enlightened gentlemen who heard the stories was John Goudie, the man Robert Burns described as the 'terror of the Whigs'. He scoffed at ideas of devils and ghosts and he reluctantly accepted a request to visit Beanscroft, with a view to solving the mystery.

He went there with the Reverend Gillies of Kilmarnock and Robert Muir, a wine merchant.

The farmer was quizzed. The property was inspected, and so were the ropes. Here was the proof, but proof of what? No one was sure. Goudie and his companions considered the breaks in the ropes. He thought that they had been burned with acid, an unlikely substance to be used by a supernatural being.

Only the farmer was told of this conclusion. The rest of the household was led to believe that the visitors had found nothing and were completely baffled. But that night, a more confident farmer settled into his barn. After what seemed like an eternity, the door opened and someone came in. The farmer watched as the figure began screaming and yelling. This was the Beanscroft Devil.

Then it was the farmer's turn to yell. The figure stood still for a moment, apparently unsure of what to do. Then he darted back to the farmhouse. But the farmer had discovered the secret. He knew the identity of the Beanscroft Devil. It was his eldest son. He had grown impatient and wanted to scare his father and the rest of the family away so that he would have the farm to himself.

Filled with shame and ridiculed wherever he went, the son soon left Scotland, and he never came back.

*

The Devil is but one personification of evil. Another is the witch. Just what was it that drove the witch-hunts of the seventeenth century? In these enlightened times no one believes in witches, except, perhaps, briefly, each Hallowe'en. But at one time, old women were hunted down and burned as an irrational frenzy swept the country. It has been suggested that this may have been a sort of mass hysteria brought on by ergot poisoning. Ergot is grain fungus and could have ended up in ale – drunk by the whole population in preference to unwholesome water – and in bread, eaten by everyone. Today, stories of witches and witchcraft may well be told to frighten children, but in the seventeenth century, it was much more serious than that. Across the country witches were strangled, hanged, drowned or burned. Once exposed, no one doubted that the person facing death really was a witch, for they nearly always confessed to their crimes.

When a witch was caught, a confession was required if the soul was to be saved. It was never easy to get the confession. The authorities often resorted to torture. Wakers were used to deprive the accused of sleep. The suspected witch was often starved. Pain was inflicted by thumbscrews. Finger nails were often torn out and pins inserted deep into the flesh. It was known that the Devil initiated his witches by sucking some blood from them, leaving a mark on the body. These marks were said to be immune to pain and so her tormentors would stab the suspect's body with needles on anything that looked like a mark until one was found that seemed to be immune to pain.

Sometimes the accused woman was hung by the arms, and weights were tied to her feet. Other horrific tortures were used. Four prongs were forced into the mouth, pressing against the cheeks, the tongue and the roof of the mouth. Metal stockings might be applied and slowly heated until the flesh began to roast. Little wonder that nearly all the suspects confessed to anything their tormentors suggested.

There is, however, little evidence to support the idea that Kilmarnock folk hunted down old women in order to kill them as witches. Perhaps the local people realised that the claims of witchcraft were ridiculous. It would be nice to think so.

The same could not always be said for other towns. Janet McNicol lived near Kilmarnock in the seventeenth century, but moved to Rothesay. In 1673 she was accused of practising the 'vile and abominable crime of witchcraft' in the Kilmarnock area for a period of twelve years.

There was no evidence to support the claim, and whatever it was that had attracted the attention of the authorities in Rothesay, seems to have been missed by the church and people of Kilmarnock. Perhaps her crime was that she had a wrinkled face or a bent back. Maybe she had a feeble mind or, alternatively, a superior one. Maybe she grew and mixed her own herbs. Whatever the circumstances, Janet was taken to the Gallows-craig on Rothesay and publicly strangled.

In 1696, an eleven year-old girl from Renfrew named Christian Shaw, is said to have been bewitched. It was the laird of Kilmarnock who was called in to investigate the case. The girl was not on trial. It was accepted that she was a victim. But seven people were accused of bewitching her. All but one ended up dead: one as a result of suicide, the others by sentence of the court. One person was found not guilty. It was the last major witch trial in Scotland. Twenty years after these events, Christian Shaw came to live in Kilmaurs and in 1719, she married the minister there, the Reverend John Millar. Just two years later, he died and Christian went to Johnstone, where she established a thread-making business, an industry that would make Paisley a wealthy town.

These appear to be Kilmarnock's only involvement with the

witch-hunt craze unless, of course, you include the curious case of the Craigie Witch. She is said to have taken a spite against the church and was determined to destroy the building. So she used her magic powers to lift a great boulder and flew with it up, up into the sky, with the intention of dropping it on the church. But before she reached her target, her apron strings broke and the stone fell to earth with a great crash. The Witch's Stone was pointed out to visitors for many years until it was finally broken up for building material.

FOUR

TELL-TALE SIGNS OF POE

THE LANDSCAPE, CULTURE AND politics of Ayrshire have inspired many great writers. The most famous, of course, were Robert Burns, John Galt and Alexander Smith. John Keats was inspired on his visit to Ayrshire in 1818, but Ayrshire may well have had a profound influence on the master of mystery and imagination, Edgar Allan Poe.

Poe was the foremost writer of 'dark literature'. But he was also a pioneer. Long before Sir Arthur Conan Doyle was writing about Sherlock Holmes, Poe had one of his characters using exactly the same techniques of observation and deduction. He is seen by many as the 'father' of an independent, American literature. He is popular on both sides of the Atlantic. His best known works include *The Pit and the Pendulum*, *The Masque of the Red Death*, *The Raven* and *The Fall of the House of Usher*. At first the idea of a significant Ayrshire influence may seem a bit strange, but we should not be too hasty to dismiss the suggestion.

Poe was born in Boston in 1809, and he died in Baltimore in 1849, having spent most of his forty years in the USA. Most – but not all! His father and his grandfather were also born in the USA. But, as an impressionable young lad of six or seven, Edgar Allan Poe lived in Irvine and spent much of his spare time visiting family and friends in Kilmarnock.

Most Poe biographers ignore this brief part of the great man's life, concentrating on his subsequent education at Stoke Newington, in England. Hervey Allen in *Israfel*, first published in 1926, chronicled Poe's time in Scotland, but skipped over the possible Ayrshire influences that may have subsequently appeared in his poetry and prose.

More recently, Robert Densmore Brill, from Pacifica, California, has taken up the challenge of researching this neglected part of Poe's life. And he has done something that other Poe biographers have not – he has paid several visits to Ayrshire. On his earliest visits he encountered communication problems. While he met enthusiastic local historians who knew Ayrshire folklore, and that Poe had spent time in Ayrshire, they were not sufficiently familiar with Poe's works to say that he could have taken an idea from here, there or anywhere else.

But gradually Bob learned more of the history and culture of Ayrshire; more of the political and religious problems of the early

1800s and more of the nature of Ayrshire. And the more he learned of Ayrshire, the more he understood Poe's works. Let me give just one example. Bob Brill, his wife Grace and I were sitting having coffee together, when Bob let out a cry of surprise: 'Look at the birds!' he called with almost child-like enthusiasm. I looked, but could see nothing unusual. 'Just some crows,' I said casually. But Bob was looking with the eyes of Poe and saw not common crows but sinister ravens. Of course, crows are not as common in some places as they are in Ayrshire.

Such subtle influences are all around Ayrshire. The more that Bob found out, the more convinced he became that the young boy's brief time in Ayrshire had an important impact on the development of his fertile imagination. Today Bob Brill argues that much of the culture, history, and even place-names of early nineteenth-century Ayrshire and Greenock, crop up in Poe's poetry and prose.

But why should an American boy, aged about six, travel across the world on a dangerous sea voyage? And why to Irvine and Kilmarnock? The answer lies in tragedy and family ties. The Poe family had its roots in Ireland and Ayrshire, and Edgar Allan Poe's ancestors can be traced to Fenwick in the middle of the eighteenth century. One David Poe is listed in the Hearth Tax register as living at Perceton, near Irvine, in the 1690s.

It was Alexander Poe, great-grandfather of the author and poet, who left Ayrshire for America in 1739. Edgar Allan Poe was very much an American and the influence of Scotland handed down through the generations from his great-grandfather to his grandfather and then to his father was probably negligible.

But fate dealt Edgar a cruel hand that was to lead him back, for a while, to the land of his ancestors. Edgar, or Eddie to his family, was the second son of David and Elizabeth Poe. Their first son was William Poe, born in 1807, but he was left with his paternal grandfather. Edgar was born in January of 1809. In 1810 Elizabeth found she was pregnant again and, in July, her husband David Poe vanished from the scene. Some say he ran off to Scotland with another woman but, in reality, he almost certainly died while in New York. In December Elizabeth gave birth to a daughter, Rosalie Poe. Elizabeth was not in good health and, in December of the following year, she died at the age of twenty-four.

Almost immediately the children were split up, and Edgar was taken in by the Allan family, John and Frances, who, although they were apparently close family friends of the boy's parents, took only one of the children. John readily paid some of the funeral expenses of Edgar's mother. John Allan was more than just a foster-parent – he and David Poe were cousins – and he had relatives in Kilmarnock and Irvine in far-off Scotland.

John Allan came from Irvine. His father was William Allan, a sea captain, who no doubt had taken John to Virginia in the first place. John had left these shores after being given glowing accounts of wealth to be made in the New World from tobacco and, in all probability, slavery. These reports came from his uncle, William Galt, another Irvine man, and Irvine novelist, John Galt. John Allan helped set up a business under the name of Ellis and Allan. The Ellis part of the name came from Charles Ellis, yet another Scotsman.

John Allan also had family in Kilmarnock. His sister had married Allan Fowlds, a merchant who sold grain and seed to farmers from all over Ayrshire. He lived in Nelson Street in Kilmarnock. Despite the great distance, and the vagaries of the postal service, the family was fastidious about keeping in touch and most of the letters sent from Kilmarnock to John Allan are now preserved in the Library of Congress in Washington DC.

Four years after fostering Eddie, John and Frances Allan went on a trip to Ayrshire and other places. They brought with them the young lad, now thought of as a son. And, of course, because of the regular correspondence the extended family in Scotland knew all about the bright and lively young lad.

However, Ayrshire in the early nineteenth century was far from what Eddie had become used to in the land of opportunity. When he arrived in Ayrshire, in the summer of 1815, Napoleon had just been defeated. War in Europe had just ended, as had the war between Britain and America. But years of fighting had meant sharply rising taxes. Many families were living in poverty. There was limited freedom of speech, and those who advocated democracy were often thrown in jail or shipped off to the colonies of Australia and New Zealand, a sentence against which there was no appeal. Agitation for reform was building, but people were living under an oppressive regime.

What would a young boy, used to a more liberal life, make of it? Attendance at church was, if not compulsory, expected, and services were long and dour. Not the sort of thing that would hold the attention of a lively young lad of above-average intelligence. Perhaps more than anything, the major influence on the boy's mind at this stage in his life were the fireside tales, some very ancient and some very recent.

Young Edgar must have been enthralled by the gory stories from the battle of Waterloo, for many Ayrshire men fought in that battle in April 1815 and the general talk was of tales of heroism by people such as Charles Ewart. What great tales of sea voyages did young Edgar Allan Poe pick up from the Allan family? What did he think of the long Ayrshire summer nights; of the cold wet winds and rain; what did he think of the many moods of Arran, which he must often have gazed at across the Firth of Clyde?

Soon, Edgar was being formally educated in Irvine. He went to the Kirkgate School in the town, next to the parish church. The churchyard was the playground. One of his writing exercises was to copy gravestone inscriptions. Schoolbooks for this work were too expensive. What did young Edgar make of inscriptions such as 'here lies an unknown sailor washed ashore' . . . and what would he have made of tales of premature burial?

Many years later when Poe had made a name for himself, one of the friends at school, James Galt, was quoted in a local newspaper as saying that he remembered the young American boy being very mature for his age, full of self-confidence and absolutely devoid of fear.

Edgar's foster parents left him with relatives in Irvine while they went on with their travels to London and beyond. Edgar hated being left on his own. Perhaps memories of the death of his real mother played a part in it. He started making plans to stow away on a boat bound for America; or, as an alternative, to run away to London. Of course, he did not have to escape from Irvine because, after only a couple of months, he was packed off to live near London.

It seems that Poe greatly enjoyed his frequent trips to Kilmarnock, where he could play with boys such as Jock Gregory and James Anderson (who in adulthood was well known as a writer of hymn tunes). The boys played around Nelson Street and on the Lady's Walk, now part of Howard Park. Poe could not have failed to discover that it was supposedly haunted by the ghost of Lady Kilmarnock.

As well as his visits to Kilmarnock, Poe was taken on a trip to Arran. Arran has been described as Scotland in miniature. And here at least Poe was impressed with the scenery and the general feel of the island. It is argued by some commentators that his poem, *The Lake*, was inspired by his trip to Arran. Bob Brill believes it could just as easily have been Loch Doon.

Events in Kilmarnock may also have inspired an interest in science and technology. The Kilmarnock and Troon Railway had been completed in 1812, and steam traction was introduced in 1816 or 1817, but there was at least one stationary steam engine in use on the line. It would be interesting to know if Poe was ever taken on a day trip from Kilmarnock to The Troon.

Poe was not just a master of mystery and imagination of the literary kind. His own life was also full of mystery. When he was twenty-seven, he married his cousin, Virginia Clemm. She was only thirteen, and yet her mother supported the wedding and had to lie about Virginia's age to allow the ceremony to go ahead. The rest of the family opposed the wedding.

Poe's death is shrouded in mystery, with claims that he drank himself to death being dismissed on the testimony of those who tended him in his last days. His writing of course is equally mysterious. In 1838 he published a macabre story of cannibalism, perhaps inspired in some way by tales of the legendary Ayrshire cannibal, Sawney Bean. In *The Narrative of Arthur Gordon Pym of Nantucket*, four survivors of a shipwreck are dying of thirst and hunger. They draw lots, and one of their number, Richard Parker, becomes a victim of cannibalism. In 1884 three survivors of a real shipwreck faced trial for murder, having killed and eaten a companion called Richard Parker. Fact following fiction?

There are other literary twists of fate: the site of the Fowlds' family home in Nelson Street became the *Kilmarnock Standard* printing works and one of the mascarons on the building is of William Shakespeare. Of course, all this adds fuel to the Poe legend. Like others versed in Ayrshire's folklore and history, I am not sufficiently familiar with Poe's works to pass judgement on its Ayrshire influences. But I was privileged to receive early drafts of Bob Brill's book on the subject and I eagerly await the publication of *Mar'se' Eddie in the Shire*.

FIVE

KILMARNOCK'S X–FILES

WE ALL LOVE A good mystery. We want the world to be a much more mysterious and unpredictable place than scientists would have us believe. Stories of ghosts, UFOs and fairy folk seem to happen all around us, but surely not in a hard-working industrial town like Kilmarnock. We are far too sensible for all that – and such things should be reserved for the popular science-fiction programme the *X–Files*. Perhaps not, because over the years, I have collected many stories that fall into the category of 'Mysterious Ayrshire'.

Some of the tales go way back into the mists of time, but perhaps the strangest of them all happened on a warm August evening in 1997. The *Kilmarnock Standard* recounted the story, which came from an anonymous reader who had been jogging on the road between Kilmarnock and Hurlford:

> I was heading from the Bellfield roundabout towards Hurlford and was near to the Kaimshill Farm entrance. I had just started running again after stopping to stroke a German Shepherd dog which was accompanied by a woman and three young children.

> When I looked further along the road I could see three figures about 50 yards ahead. The male figure was wearing a long black double-breasted coat with large buttons and he had on a shiny flat cap which might have been leather. He was pushing a wheelchair containing a woman. All I can remember about her was that she was wearing a hat, possibly with feathers on it. Alongside them was a boy aged about eight or nine who was wearing short trousers. When I think back now their clothes weren't modern day, but I didn't think anything of it at the time.

The jogger dropped his eyes to check the path ahead, and when he looked back up the road . . . the trio had vanished. He thought that they might have wandered off the footpath and attempted to go through an opening, but when he checked it, the jogger found it had been bricked up. The jogger had only taken his eyes off the trio for a moment, and yet he could find no trace of them at all. Were the figures ghosts of a time long gone or did the jogger simply see a trick of the light?

*

Other ghosts have been recorded in the Kilmarnock area. The Dick Institute, the town's library, art gallery and museum, is said to be haunted by a well-dressed lady, who has been seen by staff disappearing through a wall.

One member of staff recalled that, a few years ago, in a storeroom, the temperature suddenly dropped, while at the same time there was a strong smell of Germoline. This was also noted by the janitor who was with her. The lady staff member felt a rustle as if someone had swept past her. She turned and saw someone who looked like a nurse in a stiff grey uniform and starched white apron. Her distinct impression was that the nurse was young, pretty and had hypnotic eyes. The apparition walked down a corridor and suddenly a row of beds appeared. They appeared to be occupied by soldiers. Then, as quickly as she had appeared, the nurse vanished taking the strange vision with her. But what on earth were hospital beds doing in a library? That part of the mystery is easy. During the First World War, the Dick Institute was converted into a convalescent hospital for wounded soldiers.

Another strange tale about the Dick is more recent. A member of staff went to a store to get four festival masks, but could only find three of them. She returned later to find the fourth and as soon as she opened the door she saw a brightly coloured mask, quite unlike the other three. It was on a top shelf directly opposite the entrance door. She went to ask a supervisor if it was the one required, but when she and the supervisor went to check, there was no sign of the coloured mask. The one she was looking for turned up in another part of the building, even though no movement slip had been completed.

*

Another ghost, that of an 'old hag', is reputed to appear from time to time at the Dean Castle, Kilmarnock's most popular tourist attraction. One of the most recent sightings was in February 1995. A guide had taken a group round the castle and one of them asked the guide who the old lady in the kitchen was, the lady with the black skirt and tartan shawl. The guide hadn't seen any such person, but did know the story of the 'old hag' and her previous incarnations.

Some spooky tales concern a premonition of death. Around 1744, the Palace of the Dean Castle was a ruin. It had been seriously damaged by a fire in 1735 and because of the cost, never repaired. The main residence of the Boyd family was, by this time, Kilmarnock House in the town centre. William, fourth Earl of Kilmarnock, was in the mansion grounds. His wife and various servants were indoors. One servant was in an upstairs room sewing linen. In the room where this servant was working, there was a noise; the door creaked open. She casually turned . . . and a bloody head rolled across the floor. She screamed. The head vanished. Then it happened again. The creak; the door; the head; the scream. And again – creak, door, head, scream.

By this time the Earl was nearly at the room with his wife and others. The story was told and repeated at the time, and it was dismissed as the imaginative fancy of a young girl. But a year later the Earl found himself supporting the Jacobites at Culloden. He was captured and, because of his rank, accused of treason. He was found guilty and executed in London in 1746. Death was by the executioner's axe!

*

Something else that happened hundreds of years ago in Ayrshire leaves us wondering whether or not predictions can sometimes come true. Early in the fifteenth century, Ayrshire was still divided into Kyle, Carrick and Cunninghame, and the River Irvine was the boundary between Kyle and Cunninghame. This tale concerns a prince, Sir John Stewart, son of King Robert II. He stood out clearly from most other Ayrshire folk of the time because his hair was very red. Indeed, everyone knew him as Red Stewart. One day he and his entourage were hunting when they met an old woman. She told him that he would not die either in Kyle or in Cunninghame. Was it a threat or a warning? Was it just a playful forecast? Whatever the circumstances, Red Stewart took it seriously. People didn't travel much then and Red Stewart thought he was safe as long as he kept to the two districts of what we now call Ayrshire.

One day, some years after this encounter, Red Stewart was ambushed by bandits as he crossed the River Irvine near Kilmarnock. At the end of the day, Red Stewart lay dead. He had died neither in Kyle nor in Cunninghame, but in the river on the boundary between the two.

*

Odd lights in the sky are a regular feature of newspaper columns. The most recent spate occurred in July 1997, when several people reported seeing strange lights or an alien craft over central Ayrshire, including specific sightings over Kilmarnock and Dundonald. One witness described a craft as 'kite shaped' with white lights at the edges and a red light in the centre. In retrospect it now seems this

35

might have been something like a Stealth bomber on a trial, perhaps from Machrihanish. But who knows?

There were reports at the same time of household gadgets such as an electronic alarm clock being affected. All I know is that all such stories have to be taken with a large dose of salt. I remember driving near Sandyford at Prestwick Airport. Right in front of me, but some distance ahead, I caught a glimpse of the unmistakable shape of a Boeing 747 coming in to land. Suddenly this craft turned through ninety degrees and dispersed. It was no aircraft, just a flock of birds. But in the instant I saw it, my brain was trying to work out what it was and the closest match was a 747 coming in to the airport. I think many UFO and ghost sightings have such explanations . . . many, but not all.

Not easy to explain is another aviation mystery passed on to me by the late John Hall of Stewarton. John was an expert on Ayrshire military history. One of the strangest military tales he had in his files concerns the funeral of a Second World War RAF serviceman. The man was killed in a postwar accident and was buried at Kilmarnock cemetery. In attendance were several colleagues who were pleased to see three RAF bombers fly low over the cemetery in a final tribute. As RAF men they could easily identify the type of aircraft. Silent pleasure at the tribute turned to utter astonishment later, when it was discovered that the RAF no longer had any of the type of aircraft clearly seen by the mourners.

*

Some mysteries are not based on what we have seen but on what can be heard. In 1979 a man from Charles Street in Kilmarnock was hearing a strange buzzing noise, like a far off generator. Neighbours and visitors were also aware of it. The noise seems to have lasted about a year before fading away.

Other mysteries are based on extraordinary talents. Margaret Clelland was born in Darvel in 1845. As a child, she had a remarkable grasp of arithmetic. One day when she was about nine years old, her teacher gave her some sums and was surprised that, although she had the right answers, her workings did not appear on the slate. He gave her more complex sums and once again she provided the correct solutions with no working notes. She was then asked to calculate 123456789 multiplied by 987654321, and almost immediately gave the right answer, having worked it out in her head.

There are other strange tales from the Kilmarnock area. Since the mid-1970s there have been persistent sightings of puma-like creatures in various areas. It, or more correctly, they, have been seen in the Dean Country Park, in the grounds at Springhill House, near Dundonald, on the Fenwick Moor and near Newmilns. There is a growing body of opinion that these big cats were originally pets, turned out of their homes following changes in the laws regulating their ownership. The assumption is that they have not only survived but also have bred.

Of course, mysteries are only mysteries until there is enough evidence to establish beyond reasonable doubt what lies behind them. Something mysterious was spotted in the sky over Fenwick in February of 1999. Odd lights were seen by various people. They were not moving, but appeared to be akin to lightning. No one could explain them. However, not long after, an earthquake was felt throughout Ayrshire. Lights such as those seen over Fenwick are often seen where there is seismic activity.

Many mysteries remain unsolved simply because we do not have enough evidence and yet we tend to want the answer to remain mysterious. We want it to be a ghost and not a reflection; we want it to be aliens and not moonlight reflected from ice crystals. As the *X-Files* poster says: 'I want to believe.' In my case, I want to be convinced as well.

SIX

MURDER MOST FOUL

MURDER IS A RARE crime and in early nineteenth-century Kilmarnock it was almost unheard of. And yet, at a time when Kilmarnock was still a large and rather sleepy rural village, the people of this community had to deal with a double murder.

It happened in November 1807 and the victims were Jean Alexander and Christine Peacock. Jean kept a small grocery shop close to the Fleshmarket Bridge at the corner of what was soon to become Waterloo Street. Both women had been strangled, one with a rope and one with a handkerchief. It was soon established that three gold rings had been taken from Jean's fingers and that approximately £70 in notes and coins had been taken from the house. That was a huge sum of money in those far-off days.

Investigators soon found out that two Irish shoemakers had been in the habit of visiting the house: William Burnside and Thomas Taggart. They were quickly arrested and thrown in the jail at Kilmarnock. The two accused were put on trial at the Ayr circuit court on 24 September 1808. They pleaded not guilty to the capital charges of murder. A servant girl swore that she had seen the two accused men coming out of Jean Alexander's shop on the morning of the murder, but there was very little other evidence and certainly no proof that they had killed anyone. After due deliberation, the jury returned a verdict of not proven.

Just three months after that trial, Kilmarnock people had yet another murder to contend with. On Christmas Day 1808, a young soldier stationed in Kilmarnock was killed. He was James Miller from Perth, one of a party of soldiers in Kilmarnock on a recruitment drive. James had joined the army in 1804 at the age of fourteen and was a fifer. He was a popular young man, both in the regiment and with the people of the town that he had come to visit.

On the night of his death, he had been at a party in the home of a spirit dealer in Fore Street. About midnight Miller and a friend left and, at the Cross, Miller's companion recognised a man called William Rowan. As Rowan was a deserter, he was apprehended and offered no resistance. It appears that, at this stage, young James was left alone with Rowan. They walked in the direction of Nailer's Close, a narrow lane between the Cross and Green Street. They were going to Green Street because the Officer in Charge lived there and would deal with the deserter according to army regulations. But, just after entering the darkened close, the deserter pulled out a knife, savagely stabbed Miller several times, and made good his escape. Miller managed to crawl to the officer's quarters, where his wounds were immediately dressed. Next day he improved and was able to walk around the room. Although it seemed that he would make a full recovery, an infection set in and Miller died the next day.

The popular young soldier was buried in the Laigh Kirkyard with military honours and hundreds of townsfolk attended the funeral. A £20 reward was offered for the capture of Rowan. The murder weapon was recovered, having been stuck into a tree near Kilmarnock House. The regiment put a monument over the lad's grave, but when, in 1847, it became decayed it was removed. And as for Rowan, he slipped into the night after killing Miller, and was never traced. He literally got away with murder.

*

Another day of celebration turned sour seven years later. On New Year's Day, 1815 John Muir was killed. Was it murder? Was it a tragic accident? No one was certain. It was about 3 a.m. and in those days the new year was celebrated on 12 January. James Muir, a miner who lived in High Street, and his friend John Craig from Riccarton had been drinking together. About three o'clock they were on their way home and going down the Foregate when they saw a light on in a house occupied by another John Craig. They knew the occupants and knocked at the door. There seems to have been some history of bad feeling, because when the door was opened by Adam Logan, it was clear that Logan was far from pleased to see them. He grabbed Muir and swore at him. There was shouting and a scuffle broke out. Other people from the house came out to see what was going on. There were no lights in the street and no one saw Muir fall over.

By the time he was discovered on the ground, he was already dead and when the body was properly examined, it was found to have a small wound in the head. Was the injury caused by the fall, or was it the result of a deliberate attack? The John Craig who lived in the Foregate was charged with murder, but there was not enough evidence to convict and he was found not guilty. The case was the talk of the town until a few months later the battle of Waterloo pushed everything else from the news. Years later one of the women who had lived in the house is alleged to have made a deathbed confession that she had stabbed Muir with a pair of scissors.

*

There are some murders that seem to fire the popular imagination, whether it is because of the brutality, the circumstances of the crime or the people involved. One such case was the murder of James Young, a sixteen year-old boy brutally slain near the farm of Fortacres, just south of Kilmarnock. It was 27 May 1848 and, on the fatal night, James left Fortacres where he had been working, promising to return that same night. At about seven in the evening he arrived at his father's house at Knowehead, Riccarton. He spent some time in the company of his parents and other members of his family, but he never returned to Fortacres.

About four o' clock next morning his battered body was found not far from Fortacres by two young men. An examination revealed two gaping wounds, one in the neck and the other in the back of the head. A carpenter's chisel, covered in blood, was found near to the victim. The boy's pockets had been rifled and his silver watch stolen. A search of the area was carried out but there were few clues, and little prospect of finding the killer.

A thirty-two year-old Irish labourer by the name of James McWheelan had been seen in the area before the murder and, of course, the authorities wanted to speak to him. His description was quickly circulated. Then, at the toll at Lochwinnoch, between Beith and Paisley, a farmer saw a suspicious character leaving the toll-house. He thought nothing of it until he heard that £35 and a watch had been stolen from the tollhouse. He mounted his horse and set off in the direction of Paisley. Near the town he caught up with the man, made a citizen's arrest and managed to recover the stolen watch and money. In Paisley, police realised that the description of the man col-leagues in Ayrshire were looking for matched the man they had arrested for robbing the toll. He was indeed James McWheelan. Piece by piece, the police managed to put a case together. In a pawn shop in Beith they found the watch taken from James Young. Soon they had enough to go to trial.

The trial was held during the Ayr Autumn Circuit and was the centre of attention in the county. People were drawn by what the *Ayr Advertiser* called the 'barbarity and wantonness' of the crime. Many women may also have been attracted by McWheelan's rather exotic looks: despite being born in Dublin he was dark and handsome and, according to one report, resembled an Italian brigand. It is perhaps not surprising that the courtroom was packed with spectators anxious to hear every last detail of the murder.

The prosecution, leaving nothing to chance, pulled out all the stops for the trial. No less than ninety-three witnesses were called to give evidence against the Irishman. And it was damning. Many recalled that they had seen McWheelan near the scene of the crime or on the road to Lochwinnoch. The medical examiner's testimony revealed that bloodstains had been found on his clothing and, of course, stolen items had been found on his person. The jury was certainly convinced and took only fifteen minutes to convict McWheelan of robbery and murder. Under the law, the judge, Lord MacKenzie, had no alternative but to sentence him to death.

The story of McWheelan's execution is almost as dramatic as that of the crime for which he was convicted. At that time, executions were carried out in public, adjacent to the Prison and Courthouse Building located in Ayr's Wellington Square (where the County Buildings stand today). Accordingly, McWheelan was held in Ayr prison to await his grisly fate, which was scheduled for 26 October. During his spell there he proved very difficult to control; he cursed and swore at his captors, and constantly kicked and battered the cell door. He may have reasoned that he had very little to lose by these unruly actions.

It was only the personal intervention of prison governor McKissock that enabled McWheelan to come to terms with his fate. Showing great patience and determination, the governor spent many hours with the condemned man urging him to make a confession and his peace with God. Slowly, McWheelan grew to trust and respect McKissock and, on the night before the execution, in the company of the governor and the Reverend John Graham of the Reformed Presbyterian Church, he wrote a full confession that ran to twelve pages. In the document he expressed his deep gratitude to McKissock who, he said, 'had been like a brother to him'. He also noted with great regret that drink, and the need to steal money to buy it, had been his undoing.

When the terrible day dawned the magistrates proceeded to his cell at 7-15 a.m. where they found him ensconced with Reverend Graham and another minister; at the eleventh hour, it appears, he had also found religion. He was marched outside to the scaffold where thousands of people, including many women and children, had gathered to watch the proceedings. Although there was something of a carnival atmosphere, there was still a possibility of disorder, and so a large body of special constables and a detachment of the local yeomanry were on hand to keep the peace.

McWheelan was placed over the drop by executioner James

Murdoch of Glasgow, who tied the noose tightly round his neck. As was the custom, the condemned man was given a napkin to hold. The arrangement was that, when he felt ready, he would drop it and the executioner would pull the lever, causing the trapdoor to open. But McWheelan was clearly petrified and would not let the napkin go. A full thirty minutes passed during which time he repeated the prayer, 'Lord take me to thyself', over and over again. With the crowd growing tense and irritable, the magistrates took matters into their own hands and gave a signal to Murdoch, who caused the drop to open. Following several minutes of convulsions, McWheelan breathed his last.

The fascination with the case continued unabated for some time. Local newspapers published readers' poems about McWheelan. Ministers reminded their congregations about the part played by drink in his downfall. And the Reverend John Graham even published a pamphlet entitled *The Felon's Cell*, a best-selling account of his conversations with McWheelan in Ayr Prison.

*

Fenwick Moor can be a bleak place, particularly in winter, and in the days before much of it was drained, the land was constantly wet and marshy. Local folklore tells of a foul murder committed on the moorland early in the nineteenth century. A soldier regularly travelled the route from Glasgow to Ayr. He had to. He carried the cash to pay the soldiers who were stationed there. In those days the section of the route between Glasgow and Fenwick was lonely, windswept and without lights. But the soldier was a reliable soul, and he was strong and well trained.

Then one day the soldier failed to turn up at Ayr. A search was soon launched and his horse was found alone and unharmed on the moor. Enquiries were made and it was soon established that the soldier had called in at the inn at Kings Well. This was once an important stop on the route between Kilmarnock and Glasgow, and was close to where the Eaglesham turn-off is today. Still, there was no sign of the soldier, or the wages that he had been carrying.

Speculation was rife. Some people said that he had in all probability run off with the money; other folk darkly speculated that he had been robbed and murdered. Time passed and there was still no word; no clue. Then a man crossing the moorland was horrified to see a hand sticking out of the bog. He summoned help and the body he had discovered was soon extracted from its marshy grave.

It was identified as that of the missing soldier. By his appearance, it was concluded that there had been a violent struggle. As expected, there was no sign of the missing cash. Suspicion fell on a man who had suddenly come into some money. He was arrested and stood trial on a murder charge but, in reality, there was no strong evidence against him and he was found not guilty. He returned to Fenwick and bought a farm just off the main road to Glasgow, close to where the murder had been committed.

*

A more recent murder case involving a burial on the Fenwick Moors happened in October 1988, but the murder was not brought to the attention of police until June of 1989. Enquiries began after three people on drugs charges spoke about having killed a drug courier from Bristol. Having confessed to the murder, they admitted they had disposed of the body by burying it on the Fenwick Moor.

But, in Scotland, a confession alone is not enough for a conviction. They said the body had been moved in a hired van. The hire company was able to check records. A newly bought shovel used to dig a grave had been dumped in a refuse bin, and was recovered by police. A mattress was supposed to have been used while the body was being buried and the public were asked for help in this matter. Police received reports of 168 mattresses dumped in the area. Every one of them was checked. But still, no body was found. Eventually, the case went to trial and the three accused were found guilty and given long jail sentences. The case was unusual in that it is very rare in Scots law to secure a murder conviction with no corpse.

Another recent murder case has had a major impact on the way that fingerprint evidence is checked and dealt with. Marion Ross, a former bank clerk, was viciously attacked in her home at Irvine Road, Kilmarnock in January 1997. She was stabbed in the eye with a pair of scissors – which were then stuck in her throat – and her ribs were crushed. It seemed to be a routine case; the evidence appeared to point to one David Asbury and he was quickly arrested. The case against him was carefully assembled, and at his trial he was found guilty of murder. But it was not Asbury's conviction that was put under the microscope. It was the evidence of police officer Shirley McKie, then with the CID in Kilmarnock.

Early in the investigation she had requested, and was refused, permission to enter the crime scene. Then a stray fingerprint in the house was identified as being hers by the Scottish Criminal Record Office. During evidence at Asbury's trial, Shirley McKie denied being in the house where the murder had been committed, with or without permission. This troubled her superiors. She subsequently faced a trial of her own, accused of perjury.

But fingerprint experts from the USA – Pat Wertheim and David Grieve – were brought in and they said emphatically that the stray print did not belong to McKie. Other leading practitioners in the field agreed. In consequence, the case against her in Glasgow's High Court collapsed and she was acquitted in May 1999. As a result, the general reliability of fingerprint evidence was called into question and this led to a review of how the issue is dealt with in Scots law. The doubt cast on the fingerprint evidence has also had ramifications for David Asbury: he was released on bail after serving three years of his sentence and, on 14 August 2002, had his conviction quashed by the Court of Criminal Appeal.

The whole affair has had profound consequences for Shirley McKie. The daughter of a retired police officer – Chief Superintendent Ian McKie – she resigned from Strathclyde Police after her trial. Her life, understandably, has been scarred by the circumstances of the case. Indeed in an interview with *The Herald* in July 2002 she said that, 'I feel as if I have been assaulted, abused and raped by Strathclyde Police and the justice system.' The effect on her mental health has been considerable; she required medication, and help from a psychologist, and even contemplated suicide in the event of being convicted of perjury.

SEVEN

THE 'LIMBS IN THE LOCH' MURDER

IT SHOULD HAVE BEEN a routine exercise, but it didn't turn out like that. The plan was that the officers from Central Scotland Police who gathered on that chilly December day were to get some experience in underwater work in the cold dark waters near Rowardennan Pier on Loch Lomond. They got much more than they expected, for in fifteen feet of water they found a left arm and a leg. It was a chance discovery, but one that led to the most remarkable criminal case in Kilmarnock's history. As the full horrific details unfolded, it was a case that was to send shock waves throughout the country, and ultimately involve police forces across the world.

It was Monday 6 December 1999, and the macabre discovery in Loch Lomond made headlines across Scotland and beyond. Earlier in the day, Ian and Christine Wallace had reported that their eighteen year-old son, Barry, was missing from their home in an affluent Kilmarnock suburb. Barry was employed as a shelf-stacker at one of the town's two Tesco supermarkets. On the evening of Saturday 4 December 1999, Barry had gone to Tesco to meet a work colleague, Lewis Caddis. The two friends planned to have a few beers, before joining other colleagues for a Christmas party at the Foxbar Hotel in London Road.

It was reported that Barry, a gregarious and popular young man, had a very enjoyable night out. At about 1.45 a.m., keen to find a party, he was seen in the Foregate heading for a nightclub in the town. It later emerged that he had a short, drunken exchange of blows with another man in a taxi queue. But he did not return home. On the Sunday, Barry's parents grew increasingly concerned and started calling friends. Then, on the morning of Monday 6 December, they called the police to report their son missing.

Meanwhile a thorough search was launched at Loch Lomond and, on the day after the arm and leg were discovered, a right arm was found. On the third day a second leg was discovered. Later the torso was recovered. At this stage Barry's case was treated as a missing person. Police were concerned, but the hope was that he had decided to stay with friends for a few days. Barry's father was quoted in *The Herald* on 15 December 1999 as saying that police were 'ninety-nine per cent certain' that the body parts were not those of his son.

However, detectives dealing with the limbs found in Loch Lomond grew increasingly concerned. The limbs might have been there as the result of a horrific accident, but forensic examination quickly suggested foul play. It was apparent that they had been hacked from the corpse and dumped in the loch. It was also clear they had not been in the water for long. The mutilation of the corpse told detectives that a vicious killer was involved. Even so, police did not know if the limbs belonged to the victim of a gangland revenge killing, a serial murderer or any other kind of killer. In the early stages of the investigation the suggestion was that they belonged to a victim of a gangland feud or turf war. Even so, the apparent brutality shocked those investigating the case.

Murder is a foul deed, but it is somehow a lot worse when the victim's corpse has been mutilated and the dismembered parts dumped like pieces of old rubbish. The case was so unusual, so brutal, that the media followed it relentlessly. There were acres of newsprint devoted to the story and it featured heavily on radio and television. The papers immediately dubbed it the 'Limbs in the Loch' case.

Early on there was nothing to link the limbs from Loch Lomond with the missing teenager from Kilmarnock. Even so, police were preparing to take DNA samples from Barry's family when another horrible discovery was made sixty miles from Loch Lomond and only eight miles from Kilmarnock. On 15 December, a woman walking her dog on the shore at Barassie found a human head. The discovery was so horrible that at first she did not accept what she was looking at. The head was quickly identified as that of missing teenager, Barry Wallace, and it was also quickly linked with the limbs found in Loch Lomond. What might have been a fairly routine missing person case had become a murder hunt; a hunt for a brutal killer. Police were now deeply worried. There seemed no possible reason for the murder of Barry Wallace. He was not involved with gangs, drugs or any form of criminal activity. The worst fear was that he was the innocent, random victim of someone who got their kicks from murder.

The police wanted to know what kind of killer would cut up the body of his victim? Psychologists told them that they might be dealing with a sadistic serial killer, a predator who stalks his victims and probably tortures them before killing them and cutting up their bodies. This was a killer who might strike again at any time; someone who might have killed before. These clues led police to suspect one man in particular, a man with a frightening record of attacks on young males. His name was William Beggs.

*

William Ian Beggs was born on 4 October 1963 into a highly respectable and well-educated family from County Down, Northern Ireland. His father, William Beggs senior, was a college lecturer and his mother Winifred a teacher. The family attended church regularly, and Beggs was described as quiet and intelligent by his teachers at primary school. It seemed like the perfect middle-class upbringing. However, the family's good reputation was tarnished when a move was made from the town to a substantial bungalow in the countryside. There were reports of disputes with local farmers about their dog, and they came to be seen as outsiders.

The young Beggs attended a Quaker school in Lisburn and, as he got older, he developed hardline right-wing and unionist views. Ironically, in the light of his future behaviour, he was virulently opposed to homosexuality and helped organise a 'Save Ulster From Sodomy' campaign when legislation to liberalise the law was proposed. He joined the Federation of Conservative Students and even met Margaret Thatcher, who was then Prime Minister. These views did not endear him to his fellow pupils. He was seen as creepy, and an unsavoury incident on a Duke of Edinburgh Award Scheme camping trip cemented this feeling. A fellow male pupil, who was sharing a tent with him, found razor blades in his sleeping bag. In another incident Beggs was beaten up by the older brother of a boy he had allegedly exposed himself to.

Despite his unpopularity, Beggs did well academically. He passed nine 'O' levels and two 'A' levels, and might have considered attending college in Northern Ireland. But this door was closed when a loyalist paramilitary group, the Ulster Volunteer Force, instructed him to leave the province. It emerged that parents had become very concerned about Beggs hanging about local schools and complained to the paramilitaries. He left Ireland and decided to study public administration at Teeside Polytechnic in Middlesbrough where he graduated with a third-class honours degree in 1987. However, during his time at college his true nature began to emerge. In 1985 he was questioned by police about an indecent assault, but the matter did not reach court. There were also fourteen incidents of plying men with drink and slashing them as they slept. However, no charges were brought as the victims appeared reluctant to give evidence, perhaps because of the homosexual overtones.

Then, in May 1987, the badly mutilated body of Barry Oldham, a young homosexual from Aberdeen, was found in a country lane in North Yorkshire. His throat had been repeatedly slashed, and attempts had been made to dismember his body and cut off his head. Because of the savage nature of the killing the police assigned a team of 100 detectives to the case. Beggs was quickly arrested and, on this occasion, the matter did reach court and he stood trial for murder. The jury was told that Beggs killed the victim in his Middlesbrough flat after meeting him in a gay club. Other men testified to their own terrifying experiences at his hands. One man told the court that he woke up in bed to find two cuts on his back and Beggs pinning him down. The attack only stopped when a friend came into the room and turned on the light.

Beggs was found guilty of murder. However, there was to be a dramatic twist. The following year, he lodged an appeal, and it was upheld by the Appeal Court in London. The higher court ruled that the original trial judge had been wrong to allow the Crown to introduce evidence of earlier attacks. This, it was argued, had a prejudicial effect on his defence. The conviction was quashed and Beggs was a free man. The police were, of course, angry and bewildered at the verdict. The officer in charge of the investigation, Detective Chief Superintendent Tony Fitzgerald, was particularly concerned; he firmly believed that Beggs was a very dangerous man.

In due course, Beggs turned up in Scotland, and moved to a flat in Doon Place, Kilmarnock where he worked as an estate management officer in the housing department of the former Kilmarnock and Loudoun District Council (he was later sacked by the Council for failing to disclose details of the court case in Middlesbrough). In 1990, in a more sinister development, he infiltrated the Scout movement in Kilmarnock – a move perhaps designed to give him access to young boys. But he was thrown out of the organisation in 1991 when the story of the Middlesbrough murder charge emerged.

But it would not be long before he reverted to his former, evil ways. In October 1991 he was convicted of a razor-blade assault on Brian McQuillan, whom he had picked up in Bennet's, a gay night-club in Glasgow. Recreating his ordeal for a television documentary produced by BBC Scotland, McQuillan recalled waking up in Beggs's flat in Doon Place to find that he had been slashed, and that the walls of the bedroom were covered in blood. He leapt from the bed, but Beggs followed him saying, 'Things will be over soon. You have made me do this.' McQuillan only escaped with his life by jumping headfirst out of a window. McQuillan later said that he was sure that Beggs had drugged him by spiking a drink.

The jury at the High Court in Kilmarnock found Beggs guilty and the judge, Lord Morison, sentenced him to six years. He noted, quite accurately, that Beggs was a danger to the public and had an abnormal personality. Following the normal arrangements, Beggs was released from prison after serving only half his sentence. He returned to Kilmarnock and, in an effort to improve his education, enrolled in an information technology course at Paisley University, eventually being awarded a Master's degree in the subject in 1996. His fellow students had no illusions about him; they nicknamed him 'Fred West', after the notorious serial killer from Gloucester. Beggs was also able to find a job as a call centre manager with Sykes (Europe) in Edinburgh. This presumably provided him with the money to buy and run a car, an essential tool for his nocturnal forays. He was now ready to commit his most heinous crime yet.

*

Given this track record, it is hardly surprising that Beggs was a prime suspect in the murder of Barry Wallace. Indeed, by mid-December 1999, he was openly named as such in several newspapers, which led some commentators to argue that a fair trial would be impossible. Joe Beltrami, the legendary defence solicitor from Glasgow, took a very strong line; he thought the enormously detailed information that had appeared in the press would make it impossible 'for rational jurors to expunge all this information and prejudice from their minds'. The Crown Office – the body with the main responsibility for prosecutions in Scotland – was reportedly very angry at what some believed was a tabloid feeding-frenzy.

At this time, ten days after the limbs were found, Beggs remained calm. He casually strolled into work, unaware that police had already obtained a warrant to search his home. Officers from Strathclyde Police broke into his flat and began an inch-by-inch forensic search. They took away well over 5,000 items from the flat – all of them constituting potential evidence. The items included a handcuff key, several razor blades, a kitchen knife and a polythene bag. A strong forensic case was being assembled.

Beggs was alerted about the police action by a television news report on 17 December, and decided to flee. Despite the constant police presence outside his flat, Beggs gave the surveillance team the slip by going out through the back door. He then drove through the night to Luton Airport where he abandoned his car. The next day he travelled to Heathrow Airport, where he took a flight under an assumed name to Jersey, and then on to Dinard in France. On 28

December, accompanied by a Dutch lawyer, he surrendered to police in Amsterdam, perhaps attracted by the reputation that Holland enjoys in the field of human rights. Beggs did his best to prevent extradition, and dragged the process out until September 2000 when he lost a final appeal. Eventually, on 8 January 2001, he was extradited to Scotland to face trial at the High Court in Edinburgh. Bizarrely, it was said that he attempted to commit suicide on the flight home by deliberately choking on a bar of chocolate.

The proceedings started on 14 September 2001. The court had already rejected the plea that the accused would not receive a fair trial because of the amount of media coverage, mainly due to the length of time that had elapsed since the alleged offence took place. The prosecution's case was that Beggs had lured Barry Wallace back to his flat in Bellfield, handcuffed him to a bed against his will, and that he subsequently died from asphyxiation, or heart failure brought on by sheer terror, during a violent sexual assault, probably from behind, by Beggs.

There was considerable forensic evidence linking Barry Wallace to the flat in Doon Place. A kitchen knife told its own story. Forensic examination showed that it had been well cleaned, but there was a trace of Barry's blood between the handle and blade. There were tell-tale bloodstains on a mattress. A plastic carrier bag from Scandinavian Seaways was found in the flat – the same type of bag that Barry's head was in when it was found at Barassie beach. It also came to light that Beggs had injected Barry with a syringe, although no drugs were found in his body; this may simply have been a ghastly device by Beggs to terrify his young victim even more.

However, one problem faced by prosecution lawyers was that even the medical experts could not agree on the precise cause of death. Indeed, the advocate for the defence, Donald Findlay QC (the high-profile former vice-chairman of Rangers Football Club), put forward an alternative version of events. He argued that Barry had gone back to the flat voluntarily, perhaps because he was so drunk, agreed to a sex act that went wrong and died later because of the amount of drink he had consumed. Findlay reminded the jury that simply to dismember a body does not constitute a crime in Scots law. Although Barry Wallace's blood was found in the flat, Findlay suggested there was nothing to prove that it had been spilled before Barry died.

But there were some crucial pieces of evidence introduced by the prosecution. A Kenneth Petrie, who had met Beggs in Edinburgh (but who died before the trial took place), had given a statement to the police that Beggs told him that he liked to cruise the streets late at night and pick up young men, particularly straight men like Barry Wallace. He would then lure them back to his flat, often with the promise of more drink. In addition, Richard Balfe, a university lecturer and a good friend of Beggs, told the court how Beggs had phoned him on the Sunday that Barry died. According to Balfe, Beggs told him that he had got off with a 'young, sweet guy'.

The part played by prosecutor Alan Turnbull QC was also highly significant. Turnbull had led the successful prosecution of the Lockerbie bombers and his handling of the Beggs case was generally considered to be masterful. At one point, he showed a photograph of Barry's severed head on a court television without giving any prior warning to the jury. Many observers believe this was a major turning point and helped sway the jury against the accused.

At the end of the trial the jury weighed the evidence and found Beggs guilty of murder. He was given a life sentence by the judge, Lord Osborne, with a recommendation that he should spend at least twenty years behind bars. It appears that Beggs went to pieces in his cell below the courtroom. Witnesses reported that he burst into tears, shouted and screamed at the top of his voice and threw food at the walls.

Experts believed that if he had not been stopped at that point, many more innocent people might have died at his hands. One of them, Ian Stephen, an eminent forensic psychologist and consultant to the popular television crime series *Cracker* starring Robbie Coltrane, said Beggs had the potential to become a serial killer. He added that his methods were similar to those of mass murderers, Dennis Nilsen and Jeffrey Dahmer, both of whom were gay and also dismembered their victims. As it was, police were greatly concerned that others might have perished in the flat; indeed, blood from seventeen other men was found in his flat, along with many photographs of young men. They contacted the authorities in every country Beggs was known to have visited, asking them to check missing persons records and for any case involving mutilated bodies.

The police, of course, were pleased that a conviction was secured. It had been a complex and difficult case lasting all of twenty-two months. In addition, officers had been criticised for letting Beggs slip through the net and escape to Holland. The man in charge of the investigation for seventeen of those months, Detective Superintendent Stephen Heath, was clearly relieved that Beggs was safely behind bars, describing him as an 'evil and cunning killer'. Mr Heath also

Guilty! The front page of the *Daily Record* on 13 October 2001.

noted how unusual it was for murders to involve someone who had no connection to the murderer.

The end of the trial also meant that Barry's parents were able to speak openly about their son. Ian and Christine Wallace conducted themselves with great dignity throughout the whole process. They expressed satisfaction that Beggs had been found guilty, and that no other innocent child or family would have to suffer as they had. But they were also angry about wholly false implications in certain sections of the media that Barry pursued a promiscuous gay lifestyle. As Ian Wallace said, some newspapers had 'dragged his son's name and reputation through the gutter'. He was, his father went on, simply in the wrong place at the wrong time.

In fact, Barry Wallace was very popular and respected, with all the ambition we might expect in a young man of eighteen; in his case, that might well have meant a career in the Royal Navy. He always had time for other people, and one friend described him as 'incredibly caring'. His parents expressed their gratitude for the support they received from family and friends right through their ordeal. Another measure of Barry's popularity was his funeral; it was estimated that more than five hundred mourners turned up to pay their last respects at St John's Church in Onthank. Indeed the church was so full that many mourners had to assemble in an adjoining hall or to stand outside. His coffin was carried from the church to the sounds of the Robbie Williams song, 'Angels'.

The contrast with the evil man who murdered him could not be greater. Beggs is now universally reviled. It is even said that the Ulster Volunteer Force has put out a contract on his life, offering a five-figure reward if someone kills him in prison. Apparently the paramilitaries were incensed that Beggs displayed UVF posters and other loyalist material in his flat.

There has been much speculation about what turned an apparently well-behaved and studious child, from a highly respectable background, into a ruthless and predatory killer, or to quote a *Daily Record* headline 'From Quaker to Ripper'. Psychologists believe the key to his personality was the careful way he cut up and sliced his victims' bodies. It was the sight of blood and the use of a sharp blade that provided the key to his sexuality, and this can be traced right back to the incident in Northern Ireland with the razor blades in the sleeping bag.

William Beggs is now one of that very small band of infamous criminals whose every move or action in prison receives great attention in the media. He ranks alongside Myra Hindley, Rosemary West and the 'Yorkshire Ripper', Peter Sutcliffe, in this regard. Indeed he was referred to as Scotland's most hated man in an article in the *Sunday Mail* on 9 June 2002, and comparisons were drawn with the fictional killer, Hannibal Lecter, from the Hollywood movie *Silence of the Lambs*. And we may not have reached the final chapter in this grisly story; as this book was going to press in the summer of 2002, it was reported that William Beggs was preparing an appeal.

EIGHT

MONEY TALKS

MONEY DRIVES THE WORLD'S economy and what would money
be without the banks?

At the start of the nineteenth century Kilmarnock had its own
bank. The Kilmarnock Banking Company was established in 1802 by
a group of local businessmen who included Major William Parker of
Assloss and George Douglas of Rodinghead. Major Parker features
elsewhere in Kilmarnock's history. He was a friend of Robert Burns
and before the voting reforms of 1832 he was the only man in
Kilmarnock allowed to vote. George Douglas also features prominently
in the town's history. He helped establish and run the Kilmarnock
and Troon Railway. Indeed, the Kilmarnock and Troon Railway
Company was an important customer of the Kilmarnock Bank.
Others involved in setting up the Kilmarnock Bank were Mungo
Fairlie of Holmes, James Fairlie of Bellfield and Patrick Ballantyne of
Castlehill in Ayr.

Before the Kilmarnock Bank opened what it described as an
agency in the town on 10 June 1802, there was already a bank in
Kilmarnock. It was a branch of the Bank of Scotland, but it seems
they had some sort of gentlemen's agreement and the Bank of
Scotland promptly closed its Kilmarnock branch. Unlike many of the
other banks of the day, the Kilmarnock Bank was a purely local
affair with just one branch, although it did issue its own banknotes.

Paper money was pioneered in Scotland by the Bank of Scotland
and the Royal Bank of Scotland. Notes issued by the Kilmarnock
Bank were for one guinea and two guineas. Each was printed in
black on one side only and measured about 145 by 110 millimetres.
The notes were designed by J. Sanderson and engraved on copper
plate by Kirkwood and Son. They had the coat of arms of the town,
with the face value to the left in words.

They were numbered and dated by hand as was the practice in
those days. Indeed the notes were more like cheques than today's
banknotes. They also had three signatures each. Dealer Stanley
Gibbons points out that the notes issued by the Kilmarnock Bank are
extremely rare, and that fewer than ten of each are still in existence.

Although it traded successfully, by 1821 the partnership had
dissolved and the business passed to Hunters and Company of Ayr.
Hunter's was a considerably larger organisation and ultimately had

The Kilmarnock Bank issued its own notes.

branches in eight Ayrshire towns, including Galston and Stewarton. Hunters continued trading in Kilmarnock but in turn was absorbed into the Union Bank of Scotland in 1843. The Union Bank traded successfully for more than 100 years and became part of the Bank of Scotland in 1955. In 2001 the Bank of Scotland merged with the Halifax.

*

Not everyone puts their money in a bank, and before 1755 there were no banks in Kilmarnock in which to make a deposit. People who had spare money had to keep their coins hidden as best they could. This was particularly so at the end of the seventeenth century when Covenanters were being brutally oppressed and the army was stationed in Kilmarnock to 'maintain order'. Many people found good hiding places for their wealth. One such man was the owner of a tavern at the foot of the Foregate. He hid his money in a leather bag in a niche in the wall of one of the upstairs rooms, just below the thatch. At that time many of the coins in circulation in Scotland were European – Austrian, Dutch, French, as well as English.

No one knows what happened to the innkeeper or even his name. He vanished from the scene leaving his wealth behind him. Years went by and his secret stash remained a secret until 1863, when the old inn was being demolished to make way for a grain store for a Mr

Mather. The demolition work was being carried out by James Wallace and half a dozen men in his employment. It was about one o'clock that warm Tuesday afternoon in June when one of the workmen pulled away some of the thatch and revealed a small cavity in which there was a black substance that he could not quite identify. He prodded it with his pick and it burst into a shower of silver coins, mostly Austrian, but also of other European countries including Scotland and England.

Had this happened today, the coins would have been carefully studied but this was 1863 and the coins were simply divided up among the workers on the site, who quickly sold them for current coins of the realm. The oldest was dated 1553, and the newest 1677. The coins were not counted, but the *Kilmarnock Post* believed there were probably around 300. The *Kilmarnock Standard*, which was founded in 1863, had the story in its very first edition, and put the number of coins found at 900 with a value of at least £100. The *Standard* complained that no effort was made to study the coins and added that some of them had fallen into the debris during the demolition process, a claim that attracted quite a number of treasure hunters.

It was not the only major stash of coins found in the Kilmarnock area. About 1823 an earthenware pot containing a number of coins was found at Lochgoin near Fenwick. This, too, may have been hidden in Covenanting times as these coins dated from about 1670.

And some time around 1786 workmen demolishing a house in Green Street found an earthenware pot hidden below the floor. It contained a number of coins, again from the time of Charles II. Another old coin from the time of James VI was found in gravel on the bank of the Kilmarnock Water near Dean Castle in 1852, not long after the serious flooding that devastated the town.

But let's return to banks and the reluctance of some people to use them. One morning a sailor arrived at Christie's ironmonger's shop in Kilmarnock with an odd request. He was smartly dressed in a blue suit and he spoke with a foreign accent. He asked Mr Christie to look after five pounds for him for a few days and laid five sovereigns on the shop counter.

Mr Christie eyed the stranger curiously. 'Suppose you don't return?' Mr Christie asked. The visitor smiled saying that, if he did not return, Mr Christie could keep the money. Five pounds was, of course, a lot of money at that time. Christie agreed and a week or so later the stranger returned looking as smart as he had done on his first visit. Mr Christie laid five sovereigns on the counter for him. He lifted four, telling the shopkeeper to keep one for his trouble. But Mr Christie, being a kindly and honest soul, could not take so much for having done so little.

Mr Christie was, however, curious about why he had been asked to look after so much money for such a brief period of time. The seaman explained that, after he left the five coins at the shop, he spent a few days in the town enjoying wine, women and song. But, unlike many of his seafaring friends, he had the considerable comfort of knowing there was money to fall back on when he had finished his carousing.

*

At a time when the army wanted new recruits, the reward for joining up was a shilling – known throughout the land as the King's Shilling. Because of the war in Europe and also the conflict with America, prices had been rising sharply. A widow had gone along to a farmer near Fenwick to buy her winter supply of meal.

This farmer was well-known in the area for being quick to increase his prices and being very reluctant to reduce them. He told the lady the cost of her purchase, but she was a shilling short. They argued a while and a passing soldier asked what the fuss was about. Of course, he knew the farmer's reputation.

'How much are you short', he asked the widow, kindly. 'A shilling, just a shilling.' The soldier eyed the farmer with contempt. Then he threw a shilling at him: 'Here, here's a shilling in the name of the king.' And so, all three were happy. The farmer got his price, the soldier had done a good deed and the widow had all the grain she needed for the winter.

But the tale does not end there. Next day, the soldier returned to the farmer with two recruiting officers. Imagine the sheer horror on the farmer's face when reminded: 'You accepted the shilling in the name of the king.' And so the farmer was dragged off to the barracks at Kilmarnock, believing that he was in the army for a spell. He wasn't. The soldiers let him go home at the end of the day, but he did learn an important lesson and it is said that, afterwards, he was always that much nicer to his customers.

*

Money can lead to greed, greed to crime, crime to punishment. One man who fell into this cycle was a Kilmarnock schoolteacher named John Graham. He was born about 1734 in Perthshire and completed his education at the University of Glasgow under Adam Smith, the economist who still greatly influences political thinking today. Graham was destined to become a minister, but the death of his father left him without sufficient funds and he became a teacher at the Grammar School in Kilmarnock.

For nearly twenty years, from 1760 to 1779, he helped transform the Kilmarnock school into one of the finest and most efficient in Ayrshire. He was well respected and was also custodian of the parish records. Then he fell under the influence of a man who proved his ruin. Induced to better things in London, or so he thought, he sold all his possessions at an auction that lasted a week. Then he hired a coach to take him, his wife and eight children to London, where he spent extravagantly, too extravagantly.

Soon he was in serious debt. His solution was to engage an engraver to make a plate for a £10 note. The engraver, having been paid, tipped off the authorities and Graham was arrested. No notes were ever printed from the plate and Graham escaped with a jail sentence. He should have learned his lesson, but he did not.

No sooner was he out of jail than he was at it again. This time he got hold of notes valued at £15 and by erasing the 'een' and substituting a 'y' he passed off the forgeries as £50 notes. Such a scam could not last and Graham was arrested again. The notes had been passed off through Graham's wife. At the subsequent trial Graham and his wife simply blamed each other. They were both found guilty of forgery and sentenced to be executed. Mrs Graham was spared the gallows but the teacher who had succumbed to greed was hanged at Tyburn on 15 October 1782.

NINE

HERITAGE WRITTEN IN STONE

THERE IS SOMETHING ABOUT a lion that fascinates us. The stuffed lion's head at the Dick Institute is an icon for the museum and, at the Kay Park and the Dean Country Park, visitors can see stone lions, which never fail to attract the attention of children. These stone lions are a reminder of a major business venture in Kilmarnock, that of J. and M. Craig. The lions were a sideline. The company ran quarries, several coal-mines and they made bricks and sanitary ware, urns and all manner of fireclay products . . . and exported goods all over the world.

To find out more about this enterprising Kilmarnock company and its people, I asked Ann Amor from Bolton for help. She first came across the firm when her mother gave her some of its ornate pottery and she began researching the history of the business in parallel to researching her family tree. Her mother is Jean Ferguson Craig, a direct descendant of key players in the business. Ann has now thoroughly researched the business and has provided the information for this chapter.

Mining and quarrying in the area around Dean Castle goes back centuries, but the firm we are interested in here started working the quarry in the nineteenth century. Our story begins with Matthew Craig, senior, who was born in 1787 and started work as a labourer in Kilmaurs. He married Helen Smith in 1810 and they had ten children. Only four of them – Mary, James, Helen and Matthew – survived into adulthood.

It was Matthew, the elder, who first worked the quarry at Dean, close to the castle. This quarry produced large quantities of stone for local building work and fireclay for bricks, tiles and sanitary ware. As the business flourished, the family moved from Kilmaurs to Kilmarnock and, by 1824, they took the lease of land near where they were working but on the other side of the river, near Assloss.

In 1826 Matthew Craig was operating two quarries, one on each side of the Borland Water. It was an expensive business transporting materials from one to the other and, to save on transport and toll costs, he built a tunnel under the river to link the two quarries. It soon became a local curiosity and attracted many visitors and the attention of the Press. The tunnel was seventy feet long, twelve feet wide and twelve feet high. It was cut through solid rock and did not require any arching or other building supports. The tunnel was kept clear of water by a steam-powered pump, which was also used to keep the quarries clear of water and this was at a time when steam technology was still in its infancy. Clearly, Matthew Craig was a very enterprising gentleman.

Sasine records of 1837 show the family buying land and expanding the business in various directions. In 1840 their factory at Moorfield was producing 800,000 tiles per year. By the early 1840s, Matthew turned his attention to fireclay bricks, made from the fireclay at the bottom of the quarry. He employed only one brickmaker but the stock accumulated as the properties of fireclay bricks were relatively unknown at that time. However, brick making was something that the company returned to and today it is still possible to find bricks with the J. & M. Craig imprint in gardens and even on gap sites around Kilmarnock.

Matthew died in 1847 aged sixty and, with the death of the father, the sons, James and Matthew Craig, formed a partnership to continue the business. This was the firm of J. & M. Craig. They were soon making large quantities of bricks, tiles, drainpipes, chimney pots, decorative stoneware of human and animal figures such as the lions already mentioned. They also made baths, troughs, sinks, vases, garden urns – indeed anything that could be made of stone.

Expansion in the 1850s was rapid. In 1851 they employed twenty men at the Dean but by 1861 this had grown to fifty-eight men and twelve boys. In 1858 they leased Kilmaurs Quarry; in 1861 they bought the Hillhead works, and in 1862 took the lease of Perceton. By 1868 Matthew was also a managing partner of the Lonsdale Haematite Iron Company in Whitehaven, Cumbria. A company bill-head, dated 1869, lists the company's main products as fire bricks, flooring tiles, flue covers, glazed pipes and gas retorts, with a sub-sidiary line listing vent linings, chimney cans, ground fire clay, wall coping and cattle troughs.

By 1865 the company was producing goods totalling 20,000 tons and Matthew went to London to argue the case for extending the railway that came through Kilmarnock. He took an interest in local affairs and, in 1871, was elected as a bailie. During his time in this post he served on many committees and was also an elder at the Winton Place Church. But he died of tuberculosis when he was just forty-three, leaving a wife and eight children. Indeed, this church now has a magnificent full-length, stained-glass window, dedicated to the memory of Matthew and his wife, Jeannie, in recognition of their many years of faithful service.

James had always been very close to his brother and was devastated by Matthew's untimely death. It took him some years fully to recover from the shock of his bereavement. The business began to suffer. But James was made of strong stuff, and so was his wife, Agnes Gilmore Baird. She was the daughter of radical reformer Thomas Baird, whose name is on the Reformers' Monument in the Kay Park.

In 1872 Dean Quarry was exhausted and it closed. Three years later, with some of his old energy back, James Craig followed in his brother's footsteps and was elected as a bailie. He too served on numerous committees and in doing so seems to have reinvigorated himself.

The business recovered and started to thrive again. A report of 1880 said that fireclay bricks were the company's main business and that one man with the assistance of two boys could make between 3,000 and 4,000 bricks a day. As the business looked to a wider area for sales, its reputation grew and the company began to win awards. It was also well known for looking after employees, and provided an annual summer excursion for the workers with all costs paid by the firm.

In 1884 the company started making sanitary earthenware at what was later known as Longpark Pottery. At first the plant had thirty employees, working sixty hours a week. Longpark was to grow into one of the company's major assets. Early on it earned a reputation for producing high quality goods and became famous for decorative pottery ware. This reputation was given the royal seal of approval when the firm won the contract to provide the first flushing urinals at Balmoral Castle and also for stations on the Great Western Railway, Liverpool Docks and the Prince Alfred Hospital in Sydney, New South Wales. One of the company's specialities at this time was the glazed brick, used in toilets, kitchens and washhouses, and also for general building. Examples can be seen in some houses in North Hamilton Street, Kilmarnock.

By 1885 the business not only had sales across the United Kingdom, with agencies in various parts of Scotland, England and

Longpark Pottery, once a major business in Kilmarnock.

Ireland, but also a thriving export trade, particularly to Australia, the USA, India and China. Ships left regularly from Irvine, Troon and Ardrossan, as well as Glasgow and Greenock.

From time to time, bricks do turn up in places like Australia and people contact the Dick Institute or the *Kilmarnock Standard* in their efforts to find out more about the company. Some products end up in museums, such as the one at Rottnest Island, about a forty-five minute journey from Perth, Australia.

One of the Craig sons, also Matthew, went to Australia to look after the company's business interests there and, while in that country, married a girl from Aberdeenshire. James continued to look for opportunities to expand his business interests and in 1892 started the Moorfield Colliery. At first this was operated as a separate business enterprise. By this time Craig was employing 800 people. When the business became a limited company in 1895 the various business interests were pulled together under the name of J. & M. Craig Ltd. It remained a family concern with all the shares being held by members of the family. James retained his traditional role as Managing Director.

In 1899 Rothesay on the Isle of Bute was a popular destination for folks from Glasgow and the west of Scotland who were 'gaun doon the watter'. In consequence the local council decided to build new gentlemen's toilets to serve the increasing number of visitors. The firm of J. & M. Craig Ltd provided tiles to decorate the new toilets and today they are rightly considered an outstanding example of Victorian workmanship. A tile bearing the company name is included in the decorations there.

In a letter to me about the toilets, Ann Amor tells me of her expedition to Rothesay to photograph the J. & M. Craig products:

> I thought the super-loos at Rothesay were well and truly spectacular. I managed to get into the gents long enough to take photos – along with an eighty-year-old lady who giggled loudly at the thought of her being in a gents for the first time in her long life! We were all suitably impressed . . . I did get some queer looks, however, when I spent time photographing the Craig brick evident at the back side of the building away from all the splendour.

The year 1899 was also the year when James celebrated his golden wedding anniversary and he certainly celebrated in style. He had travelled extensively and had a great many business contacts. His celebration tea dance at the Agricultural Hall in Kilmarnock served 1,200 guests.

But suddenly, it all went wrong. In 1906, for reasons that are far from clear, James, who was then eighty-three, decided to put the entire business into liquidation. This was an odd decision for the company does not appear to have been in any financial difficulties at that time. Even while the future of the business hung in the balance, James died. It was January of 1907. The town recognised the enormous contribution he had made to the prosperity of the area, and he was given a civic funeral. The town bells tolled for an hour and there was genuine grief throughout Kilmarnock.

James had left no family of his own and the task of running the business fell to Matthew's sons. The business of liquidating the company had already started. The main fireclay works were sold in 1907 along with other buildings and stock. But the business still had a bit of life in it yet. Before 1907 was out a new company was formed under the name of J. & M. Craig (Kilmarnock) Ltd, with its head office in Hill Street.

The new business found trading difficult. The nephews lacked the exceptional leadership and strong management of James Craig. The world had also changed and was continuing to change rapidly. Yet the business produced illustrated catalogues and continued to have good international links; it even boasted offices in Hamburg and Buenos Aires. But, by the time of the First World War, the company was getting into serious difficulties. In 1916 the new business was put into liquidation, and eventually the assets and name were sold to Shanks in 1919.

By this time all that remained of a once extensive business enterprise was the pottery at Longpark. Shanks continued to manufacture goods at Kilmarnock into the second half of the twentieth century but, ultimately, the Kilmarnock side of the business was closed and transferred to Barrhead, thus closing an important and largely forgotten chapter in Kilmarnock's industrial heritage.

TEN

THE SPIRIT OF KILMARNOCK

HIGH ON THE EASTERN slopes of the Southern Alps on South Island, New Zealand, there is a glacier by the name of the Kilmarnock Glacier. It feeds the Kilmarnock Falls, a spectacular waterfall, which has water cascading down 152 metres. Why the Kilmarnock Falls and why the Kilmarnock Glacier? Well, the story goes that the glacier and the falls were named around 1900 by a character named James O'Malley who worked for the nearby Bealey Hotel. Part of his duties was to take the guests to see the falls. It is said that he always kept a bottle of fine Scotch whisky at the foot of the falls, strictly for emergencies of course! At this stage the spectacular features did not have a name, but when Mr O'Malley was asked what they were called he said the first thing that came into his head. He answered they were the Kilmarnock Glacier and the Kilmarnock Falls. Of course, O'Malley had never been to Kilmarnock in his life and probably had no idea where the town was, but he had seen the name on the bottles of his favourite whisky.

And so, as a result of Kilmarnock's most famous export, it can be said that there is a little piece of Kilmarnock in New Zealand. In some ways though, there is a little piece of Kilmarnock in almost every country in the world. No matter where you travel, people are familiar with the name of Johnnie Walker. Some folk even say that he invented whisky. But that is a claim that really cannot be made for the best-known son of Kilmarnock.

Johnnie Walker was a real person. He was born at Todrigg Farm on the outskirts of Kilmarnock in 1805. There's a fine statue to him in his home town, in the shadow of the Laigh Kirk, looking towards buildings that the whisky company once owned. And yet it was not Johnnie Walker who built the business into a vast international empire. That was the work of his son and grandson. They transformed a small local business into a company that produced one of the world's first global brands. Think about it. Whenever you watch a film or a television drama, whether it's been made in Britain, the USA or Australia, if someone reaches for the whisky, chances are you will recognise the square bottle and slanting label.

In the 1958 British film about the sinking of the *Titanic – A Night to Remember –* the steward drank Johnnie Walker whisky as the great ship went down. Superman looked for comfort in the square bottle with a slanting label and, in the legendary film *Whisky Galore*, when legitimate whisky arrived on the island it, too, was in square bottles with slanting labels.

In Scotland, the making of whisky, or *usquebaugh* – the water of life – goes back to at least the fifteenth century. Like many things Scottish, the art seems to have come here from Ireland. Laws on whisky making were difficult to enforce, but after the Act of Union in 1707, various laws were passed which seriously discriminated against Scottish products. Spirit production was targeted and anti-Scottish legislation towards the end of the eighteenth century forced many distilleries to close, nearly killing off the legal spirit trade. The start of the nineteenth century was also a tough time. Heavy taxes were imposed to help pay for wars, and restricted grain imports together with bad weather affecting harvests combined to put whisky production into a state of near crisis.

Of course, none of this concerned the young lad who was then growing up at Todrigg Farm. When Johnnie Walker was just fifteen the trustees of Alexander Walker, his father, set him up in a grocery shop in Kilmarnock, considering that this would at least keep body and soul together and secure the lad's future. As with other grocers of the time, Johnnie Walker sold exotic items from far-off countries and one of his specialities was tea. Spirits, also from abroad, were popular with customers. Of course, whisky made in Scotland was purely a sideline, and Johnnie could never have guessed it would transform the course of his family history as well as that of the town of Kilmarnock.

In the first half of the nineteenth century, grocers bought whisky from distilleries. Transport was starting to open up the country and the distilleries in the north and south of the country were eager to exploit the new markets of the central belt. There was a distillery at Old Rome near Gatehead until 1840, and William Wallace & Company had one in Low Glencairn Street, although the dates that it operated are now uncertain.

Grocers like Johnnie Walker soon discovered that casks improved the flavour. The great problem in whisky production was that the flavour, even from the same distillery, could vary from year to year. The grocers bought in bulk and stored the whisky in casks, which had previously held brandy, port or sherry. Grocers soon discovered they could mix various whiskies and come up with a consistent taste. The art of the blender was born, but it is not clear exactly when Johnnie Walker started to blend his own whisky.

As the industrial revolution gathered pace, the economy of Kilmarnock boomed. Carpets, textiles and shoes were of particular importance and, with the development of the railways, merchants were soon coming to Kilmarnock to inspect the town's wares. They quickly acquired a taste for the whisky sold by Mr Walker. One story has it that when merchants bought carpets from Kilmarnock manufacturers, they often found a bottle of Walker's whisky with their goods.

Such an innovative marketing ploy is unlikely to have been implemented by John Walker. But his son . . . well, Alexander never missed a chance to sell more whisky. One of the first things that he did after joining the firm in 1856 was to initiate the move from retail sales to wholesale. The year after Alexander joined the business his father died, but such was Alexander's incredible drive that he would turn a local grocery shop into a global business.

He set about promoting his brands in a way that no other whisky was being promoted. In 1867 he introduced the slanting label, which any whisky drinker today would instantly recognise as the Johnnie Walker brand. It is not certain when the square bottles were introduced. It was certainly before 1896 but, interestingly, it was to save space when cases of whisky were being transported and not as a marketing tool. The Walkers could never have imagined that square bottles and slanting labels would become a twentieth-century icon. An interesting aside is that the square bottles also became an instant hit with those who liked to build ships in bottles; the Exeter

Workers at Johnnie Walker, c. 1900.

The original design for the figure of

JOHNNIE WALKER

BY THE LATE TOM BROWNE

Maritime Museum has an impressive collection, and many are instantly recognisable as Johnnie Walker bottles.

In the 1860s Alexander also pushed his blenders to create better blends. They came up with something that is very close to today's Black Label. Export trade was haphazard and relied on a system known as Adventure Merchant Business. Ships with spare cargo space would take any goods that could be sold. Sales were dependent on the captain getting a good price. Despite the risky nature of the system, it was here that the company built up international markets that were to make the name of Johnnie Walker known across the world. By 1880 it was necessary to open an office in London. Ten years later, an office was opened in Sydney. A new generation of Walkers came into the business including a younger Alexander Walker and George Paterson Walker.

New marketing methods were introduced and, in 1908, Tom Browne, one of the most prominent artists of the day, was commissioned to produce a portrait of the founder. The striding-man figure was an instant success and in modified form is still used today. At the time the company produced three blends: Old Highland Whisky with a white label; Special Old Highland Blend with a red label; and Extra Special Old Highland with a black label. It had become common for customers to ask for brands by the label colour, and the re-branding exercise reinforced the ideas.

After the First World War the company was in a good position to find new markets all over the world. Even in the USA, prohibition was not a serious barrier to sales. Bottles of whisky were shipped to deserted islands and entered America through neighbouring countries. Indeed, prohibition led to Scotch whisky overtaking sales of American and Irish whiskey. All true Scots will know of course, that whisky comes from Scotland; whiskey comes from other countries. The quality of brands like Johnnie Walker was far more reliable than anything produced illegally in the States. By the time prohibition was lifted, Johnnie Walker was well established in the USA.

Just as his father had created Black Label whisky, the younger Alexander Walker was responsible for developing Red Label and turning it into a world brand. His notebooks, specifying to his blenders precisely what he was looking for, are now preserved at the company's archive in Menstrie in Clackmannanshire, along with hundreds of other documents such as company minute books, wage records, ledgers and blend sheets. Many of the documents originate from the twentieth century, but some go back to the nineteenth century.

The years after the Second World War were boom years. By the 1950s, the company was at last able to get out of the cramped property in the town centre and move to Hill Street. This move had been planned in the 1930s, but the new buildings were commandeered by the Ministry of Food for the duration of the war and for some years beyond.

Alexander Walker paid great attention to detail. He introduced a blend called Swing, specifically aimed at customers on transatlantic liners. The bottle base was slightly bevelled so that as the ship rocked, so too did the bottle, and in such a way that it stayed upright. Swing is still produced today.

Towards the end of the twentieth century, the world was changing and even big companies had to think in terms of mergers to compete. Johnnie Walker, then part of the Distillers Group, was the subject of a bitter take-over battle that was ultimately won by Guinness. Today the Johnnie Walker brands are owned by multi-national giant, Diageo plc, which also owns Smirnoff Vodka, Bailey's Original Irish Cream Liqueur and the Burger King chain of hamburger restaurants. According to the Diageo website in June 2002, Johnnie Walker is one of its 'global priority brands' and holds a very strong position in the best-performing markets.

Even after the last of the Walkers no longer had connections with the business, innovation and attention to detail remain key elements. Red Label and Black Label are crucial to the business, but the range of brands under the Johnnie Walker label is now much wider than ever before. Blue Label, introduced in 1992, was an ambitious attempt to recreate Johnnie Walker's original blend, using fifteen whiskies from distilleries Walker probably used himself. Gold Label was introduced in 1995 and was created from notes and experimental blends left by the younger Alexander Walker. In addition there is Premier brand and a Johnnie Walker malt.

Today Johnnie Walker whiskies are sold in every country in the world, except for two, where alcohol is prohibited. Some blends are sold only in one market, and some are slightly altered to suit individual markets. Attention to detail is still of paramount importance. The famous slanting label has hundreds of varieties to suit local languages across the globe. Blending is now kept to a minimum at Kilmarnock, but more than ninety million cases of whisky are bottled there each year and 90 per cent of that goes for export.

ELEVEN

THE 'GLEN': WORKSHOP TO THE WORLD

GLENFIELD AND KENNEDY LTD was perhaps the archetypal Kilmarnock business. An engineering firm at the cutting edge of technical innovation, it was founded by local men in the Victorian period and became known throughout the world for its high quality products. Indeed such was its success that it became one of the biggest companies of its type in the world and, at its peak, employed around 2,500 people in its premises in the town's Low Glencairn Street. The company will forever be known locally by its nickname – the 'Glen'.

Despite its many local connections the story begins in Argyll with one Thomas Kennedy, born in 1797, and known as 'Tobermory' by his friends. He ran a clock and watchmaking business in his native county, but found it hard to make the business pay in such a remote and sparsely populated area. He decided to move to a more promising place and arrived in Kilmarnock in 1824, where he set up in the same line of work. He was also a crack shot and his hobby became part of his growing business as he also carved out an excellent reputation as a gunsmith. Such was his expertise that he had the great honour of being appointed Court gunmaker to the Prince Consort, Albert, the husband of Queen Victoria.

'Tobermory' Kennedy was devoted to his church and it is said it was on a Sunday school picnic outing that his interest in the device that was to make his fortune – the water meter – first came to light. The picnickers came upon a wall fountain from which water was flowing freely. Kennedy exclaimed, 'Damned waste', and immediately realised that a device to control and record the distribution of water could be a valuable commodity in many of the industries that were springing up in Scotland and elsewhere. For some time thereafter he wrestled with the technical problems inherent in making a water meter. He called on, among others, his friend and fellow watchmaker, Thomas Cameron of Kilmarnock, to assist him. It is argued by many that it was Cameron, and not Kennedy, who deserves most of the credit for the invention of the meter. Others say that Andrew Barclay (whose story is told in chapter twenty of this book) also played a major part in the development of the meter.

The story of Cameron's breakthrough is intriguing. One Sunday morning he was sitting in King Street Church listening to the sermon when his mind started to wander to the subject that had come to obsess him: the water meter. He began to draw technical diagrams in the flyleaf of his bible when, suddenly, the answer flashed through his mind. Cameron leapt from his pew, exclaiming excitedly, 'By God, I've got it now' and like a man possessed ran from the church to write out the full solution. However, despite the important part he played in the invention of the water meter it was Thomas 'Tobermory' Kennedy who applied for, and was granted, the patent in 1852. And it was Kennedy who founded the Patent Water Meter Syndicate in the same year for the purpose of manufacturing the device. Cameron was not part of the syndicate, an omission that caused much comment in Kilmarnock.

In any event, the venture proved extremely lucrative and a few years later the company moved to larger premises in Low Glencairn Street. By 1865 it had become a limited company (the Kennedy Patent Water Meter Company Ltd). 'Tobermory' Kennedy had no children of his own and, in 1866, he brought his nephew, also Thomas Kennedy, into the business. The young Kennedy, a highly qualified engineer, rose to become managing director. He remained at the helm until 1909 and it was under his leadership that the company became a leader in the field of hydraulic engineering. The workforce grew substantially. In 1866 it had around 60 staff; by 1888 the figure had risen to 800 and, by 1904, 1,700 were employed. The company's rapid growth was boosted by the increasing demand for meters and other hydraulic equipment. Sadly, 'Tobermory' did not live to see the day when the company he founded became a world leader: he died in 1874, aged seventy-four, and is buried in the grounds of the Old High Kirk in Kilmarnock.

Nearby, the Glenfield Iron Company had been established in 1865 and the two companies found they had much in common. So much so that in 1899 they merged to form Glenfield and Kennedy Ltd. The new company was also very successful and continued to sell its meters and valves all over the world. The size of the works expanded considerably: in 1900 a twelve-acre field on the east side of the River Irvine was purchased to construct new production capacity; and plush new offices, befitting a world-class business, were opened in 1910. Thomas Kennedy became managing director of the merged business and his dynamic leadership saw Glenfield and Kennedy go from strength to strength. Apart from a short spell on Kilmarnock Town Council in the late 1870s, and his duties as an elder at Kilmarnock High Parish Church, he was completely devoted to the firm, although he was not rewarded with a salary comparable to other leading businessmen. He retired from the 'Glen' in 1913, and died at his relatively modest home in Howard Street in 1917.

In 1938 Glenfield and Kennedy took a large pavilion at the Empire Exhibition in Glasgow and above the doors was a sign with a proud, but justifiable, boast – 'Hydraulic Engineers to the World'. The exhibition included a wave-making machine, in whose design and manufacture the company excelled. In fact, there is an amusing anecdote told about the wave-making machine installed at Kilmarnock Baths, which was a gift from the company to the town to thank its people for making the 'Glen' such an outstanding success. About 1980, for the first time in forty years, the machine failed. It just happened to be the day that a couple of ladies from Canada called to see the wave-maker in action. They were the wives of executives from the Crane Group, by this time the owners of Glenfield and Kennedy. Engineers were duly sent from the 'Glen' to repair the machine. When they isolated the faulty part, the older of the two turned to his mate and smiled broadly. 'By here', he said, 'We've had twa o' thae doon by for forty years and never kent whit they were fur.'

The managers of Glenfield and Kennedy prided themselves on the way they looked after their workers. They set up a Welfare Association – said to be one of the first of its kind – for the benefit of staff at all levels in the organisation. Among an incredibly wide range of activities workers could enjoy a library, physical training, crafts, indoor and outdoor games, baking and music. There was also a thrift and savings bank and assistance with health care. Of course the company had also helped to form the renowned Kilmarnock Glenfield Ramblers Society. There was a generous non-contributory pension scheme, and employees could invest in a loan scheme that tied the rate of interest paid on savings to the company's profits.

While life in the factory was invariably routine, there was one event in November 1944 that sent shock waves through not only the 'Glen' but also the whole town. It occurred on a Friday morning – wages day. Without warning, two masked gunmen burst into the company's offices with the intention of stealing the payroll. But they reckoned without the pluck of two members of staff: Robert Stalker of Riccarton and William Weir of Fairlie Avenue in Kilmarnock. Without any consideration for their own safety both men immediately tackled the intruders, one of whom fired his revolver, hitting

Mr Stalker in the shoulder. Realising that the game was up the two robbers fled and, although closely pursued by other members of staff, they made good their escape.

The robbers hid out in a hay-shed but were quickly apprehended by police. It transpired that the two desperadoes were seventeen year-old James Smith of Barnweil Road in Kilmarnock and a sixteen year-old boy, also of Kilmarnock, who could not be named for legal reasons. Smith was an apprentice at Glenfield and Kennedy who often helped out in the wages office, and therefore knew the routine. He had stolen the guns and ammunition from Prestwick Aerodrome (as it was then known). The Sheriff sent both boys to borstal for three years. There is an ironic twist to the story. The car delivering the wages was late that Friday and there was no money in the office at the time the two boys burst in.

The company went from strength to strength after the Second World War and was the biggest employer in Kilmarnock. There are so many individual stories to tell of its dedicated and highly skilled workforce: among them, pattern-makers, moulders, turners and fitters. One that seems to epitomise Glenfield and Kennedy is that of Gilbert 'Gibby' McWilliam who, in 1914, joined the company straight from school in Irvine aged fourteen. 'Gibby' started as an

The finished product: valves ready for market.

apprentice moulder on the princely sum of 6s. per week. In 1961 he was still there and able proudly to reminisce about the many important jobs he had worked on: sluices for docks in Southampton and Calcutta; huge irrigation schemes in Africa; micro-sluicers for the USA and Japan. He was pleased about one change over the years – the ending of Saturday working meant he was able to get to his beloved Rugby Park on match days. 'Gibby', like many of the workers at the 'Glen', was a highly respected member of the wider community. He lived in Langside Avenue and attended Shortlees Church with his wife Catherine, where he was Session Clerk and an elder.

It seemed that Glenfield and Kennedy would continue to prosper and that men like Gilbert McWilliam would always have a trade to earn them a living. In 1961 the company opened a new hydraulics laboratory at a cost of over £100,000. It was the biggest and most advanced in Europe. More major investment followed. In 1968, a new automatic moulding-plant, capable of producing 150 moulds an hour, was installed at a cost of £750,000. With investment on this scale, what could possibly go wrong?

However, by the end of the 1960s things began to go awry as both profits and orders slipped. The 1970s were of course times of great economic difficulty for countries all over the world and, although now part of an American concern, Crane (UK) Ltd, the writing was clearly on the wall. In June 1977, just before the start of the Kilmarnock Fair, came the shattering news – the owners did not have the money available to sustain the losses being incurred and the works would have to close. A receiver was appointed and redundancy notices were sent out to the workforce, which then numbered 1,072. But the workers did not take the news lying down. Led by the formidable convener of shop stewards, Ian McLaughland, they did everything in their power to keep the plant open. Help was sought from the local Member of Parliament, Willie Ross, and from the government. The workforce was trimmed to 400 and the receiver acted to ensure that existing orders were met. By December a buyer was found: the Neptune International Corporation of America. Since then the business has gone through various changes of ownership including a period as part of Biwater Valves Ltd.

TWELVE

MARK OF THE POST

KILMARNOCK WAS ONE OF the first Post Towns in Scotland, not because it was a place of any importance but due to the fact that, in 1662, it was a convenient stop on the route from Edinburgh to Port-patrick and on to Ireland. The other stops on the route were at Linlithgow, Kilsyth, Glasgow, then Kilmarnock, and on to Dumboag, Ballantrae and Portpatrick. (I have been unable to discover the location of Dumboag. It was probably an isolated farmhouse or country mansion.)

At first the mail was brought through Kilmarnock once a week, but towards the end of the seventeenth century, an expansion in commerce and in literacy created the need for an efficient and secure mail service. Therefore, by the start of the eighteenth century, the service coming through Kilmarnock was increased to three times a week.

The location of the earliest post office in Kilmarnock is unknown. It would have been in the place of business or even the house of the postmaster, who only conducted postal business as a sideline. It was situated at the Cross from at least 1750 when the postmaster was John Fairlie, a hardware dealer. He was postmaster until about 1780. When he died the business, including the position of postmistress, passed to his widow, Agnes. Their daughter, Jean, also seems to have assumed the position of postmistress, at least for a while. She married John Muir, a merchant who ran his grocery and wine business from the property at the Cross which was later known as the Portland Arms, but it is not known if Muir used the same building as his predecessor. This John Muir was related to Robert Muir, a friend and patron of Robert Burns. Muir was active in local civic affairs. He was a magistrate, town treasurer in 1788 and became a bailie in 1795.

Eventually Muir's business passed to William Rankin, but it is not clear whether this was an inheritance through family connections or a simple business sale. In either case, when Rankin took over the wine and spirit business, he also took over the postal contracts, and he and his son would retain them well into the nineteenth century.

In 1787 the Town Council successfully persuaded the Post Office to send the Carlisle to Glasgow mail coach through Annan, Dumfries, Sanquhar and Kilmarnock instead of the route that encompasses Lockerbie, Moffat, Douglass Mill and so on. The revenue from the postal service in Kilmarnock in the 1790s was about £400 per annum and this included the neighbouring parishes that were served from the Kilmarnock office. By that time, the Glasgow to Ayr mailcoach passed through Kilmarnock and, by the end of the eighteenth century, there was a daily service on that route and one between Ayr and Edinburgh.

Postage rates were fixed according to the number of sheets, and the distance a letter was to be carried. Postage, however, was seen as a form of tax and levels were fixed in accordance with the need for revenue and not in line with the cost of mail services. At the time of the Napoleonic Wars in the first fifteen years of the new century, postal rates were increased sharply. By 1814 the cheapest letter was 7d. and by 1839 a letter from Kilmarnock to London cost 1s. 3d. Seven old pennies was almost three pence in today's money, and 1s. 3d. was little more than six pence, but this was a day's pay for a miner.

Perhaps inevitably, the existence of a regular mail service proved irresistible to the criminal fraternity, and at least one attempt at robbing the local mail resulted in a hanging. In 1814 Robert Gibson, a miner from Kilmarnock, intercepted the foot-post between Kilmarnock and Tarbolton, robbing the postman of his letters, including £30 in cash. The robber's accomplice was a James McCormack and he gave enough evidence to ensure that Gibson was executed.

In 1820 the country was in turmoil. Demands for the reform of an unfair and undemocratic political system reached fever pitch, but so too did the resistance of the ruling classes. Rebellion was in the air and Kilmarnock folk were at the forefront of it. The date for armed revolution was fixed as Saturday 1 April 1820, and posters announcing this were even displayed around the town. No one was sure if the whole thing was a serious attempt to force change or some bizarre April Fool's Day joke. But preparations were made and arms were stashed. Other towns were in a similar state and in Kilmarnock the signal that the rebellion had started was to be the non-arrival of the mail coach. However, on the morning of 1 April, the mail arrived on time, much to the relief of many.

For most of the nineteenth century there were only two postmasters in Kilmarnock. They were father and son, William, and later David, Rankin. William Rankin was the postmaster who followed John Muir. He also carried on Muir's grocery and wine business. Mr Rankin moved his business and the post office to Market Lane in 1834, but it was only there for a few years. The major changes that came about in 1840 meant another move was required and Rankin took property on the north corner of the junction of King Street and Queen Street. When the office was moved from Market Lane to the Queen Street corner, there came another significant development. For the first time, the office was managed by staff who had no connection with other businesses.

David Rankin was also heavily involved in the local community. He was one of the key organisers of, and a singer at, the Burns Centenary celebrations in 1859. He was Captain of the 5th Company of Ayrshire Artillery from its inception in 1860. His local command was given up on his promotion to Major. He was also a keen bowler and a founder member of Portland Bowling Club and, in 1868, he became the president of the Kilmarnock Curling Club.

Postmarks were used long before stamps, as a means of checking when letters had gone through a town. With the introduction of stamps in 1840, postmark cancellations were introduced and many towns adopted a Maltese Cross. One used at Kilmarnock was unique to the town and is much sought after by collectors. In the 1850s post boxes started to appear and again Kilmarnock had an early one that was of unique design.

At just about the same time that postage stamps were introduced in 1840, Kirkpatrick Macmillan invented the bicycle. An anecdote about Pate, as he was known, and the driver of the Glasgow to Carlisle mail coach is told in an entertaining little book, *The Devil on Wheels* (1946). The author, Gordon Irving, relates how in June 1842, Macmillan, eager to show off his invention, cycled from Thornhill near Dumfries to Glasgow. While in the city he met an old pal, Jock Davidson, the driver of the mail coach and they laid bets on which was faster. They agreed on a race from Glasgow to Sanquhar.

So, off they went, and it was a close run thing all the way to Kilmarnock. But Macmillan did not have to stop to pick up passengers. By New Cumnock, Macmillan was a few miles ahead and he rode into Sanquhar an easy winner.

While the post office was at the corner of King Street and Queen Street, there were still only two delivery men. In its early days the Post Office was largely a letter carrying service, but the government also used it as a means of raising tax. Gradually the Post Office became responsible for functions other than just postal matters. In 1869 the telegraph services were nationalised and handed over to the Post Office. This involved the Glasgow & South Western Railway Company's telegraph which had operated at Kilmarnock station since 1855. It passed to the Post Office on 1 January 1870 when the telegraphic code KK was adopted. Telegram facilities were withdrawn in 1982.

After David Rankin's retirement in 1872, a Mr Dickie took the position of postmaster. Post Office work continued to increase through the introduction of postcards, invoice wrappers, and various other products and services. In 1877 the Post Office delivered 42,285 letters each week in Kilmarnock, justifying the establishment of a Crown Office in the town. In 1878, the post office moved into property at the corner of John Finnie Street and Bank Place and, the following year, William Bryson, an overseer from Inverness, was appointed as Kilmarnock's first full-time professional postmaster.

When the post office moved to the new premises in John Finnie Street, there were the postmaster, a chief clerk, eleven clerks, eight town postmen, four stampers, nine rural post-runners and five telegraph messengers, making thirty-nine in all. This was more than double the number of staff employed in the middle of the 1850s when the complement consisted of the postmaster, three clerks, four letter carriers, one messenger, six country runners and three mail gig operators. This greatly enhanced staff group was able to service a wider range of destinations: Hurlford, Galston and Newmilns; Mauchline and Cumnock; Irvine and on to Ardrossan.

In the 1870s all the mail leaving Glasgow for Ayrshire was sent at midnight in a one-horse gig, described as being broad at the bottom and very narrow at the top. At first the Post Office occupied only the ground floor of their new premises, but space was always at a premium. Before long, rooms upstairs were required, and as business continued to grow, more and more space was needed.

The Post Office is nothing without the men and women who provide the service and many of those who joined gave a long number of years to it. There were men like Robert Badger. He joined the staff at Kilmarnock as a boy in 1873. By 1881 he was a clerk, then chief clerk and by 1889 superintendent, all at Kilmarnock. He stayed in the town until 1909, serving under seven postmasters. He then moved to Castle Douglas as postmaster. When he left Kilmarnock, colleagues presented him with an inscribed coffee service.

Parcel post was started in August 1883 and postal orders in 1885 and, together, these new services produced a big increase in mail order business. By the time the present office was opened in 1907, the post office was delivering 112,353 letters a week in Kilmarnock and handling a further 16,330 a week for forwarding to other towns. At this time all mail in Kilmarnock was still being hand-stamped.

Mechanised stamping was introduced in 1912. Kilmarnock's first phone had been installed in 1880 at Johnnie Walker's whisky plant. In 1912, phone services were nationalised and became part of the Post Office, remaining so until the establishment of British Telecom in 1982.

The introduction of first and second class mail in 1967, and the consequent drive to reorganisation, meant that Kilmarnock sorting office became responsible for a wider area and mail from other towns, which once had their own stamping machines, came to Kilmarnock for sorting and stamping. The areas which gradually lost their own sorting work to Kilmarnock included Stewarton and Dunlop, the Irvine Valley towns, Irvine and Kilwinning, Mauchline, Ardrossan, Largs, Millport and even Arran, though a few items of local mail continue to be stamped in some of these places.

Then came postcodes. It took coders twenty months to devise the Ayrshire scheme of postcodes, which incorporated 205 postal areas and 10,000 codes from KA1 (central Kilmarnock) to KA30 (Largs). Coding was introduced in Ayrshire on 1 November 1971. The KA area includes Arran and the Cumbrae Islands, but excludes Skelmorlie. Postcodes are read by machines, such as those at Springburn in north Glasgow, where most Ayrshire mail now goes for sorting. It is at Springburn that the scale of the operation becomes obvious. Here 1,100 employees handle 3.5 million items of mail a day. Scanners check mail and read not only postcodes, but also whole addresses at the rate of 35,000 items per hour.

Despite the centralised nature of the service, much local mail is still sorted in Kilmarnock. In 2000, the Post Office announced its intention to move the sorting of local letters out of the cramped building behind the John Finnie Street office to custom-built sorting offices at Queen's Drive in Kilmarnock and at Galston. Both buildings were actually constructed but, by 2002, the Galston building had been sold on and doubt hung over the future of the Queen's Drive facility.

THIRTEEN

MAILSHOTS: THE BATTLE FOR THE BURNS STAMPS

ROBERT BURNS WAS BORN in 1759 and, as the bicentenary in 1959 drew near, many groups and individuals across Scotland began to consider how this important anniversary could be celebrated. The International Burns Federation, which has its headquarters in Kilmarnock, believed that the issue of a special postage stamp by the Post Office would be an appropriate commemoration. Accordingly, their conferences started talking about just such a stamp as early as 1954 and informal approaches were made to the Post Office.

Perhaps predictably, these tentative approaches got absolutely nowhere. Eventually, fed up with being fobbed off with replies showing a remarkable level of indifference, the Burns Federation went directly to the top of the tree. A formal request was penned to the Postmaster General – normally a Minister of cabinet rank, appointed by the Prime Minister, and based in London – in May 1957. The proposal was quite simple – a special stamp should be issued in January 1959 to honour the work and life of Scotland's national bard. The Federation even included artwork with suggested designs for the stamp.

In taking this step, the Federation set in motion a chain of events that would go on down through the years, and ultimately would help to change Britain's outdated and restrictive stamp issuing policy. It is not clear if the Postmaster General even responded to the formal suggestion for a Burns stamp, but the matter was far from dead. The idea was now firmly in the public domain and the people of Scotland loved it.

Kilmarnock, of course, is in the heart of Burns country. A measure of how important Burns is to Kilmarnock can be seen in the fact that the town has not one, but two, statues to the poet. In the Kay Park there is a statue of Burns set into the red sandstone monument and dedicated to his immortal memory. And, at the Cross, the very heart of the town, there is a monument both to Robert Burns and to John Wilson – the man whose many achievements include first setting the young poet's works in *guid black prent*.

Burns, of course, was not born in Kilmarnock. He did not live, or work, or die in Kilmarnock. And yet Kilmarnock was a very important part of his life. As a farmer, he turned to Kilmarnock to buy seed and materials and, on market days, he often came into

Kilmarnock to sell his produce. As a poet he looked to Kilmarnock for a printer to publish his work in book form. In Kilmarnock he found friends, and often inspiration for some of his great works. Burns is as much a part of Kilmarnock history as any other local hero. Kilmarnock is also home to the International Burns Federation.

And so with the town so deeply involved in the Burns story, the *Kilmarnock Standard* took an interest in the proposal that the country should honour the two-hundredth anniversary of his birth with a special stamp.

It should not really have been a major debating point but, in the 1950s, Britain was very reluctant to issue special stamps. The policy was that only subjects relating to the royal family or important current events, such as the Olympic Games, could be featured. In 1953 four stamps were issued to mark the coronation of Queen Elizabeth (the first of the United Kingdom, the second of England). There were no more special stamps until 1957 when three were produced to mark the World Scout Jamboree. In the same year, one special stamp was issued to commemorate the Parliamentary Union Congress.

It seemed that Burns didn't stand a chance, but the Burns Federation was determined and the *Kilmarnock Standard* was enthusiastic in its support. In the 1950s, the *Kilmarnock Standard* was considered to be a serious, heavyweight newspaper. It did carry influence and it also published a weekly leader on matters of local or national importance. A leader was published on 21 September 1957 asking the pertinent question, 'Why not a Burns Stamp?' It outlined a highly convincing case for such a stamp, noting that the poet had already been honoured on the postage stamps of the Soviet Union.

The Burns Federation moved its campaign up a gear in November 1957 by writing to all Members of Parliament and, for good measure, they enclosed a copy of the *Kilmarnock Standard* leader along with a batch of other material. Other mailshots followed, all aimed at persuading MPs to put pressure on the government to force the issue – in more senses than one. The Postmaster General, a member of the then Conservative government, announced his decision to the House of Commons. He made it clear to Parliament, the nation and those advocating a Burns stamp that the Government's view was that the Post Office could not possibly issue a stamp for a person they described as a 'mere poet'.

The insult infuriated many people not only in Scotland, but also in many other countries. Just a few years before, nationalist groups in Scotland had defeated the Post Office over the use of the EIIR cipher on post boxes – today Scotland uses a crown. Still the matter was kept alive. Questions were asked in the House of Commons. Letters were sent to influential people. The Prime Minister became involved, but still the answer was the same. No stamp would be issued for a commoner. The official verdict was eventually accepted with good grace by some. Others, however, decided to take matters into their own hands and print their own Burns commemorative labels as a means of letting the Post Office know how they felt.

As the anniversary drew closer, some people suggested that if a special stamp could not be produced, then at least a special postmark could be used at Alloway on the date of the anniversary, but once again the Post Office procrastinated. A number of possible designs were produced, but the Post Office rejected them because they included a portrait of Burns. The basis for the refusal was that the representation of a commoner could not be allowed to obliterate the portrait of the Queen on stamps. There were also arguments about who should pay for a special postmark. The Post Office made clear it would not meet the cost. When the two-hundredth anniversary came around, the dispute had not been solved, but something remarkable happened in Alloway. Although 25 January 1959 fell on a Sunday, the little post office at Alloway was opened and eight men and the postmistress stamped no less than 27,000 items by hand!

The Post Office should have realised at once that, if 27,000 people wanted a standard postmark from Alloway on the date of the anniversary, there was a clear demand for something more. But there was still strong official opposition to commemorating mere poets, commoners and other lesser mortals and, as far as the Post Office was concerned, the anniversary was over and that was the end of the whole silly idea.

However, it was not quite the end of the matter. In 1964, not long after the complete rejection of the very concept of issuing a stamp for 'a mere poet', the Post Office announced that it would issue an unprecedented five stamps and other commemorative material for William Shakespeare. The designs even incorporated Shakespeare's portrait. Had Shakespeare suddenly been made an honorary member of the royal family?

Asked about the apparent contradictions between the attitude to Burns and to Shakespeare, the Post Office came up with two very spurious answers. In the first place, it was argued, the stamps planned for Shakespeare did not commemorate the man or his work, but the Shakespeare Festival, a major international event. And, secondly, the portrait was not a portrait at all but merely a symbol that looked nothing like Shakespeare. The mounting anger in Scotland was quickly followed by action. New stamp-like labels were printed with a portrait of Burns and people were urged to use them alongside the Shakespeare stamps, in breach of Post Office regulations. Some used them instead of official stamps and people were also asked to boycott the Shakespeare stamps. This was now a very hot political potato.

And then, in 1964, there was a general election and a change of Government. The new Postmaster General was Anthony Wedgewood-Benn, better known today as the maverick left-winger Tony Benn. He was immediately lobbied by the pro-Burns groups, who made clear their strong feeling that the whole of Scotland had been treated unfairly. To their surprise, the new Postmaster General agreed. Within a few weeks of taking office he announced that Britain would honour Burns with the production of two stamps in January 1966. This marked no particular anniversary, but was belated recognition for the man who was, without doubt, Scotland's greatest writer. The announcement marked the end of a very restrictive stamp-issuing policy by the British Post Office.

When the time came, the two stamps were generally accepted as being fine designs. The lower value stamp had a portrait of Burns with the Saltire in the background. The higher value stamp had a different portrait of Burns, with his signature in the background. Both stamps, of course, also had a portrait of the Queen. In addition to the stamps, there were eight special postmarks used on the first day of issue at Ayr, Alloway, Kilmarnock, Mauchline, Dumfries, Edinburgh, Glasgow and Greenock.

There came another important change. The Post Office was starting to realise the value of dealing with collectors through a Philatelic Bureau. The new Bureau had been set up in London, but to cope with the expected demand for Burns stamps, it was temporarily moved to Edinburgh. This was so successful that the Bureau was soon transferred to Edinburgh on a permanent basis. It is still there.

Several other items were produced over the years both by the Post Office and private concerns. A special Burns air-letter sheet was produced by the Post Office in 1975 and, in 1986, the two-hundredth anniversary of the printing of the Kilmarnock Edition was commemorated by the *Kilmarnock Standard*, the newspaper that had advocated the production of Burns stamps in the first place. The *Standard's* commemoration was in the form of a special cover with

It was quite a struggle to get the Burns stamps, but well worth the effort.

a pictorial hand-stamp showing the chair that was made out of the wooden parts of the old Wilson printing press.

When the two-hundredth anniversary of the death of Robert Burns in 1996 came around, there was really no doubt that the Post Office would mark the event. By this time they were aggressively marketing stamps, postcards, postmarks and all manner of other material. The Post Office was producing stamps showing anyone and everyone they could think of, including cartoon characters, and the representation of the Queen on British stamps had been reduced from a portrait to a small, almost unrecognisable silhouette.

Four stamps were issued to mark the two-hundredth anniversary of the death of Burns. The 19p stamp incorporated the opening line of 'To a Mouse' and the design was based on the actual type used in the Kilmarnock Edition. The 20p had an extract with the words, 'O, my Luve's Like a Red, Red Rose'. The forty-one pence stamp had the words 'Scots, Wha hae Wi' Wallace Bled', and included a portrait of Wallace from a window in the Wallace Monument in Stirling. Finally, the 60p had the words 'Should Auld Acquaintance Be Forgot', now the international anthem of parting. The new stamps went on sale with first day covers, postcards of the stamps, a presentation pack and a series of new commemorative postmarks.

From the two-hundredth anniversary of the poet's birth to the two-hundredth anniversary of his untimely death, there had been a sea change in the policies of the Post Office. Thanks to the sterling efforts of people in Scotland, and in particular Kilmarnock, it had changed its whole attitude from one of dismissive indifference to one of great enthusiasm. For its part, the Philatelic Bureau, which had been relocated to Edinburgh following the success of the Burns stamps of 1966, produced a souvenir booklet, recounting the story of Burns stamps, including those of the USSR and Romania. But it chose to ignore the intense battle that had gone on in the 1950s over the Burns stamps.

FOURTEEN

WHEN TRAINING BEAT COACHING

MANY CLAIMS ARE MADE about the date of the first regular railway-passenger-service. Kilmarnock folk have long known that the honour goes to the Kilmarnock and Troon Railway, which had a passenger timetable as early as the summer of 1812.

But the story really starts in 1796, when a new landowner appeared on the scene in Kilmarnock. He was William Henry Cavendish Bentinck, Marquis of Titchfield and later the fourth Duke of Portland, a powerful man with powerful connections. Indeed, his father was Prime Minister when the railway was being built.

William Bentinck acquired the lands around Kilmarnock when he married Henrietta Scott in 1796. He wasted no time in exploiting the rich coal deposits of the area. The biggest problem was transporting the coal from Kilmarnock to the coast, for much of it went to Ireland. At the end of the eighteenth century, coal from Kilmarnock was taken by road to Irvine for export to the Emerald Isle. In those days the roads were poor. Transport was slow and sometimes, in bad weather, highways were almost impassable. The only practical alternative was a canal.

Bentinck owned land at Troon and was eager to build a canal from Kilmarnock to Troon. He had a company called Flint and Dickens survey the land to find out not just the best route, but also the most effective method of transporting coal. The instruction to Flint and Dickens advised them to establish the best means of 'providing the least expensive conveyance of the coal to the sea by railway, other land carriage or by canal navigation'. Building a railway was an out-side possibility even at this stage.

Railways had already been built in Scotland, but nothing on such a grand scale as the distance between Kilmarnock and Troon. Most of the earlier railways, or waggonways, were built at colliery pit-heads and ran for just a short distance. But it didn't matter much, not at first, anyway. The survey seems to have backed the idea of a canal and a plan was drawn up. Because it traversed land owned by more than one person, it went to the government in London for consideration. The proposal was to build a canal that was forty feet wide at the sur-face, twenty-four feet wide at the bottom and five feet deep. It was suggested that water could come from the moors above Kilmarnock. The total cost of construction was estimated at nearly £37,000.

It is not clear why the canal Bill was never passed, nor why it was replaced by even more ambitious plans to build a railway. A company was formed and an Act of Parliament obtained – two Acts, in fact, because a second Act was approved for the creation of a harbour at Troon. It was the first Act of Parliament that facilitated the construction of a railway in Scotland. However, the proprietors had no thoughts of passengers at that time, and no mention of carrying passengers was contained in the Act.

The construction of the railway posed several technical problems. Spanning the River Irvine at Gatehead required a bridge of four arches – the world's first railway viaduct. After nearly 150 years of neglect the bridge was restored in 1996 and plaques were mounted explaining its historic significance. Shewalton Moss proved another tricky area, but the engineer was William Jessop, one of the finest of his day and he solved all the problems the project threw up. For four years between 1808 and 1812, the good people of Kilmarnock watched with interest as work progressed. It was a major undertaking, one of the most ambitious engineering projects of the day.

Not long before the construction was completed, the railway proprietors were approached by a William Paterson, an ambitious businessman from Kilmarnock. He wanted to run a passenger service on the railway. They approved the plan. By June of 1812 Mr Paterson was ready, although the railway was not. The terminus at the offices of Kilmarnock House had yet to be completed. But it was agreed that the passenger service could start at Gargieston, two miles from Kilmarnock and run from there until the Kilmarnock end was completed. Mr Paterson agreed to take people and their goods from the town to Gargieston and so, on 25 June 1812, the *Ayr Advertiser* carried an advert announcing the start of the service 'to carry Passengers and Goods from KILMARNOCK to TROON upon the iron Railway'.

The first trip was not a big event. No fanfare, no celebrations, perhaps because the coaches were pulled by horses and not a steam engine. In many ways, it was simply the start of a new coach service. Nevertheless, when the whip cracked and the horses pulled the Caledonia away, a new era in public transport was born. It was 27 June 1812 and the passengers making their way from Kilmarnock to Troon didn't know they were making history, and probably didn't care. But what happened that morning was the beginning of something new, something very special. The journey marked the start of regular railway passenger services in Scotland. It was a good service.

It ran three times a week and the run was smooth and reasonably swift. All things considered, the fare of one shilling (five pence) wasn't too bad.

The driver's name was Willie Wight, sometimes referred to as Willie Wright. He was the first driver of a passenger train in Scotland, though he drove horses, not an engine. He must have made a bob or two at this service, because he later purchased it.

The passenger traffic that first summer proved that there was a demand for people to travel on railways and that the service was economically viable. So the following summer it ran again, following the same pattern as before. Three return trips were made each week, on Tuesdays, Thursdays and Saturdays. In this second year the service was extended into spring and late summer. The Caledonia carried goods as well as passengers and it left Kilmarnock at 9.15 a.m. The return journey started from Troon at 6 p.m. It doesn't seem much by today's standards, but the services were adequate for the time.

Troon in the early nineteenth century was a scattered community. Certainly, the harbour was becoming a busy place and people wanted a jaunt to the coast, but there were still few houses. However, the Duke of Portland had ambitious plans for Troon that not only included the harbour and railway, but also a whole new town.

Fares were adjusted too. In 1813, a day return for an inside passenger was two and sixpence. A single journey was one and sixpence. Outside passengers paid one and sixpence and one shilling. Tickets were sold by William Patterson in Kilmarnock, and by a Mr Thomson in Troon. A claim has been made that the Kilmarnock and Troon Railway was the first railway ever to have a booking office.

One feature of the journey was a stop at Drybridge, where both men and horses were refreshed. Because of this stop, and with the horses jogging along at seven miles an hour, the journey took between one and a half and two hours. The original Kilmarnock terminus was at the offices of Kilmarnock House, but the exact location is unclear. It was probably on a site that later became the Bank Street Police Station and is now a car park. This terminus was moved down the line in 1821 to allow developments on the Duke's land. As a general rule, the passengers in those very early days did not go all the way into the Troon terminus at the harbour. Instead they preferred to disembark at Johnnie Hay's pub, the Bottle and Glass. It was an easy walk from there down through the fields to the sea.

Other people soon realised that running a passenger service on the railway could be profitable and asked the Kilmarnock and Troon

Railway Company for permission to run a service on its line. One such venture was known as The Boat, and was no more than an open truck. According to the minutes of the Kilmarnock and Troon Railway, a Mrs Jean Brown of Troon was given permission in 1830 to run a jaunting car on the line. At the same time Willie Wight was allowed to run an additional vehicle.

*

It is strange that the achievements associated with this line, such as the first scheduled passenger service and the first railway viaduct, have been ignored, even by serious railway historians. There was another important achievement on the line. While the early traffic was horse-drawn, the Kilmarnock–Troon line saw the first use of a steam locomotive in Scotland. Steam engines were used in Ayrshire at the time the railway was built. But at the start of the nineteenth century a steam engine really meant a stationary engine.

It is something of a mystery that so little is known about that first steam locomotive in Scotland. Some reports say it had four wheels; some that it had six. No one is certain when it was used. Some reports state that it was only ever used on unsuccessful trials, while other accounts say it worked for more than twenty years. Indeed, there are tantalising hints that more than one steam locomotive was used on the Kilmarnock and Troon Railway.

The truth is difficult to determine. Official records of the company hardly help. Nowhere is there a clear record saying that a steam locomotive was purchased and tried on the line. That is probably because the locomotive, or locomotives, would have been the property not of the railway company, but of the individuals who used the line.

But there are clues elsewhere and from them it seems almost certain that the first locomotive to work in Scotland was purchased by the Duke of Portland himself early in 1816. It was a six-wheeled vehicle and patents for it were taken out by Losh and Stephenson in 1817. Scaled patent drawings show a vehicle designed for a gauge of four feet – the gauge of the Kilmarnock and Troon Railway. This was the era before a national standard gauge was introduced.

The Duke had long been interested in the new steam technology. In the summer of 1812 he bought a small steam engine from William Jessop. This was almost certainly a stationary steam engine. But in the spring of 1813, the Duke was studying reports from William Jessop on the performance of 'a steam engine for drawing coals on the Iron Railway'. Jessop's letter referred to one in operation at Leeds.

It is odd that that such a momentous event as the first steam loco-motive did not attract the attention of the press. It does not seem to have been recorded in the records of the Kilmarnock and Troon Railway Company, nor in the personal papers of the Duke of Portland himself. Evidence backing the claim for the use of the loco-motive in 1816 is largely circumstantial. The sole eyewitness account of the first trial comes from Kilmarnock artist, John Kelso Hunter, who penned his colourful account many years after the event. Although he gives a very graphic description, many of the details have been consistently dismissed by certain railway historians, including the claim that the trial of the locomotive was early in 1816. But there is other evidence. In February 1816 the company paid £2 5s. for lodgings at Old Rome. Could this have been for George Stephenson, the great engineer and inventor, who it is said travelled to Kilmarnock to assemble the engine?

There are other relevant facts. Starting in July 1816, the company was buying a substantial number of replacement rails from the Kilmarnock Foundry. Payments went on for eighteen months. Was this to replace the ones broken by the 'horse that eats coal instead of oats'? Furthermore, on 1 March 1816, a landowner named James Jack intimated a claim for damages against the railway, although details are not given in the company letter book. But, at a meeting on 16 October 1821, the company again considered a claim for compensation from Jack who said that his fields had been set on fire by the cinders from 'a steam engine waggon going along the line'. Could this have related to the same incident?

The meeting refused to meet the claim, as any compensation was the responsibility of the owner of the vehicle. The use of the indefinite article may or may not be significant. It is also curious that the matter was referred to the owner of the locomotive and not to the Duke of Portland, who was at the meeting.

FIFTEEN

TRANSPORTS OF DELIGHT: KILMARNOCK'S TRAMS

THEY SHOOGLED, THEY RATTLED and if you were a passenger on the upper deck, you were exposed to wind, rain and anything else the Kilmarnock weather could throw at you. The Kilmarnock tram system was a small one – just over four miles of track and only fourteen cars. It was short-lived, lasting only from 1904 to 1926, and was never much of a financial success. To add to its problems, the system was often something of a political football. Yet despite these many difficulties, there was something magical about the old green cars.

One of the earliest suggestions that Kilmarnock should adopt a 'street tramway' came in a letter published in the *Kilmarnock Standard* in June 1887, signed simply 'A Native'. The letter proposed there should be a tram system laid from the railway station, stretching along West George Street, Portland Street, King Street and down to Riccarton Bridge, with a branch at the Cross going along Duke Street and London Road as far as the old toll. The letter also suggested a branch line for St Marnock Street, going as far as the railway bridge.

The response was less than enthusiastic and nothing happened for several years. However, as time passed, a growing number of people felt it was a good idea. The proposal was not without its critics and, as things turned out, the question of whether or not there should be a tram system was one of the most fiercely debated issues in the town's history. To further complicate the situation, many who supported the idea were opposed to the suggestion that the trams should be run by Kilmarnock Town Council.

In the end the debate hinged not on the transport needs of the town but on the needs of power – electric power. At the close of the nineteenth century Kilmarnock was the industrial hub of Ayrshire. Carpet making, whisky blending and bottling, and the making of boots and shoes were important, as were engineering and locomotive building. These industries needed a power station to generate electricity.

There was again an argument about private versus public service, but Kilmarnock Town Council already ran the gas works and there was a general feeling that the town could quite easily run an electric power-station as well. By 1898 the decision had already been taken to build a power station and, at the same time, the proposals for a tramway system were revived. British Electric Traction was first off the mark with a proposal to run tram services to Hurlford, Beansburn and Riccarton in return for one-third of the annual revenue.

However, Kilmarnock's elected representatives rejected the proposal. They wanted the prestige of running their own tram system, despite a detailed report that questioned the financial wisdom of having one at all. Opposition to a council-run scheme mounted, on the grounds that the financial risk of the enterprise should be borne by private companies and not by the ratepayers. It became a hot election issue. A local referendum was held in January 1903. The referendum attracted a highly respectable turnout of more than seventy per cent. The vote was apparently clear. Only a fifth of ratepayers supported the municipal scheme. But politics is politics. The question had been ambiguous and the town councillors decided that the people of Kilmarnock had approved their scheme.

The wheels, as it were, were set in motion. People quickly accepted that, like it or not, the system was to go ahead. Better make the most of it. In Hurlford and Crookedholm, the opinion was to press for inclusion. They won their case. But a proposal that the initial scheme should be extended through the Irvine Valley to Darvel was not. A similar proposal from Irvine that the trams should run through Crosshouse, Springside, Dreghorn and into Irvine, was also rejected. Had the two extensions gone ahead, it would have meant an impressive North Ayrshire scheme stretching nearly twenty miles from Irvine to Darvel.

Soon just about every councillor was suggesting that the trams should run through their ward. The Vigilance Committee, which represented ratepayers, made a last-ditch attempt to stop the scheme at a public inquiry but the momentum in favour had built up. The carrot was that neither a tram scheme nor an electric power scheme seemed viable on its own; but together they would be of benefit. Kilmarnock could get a transport system, electric power for lighting and a whole range of other things that clever folks were thinking up. The dual power and tram system was subsequently approved, and an Act of Parliament allowing the scheme to go ahead was passed in 1904.

Apart from the obvious need to lay track and install overhead wires, there was much other work to be done. The bridge over the River Irvine at Hurlford had to be widened, some roads had to be resurfaced and some needed lighting – powered not by gas, but by electricity. A tram depot was required and it was built near the new power station at Greenholm Street. And, of course, the cars had to be bought.

The Kilmarnock system was based largely on the one already in existence at Kirkcaldy. Professor Alexander Kennedy was the consulting engineer for the tram systems in both towns. The main difference was that Kilmarnock adopted a standard gauge of 4 ft 8½ in. An initial batch of eleven open-topped cars was ordered in July 1904 from Hurst, Nelson & Co. of Motherwell, each capable of accommodating about fifty passengers. They cost £520 each. In March 1905, three more cars were ordered from the same Motherwell company. One was open-topped like the others, but two were closed.

The cars were painted green. One oddity is that many old colour postcards show them as maroon. The reason is that the pictures were taken in black and white and artificially coloured. It seems that many of the artists who did this work were based in Edinburgh. What colour should a tram be? If they looked out of the window they saw maroon trams. Hence Kilmarnock trams on colourised postcards became maroon instead of green.

Track-laying work began in June 1904 and, by the end of the summer and the onset of autumn, overhead cables had been put in place along with new electric lamp standards for street lighting. In the first week of November 1904, the lamps were turned on and at night Kilmarnock folk saw their town in a new light – literally.

After a final inspection to approve the scheme, the new green tramcars, emblazoned with the town's coat of arms, were rolled out. The first one was driven with full ceremonial honours by Lord Howard de Walden on Saturday 10 December 1904. The tram was taken from the sheds at Holmquarry Road, up Low Glencairn Street and paused briefly at Glencairn Square for a photo-call; just two hours later the picture was in the window of the offices of the *Kilmarnock Standard*. The car was driven on through King Street and Portland Street and on to Beansburn, where house building had been going on, on the strength of the coming of a tram service. It was followed at two-minute intervals by four other cars. One of them had the Burgh Band on the top deck. This was something that would be repeated for other events in the future.

By the evening a limited service was in operation. There was initial enthusiasm for this swift, cheap and reliable mode of transport; after all, there were few alternatives other than walking. At first things looked so good that more double track was laid to improve the service and extra cars were ordered from Hurst, Nelson & Co. In the first

A 'shoogly' in action. Tram no 6 in Duke Street, heading towards Hurlford.

partial year of operation, from December 1904 to May 1905, the system carried more than 900,000 passengers and made a profit of £86. But it was the only time the system was profitable.

Special arrangements were made with some of the town's largest employers, such as Glenfield and Kennedy, and workers-only trams were in operation at peak times. The town was very proud of its new asset and, when the trams started to get dirty, the members of the Streets Committee were instructed to keep the roads on the tram routes cleaner than the other roads.

Soon the tram cars were just part of the scenery and they gradually faded from the news, until the events of Saturday, 27 July 1907 – the darkest day in the history of Kilmarnock's tram system. It was the start of the Grozet Fair and Kilmarnock was in holiday mood. About 8 p.m., five-year-old William Rowland, the son of a lace weaver from Fore Street, had been to the shows. He was hanging on to the back of a lorry in High Glencairn Street near the junction with James Little Street. He jumped off, straight into the path of a tram travelling to Riccarton. The *Kilmarnock Standard* reported that the boy was killed instantly and was 'literally cut to pieces'. It was the first fatal accident involving the Kilmarnock trams.

Incredibly, less than three hours later there was a second fatal accident. It happened on the road to Hurlford. John Campbell, a miner from Galston, stumbled, was hit by a car and knocked down. He was taken to Kilmarnock Infirmary where his injuries were said not to be serious. But he suddenly became very ill and died the following afternoon as a result of cerebral haemorrhage.

By this time the system was in financial trouble. More than two million passengers were carried in the year to 15 May 1906, but it still lost money. Over the years, although the passenger numbers rose to about 2.3 or 2.4 million, and peaked at 3.1 million in 1919, losses continued to mount. Proposed improvements and short extensions were cancelled. The fare structure was reviewed but other difficulties beset the system. To add to the financial woes, subsidence caused by old mine workings resulted in frequent track repairs in places such as London Road and Dean Terrace.

The First World War caused more problems, particularly as many men left to go to the front. The town took on its first eight female conductors, but they had a struggle to get equal wages. There were blackout regulations, even in the First World War, and in the darker streets accidents became more frequent. The track condition continued to deteriorate and motor vehicles became more numerous. Services began to be curtailed as competition from motor buses intensified. By 1925 the system was in serious trouble and, in January 1926, the Tramways Committee decided to close what remained of it. This would have required the authority of Parliament, just as it had done to start the system, but as things turned out the 'shooglies' closed a little earlier than expected. Tram workers joined the 1926 General Strike and the Town Council took the opportunity of closing the system in May of that year.

By then Kilmarnock Corporation was already operating some motor buses on the basis that they were more flexible, and Kilmarnock was one of the first towns to abandon its tram system. It is ironic then that so many towns and cities across Europe and elsewhere are again looking at trams as the best and most environmentally friendly system of mass transport. And it could just be that one of the businesses that will benefit from the boom is Hunslet-Barclay of Kilmarnock, which has a fine track-record in the business.

SIXTEEN

UNDER THE WEATHER

WEATHER HAPPENS ALL AROUND US. Despite our many impressive advances in science and technology, it is a subject that constantly reminds us that nature is still full of surprises. It's not surprising, then, that it is one of our favourite topics of conversation. Ours is probably the first generation to really understand the weather, but it wasn't until the dawn of the space age that weather forecasting moved from being an art to a precise science.

In the early years of the twentieth century James Kilmurray from Kilmarnock was a man with a reputation as a 'weather prophet'. This was long before it was either fashionable or, indeed, scientifically possible to predict weather patterns with any degree of accuracy. Kilmurray was born in the middle of the nineteenth century, but little is known of his early years. His first job was as a miner, and he became fascinated by the different atmospheres that he found in the coal pits. Later he studied the atmospheres above ground, and began to make predictions about the weather. His views were well respected and many folk who were planning events consulted him. His forecasts – or predictions as they were then called – were used in the Glasgow *Evening Times*. The editor preferred Kilmurray's forecasts to weather information from any other source.

Indeed, Kilmurray's reputation in Kilmarnock was so great that the Town Council gave him the free lease of the old astronomical observatory in Morton Place. This seventy-foot tower had been built 100 years before in 1818. It was ideal for astronomy . . . and weather forecasting.

While Mr Kilmurray might well have been able to forecast general trends in his time, some freaks of nature could not be predicted. For example, enormous hailstones fell on the farms of Artnock, Meadowhead, Greenhill and Tayburn near Waterside and Fenwick on 7 August 1856. Many of them were 3½ inches in circumference. They broke panes of glass and went down through cabbage stalks like bullets. The summer had been uncommonly cold and wet up until 30 July, when it changed to a fiery heat, which continued till 9 August.

It is rare to get a tornado in Scotland, but one hit Kilmaurs on the morning of 4 January 2000. There was a tremendous single flash of lightning and a terrific clatter of thunder, followed by an unusually heavy shower of hailstones, though this appears to have been restricted to a small area. Some areas lost electric power for a short time. The Meteorological Office recorded that a mini-tornado had hit Kilmaurs at that time. There were no reports of serious structural damage, but the roof of a farm shed was blown off. The tornado was restricted to a small area near the village, but radio and television reported that Kilmarnock had been hit by a tornado, something that surprised those in the town who heard the reports. After such news broadcasts, many people from across Scotland and beyond phoned friends and relatives in Kilmarnock to make sure that they were safe.

Storm force winds happen more often than we realise, but it's only when there is serious damage that we take much notice of them. The most severe storms to hit Kilmarnock appear to have been those of 1879, 1911 and 1968. Of course it wasn't just the Kilmarnock area that suffered.

The great storm of 1879 claimed the Tay Bridge. In Kilmarnock there was extensive damage and at least one casualty. On the afternoon of 28 December 1879, the Reverend William Bathgate of Winton Place Church, preached with his usual inspirational power. A few hours later he breathed his last, having been blown over and fatally injured by the great gale. Another victim of the same storm was Archibald McKay, best known as the author of *The History of Kilmarnock*. He was blown down by the violence of the wind while walking in the street, and sustained such severe shock and injuries that he never completely recovered. He died in his little house at the head of Titchfield Street on 14 April 1883, aged 81.

The gale of Sunday 5 November 1911 was, at the time, deemed comparable with that of 1879. Trees in Dundonald Road, London Road and Dick Road came crashing down; palings and fences were flattened; chimney cans, slates, ridging, whole chimney heads and some entire gables were sent flying. Hen houses and light sheds whirled over fields. Those who worshipped in Henderson Church in London Road could not come out by the main door as the danger from flying slates was too great. Two hundred trees were blown over at Coodham and, all over Scotland, tens of thousands of trees were uprooted.

The January gale of 1968 claimed twenty-one lives across the south-west of Scotland. In Kilmarnock, forty people had to leave their homes because of the danger of damage to buildings. Roofs were blown off buildings, houses under construction at New Farm Loch were damaged and a hutted classroom at James Hamilton High School had the roof torn off and scattered across the school playground. Fortunately the storm was at night.

More recently, in 1986, what was described as a hurricane smashed a new Scout hall in Grassyards Road and caused damage to other buildings and garden sheds. One victim was the town's 'bubble' sports centre housed in an inflatable building. The storm literally burst the bubble.

*

Harsh winters are often reported. The winter of 1740 was particularly severe and the Cross was flooded to make an artificial curling pond. The weather was so cold that the game was played for twenty-three successive days – except on Sundays, of course.

With winter comes snow which, in Ayrshire, is rarely of great severity. However the snowstorm of 1827 went down in the annals of the county as exceptional. It started to snow at about nine o'clock on the morning of Saturday 3 March. No one had an inkling that this would be a remarkable snowstorm, and people went about their daily business. It continued to snow all day and all night. Then strong winds started to whip up the snow into deep drifts.

At that time, of course, the only conveyances on the roads were horse-drawn coaches, and they were seriously affected. The Ayr Telegraph coach had passed through Kilmarnock on its way to Glasgow, but despite the efforts of six horses it became stuck between Laigh Fenwick and High Fenwick. On the same route the coach from Glasgow to Ayr became stuck near Drumboy Hill, and another coach had to stop at Logan's Well. The Glasgow to Kilmarnock coach had to stop at Mearns. A coach that had set off for England came to a halt at Mauchline.

But the most serious problems were faced by the Telegraph Coach from Glasgow. When it could go no further than Drumboy Hill, the guard joined the five passengers inside the coach, while the driver and three outside passengers decided to try to make their way to King's Well about a mile and a half away. This is close to where the Eaglesham turn-off is today. But they became separated. The driver eventually reached the inn at King's Well with some of the horses, but by the time he got there, the weather was so severe that no help could be given. At about midnight, two of the outside passengers, having wandered for six hours in a large circle, came across the coach, which at first they thought was a house. The third outside passenger was John Brown, a Kilmarnock shoemaker. He had become separated from the group, lost his way and died in the unprecedented snowstorm.

On the Sunday morning the weather cleared, but there was deep snow in all the streets. In some places the drifts were between twelve and twenty feet deep. Few people managed to get to church that morning and those who ventured out of their homes had to cut paths through the snow. The snow in many streets was so deep that it was up the eaves of the cottages.

Nothing quite like the 1827 storm has been repeated since. The most severe snowstorms in recent times were in January 1987 and February 2001. In 1987 roads were impassable, bus and train schedules were in chaos, children were sent home from school and the banks, offices, shops and factories advised workers not to come in. The snow started on Monday 12 January. One of the earliest routes affected was the A77 road to Glasgow. Early in the day, conditions on that road became treacherous as traffic slithered to a halt. In some cases it took buses five times their normal travel time to reach Glasgow.

It was a similar story in February 2001, when snow also blocked the railway line between Kilmarnock and Glasgow. A commuter train became stuck in a snowdrift and about 100 passengers spent nearly ten miserable hours waiting for rescue. Despite the advanced technology of the twentieth and twenty-first centuries, it seems we are still vulnerable to extremes in the weather.

The weather, of course, is something we are used to coping with in Scotland. But nature has other, more severe, tricks. Earthquakes demonstrate nature's awesome power but are not usually associated with Ayrshire. And yet, earthquakes have been felt in Kilmarnock. A powerful earthquake shook Kilmarnock in 1732 and was briefly recorded in the Laigh Kirk session minutes: 'Sabbath, 9 July 1732 – This day a sensible shock of ane earthquake was felt here, and several other places, a little before two in the afternoon.' On the eleventh of the same month, a shock was felt at Glasgow between two and three in the afternoon.

Tremors were also felt in the Kilmarnock area on January 27 1927, with the strongest effects being experienced at Newmilns. In December 1978, a tremor was felt in Glasgow and Kilmarnock. It shook buildings but there was no serious damage. More recently, on 4 March 1999, an earthquake of magnitude 4 on the Richter scale shook much of the west of Scotland. The epicentre was between three and four miles south of Arran.

Finally, some strange weather that could have been recorded in the X-Files chapter. Kilmarnock people witnessed something very odd during the last few days of July 1908. Each night as the sun went down, the darkness didn't come. At eleven o'clock at night, lights were not needed in houses, and at midnight people could read newspapers out of doors in the natural light. The *Kilmarnock Standard* of 4 July 1908 reported there had been a broad band of translucent pearly blue merging into a clear sky, in which was set the slim curve of a new moon. It soon became clear that this was no local incident. No one could explain it, and the odd event was recorded and left for others to investigate.

Then reports started coming in from Russia, telling of a huge fireball which had exploded in a remote part of Siberia with unimaginable force. The dates matched the odd weather seen here. With the benefit of modern scientific knowledge, it can be concluded that the explosion was almost certainly caused by the impact of a piece of a comet. There was so much dust in the sky and over such a wide area, that reflected sunlight turned night into day 6,000 miles away.

SEVENTEEN

DEVASTATION: THE DRY FLOOD

THE EMBERS OF THE bonfire were still glowing brightly, but the flames had died down and the people who had earlier formed a large crowd were drifting away from the Cross. Among those who had gathered that warm summer evening was a young man who now made his way back down King Street to his lodgings in Princes Street. We don't know his name, but forty years later when he recalled the events of the early hours of 14 July 1852, the *Kilmarnock Standard* referred to him as 'an old correspondent'. For the purposes of this narrative, we'll call him Andrew.

The bonfire had been lit because of the election, an election in which a good number of the men of the town were able to vote. It had been a hard fight to win this right to vote. It was a long way from the universal franchise that some had hoped for, but it was better than the time, twenty years before, when only one man in Kilmarnock could vote. In the election, the Honourable E. P. Bouverie received 558 votes and Mr J. A. Campbell only 302. And Mr Bouverie did seem to be just the right sort of person to represent the town in far-off London.

Andrew reached home and soon settled into a comfortable sleep. He was pleased that he had been at the celebration of this new age of democracy. Just after three in the morning, Andrew was snatched from sleep by the noise of a terrific thunderstorm. It was so loud, so close, that the building shook with each clap of thunder. He had never heard thunder as loud, and the flashes of lightning were so intense that they penetrated the blinds at the window and his closed eyes.

Between each of the claps of thunder there was an eerie silence, sometimes brief, but sometimes disturbingly long. Andrew expected to hear the rain battering down. He strained to hear it. But he heard nothing. It was as if the loudness of the thunder had dulled his ears. He looked out of the window. There was no rain. The commotion in the sky was very close; too close for comfort. It lasted for nearly an hour, but then it ended suddenly, leaving a silence that Andrew described as 'ominous and depressing'.

Andrew lay on his bed thinking about the unusual weather of the last few days. The heat had been oppressive and now this strange, powerful thunderstorm with no rain. He lay listening to the strange sound of nothing outside. Gradually his ears became aware of something. For a moment he wasn't quite sure what it was. The wind, perhaps, or maybe the rain starting at last. It certainly sounded like water. He heard it only for a moment when a sharper and more urgent sound reached his ears. A more familiar sound. The bells on the King Street Church had started ringing. It could mean only one thing. A fire. A big one. Extra help was needed to fight it. The lightning must have started a fire at some important building.

Andrew's landlord started knocking furiously at the door, calling Andrew to get up as there was a fire somewhere. Before Andrew was fully dressed, the landlord returned with startling news: 'It's no' a fire. It's watter, an' the hail toon's salin'.' Minutes later, Andrew was out of the building in time to see his landlord piling turf cut from the back green on to the doorstep. This was bizarre. They were not close to the river. The door was three steps higher than the pavement. The storm had passed without rain. It still wasn't raining.

Andrew, still standing on the top step, strained to look at the street. There was something not quite right about how it looked. Suddenly the last remnants of a disturbed sleep were shaken away and he could see that Princes Street sparkled like a river. Then he realised that the sparkling that resembled a river was indeed water gushing along the street. Princes Street was flooded. Andrew could see, but still he didn't understand where all the water had come from.

It was pouring into Princes Street from the surrounding streets. Andrew waded in, knee deep. He struggled towards King Street and could hardly believe his own eyes. King Street was a raging torrent that carried away boxes and barrels, bottles, chairs and other furniture and goods from shops. Andrew tried to estimate the depth of water . . . a pump near the corner with Fowlds Street was almost covered. It must be nearly two feet deep there, but it was rushing at such a speed that it was not safe to stay where he was.

Andrew turned back. Cautiously he made his way back along Princes Street and into Queen Street, where the water was shallower and much safer. Here he met others who had also come out of their homes to see what was going on. With a sense of amazement, they watched the destruction all around them.

Soon the flood began to subside, and it did so as rapidly as it had risen. By keeping to the high side of the pavement, Andrew was soon able to make his way to the Cross, where the bonfire had been just a few hours before.

The doors of some shops had been burst open by the force of the flood. People, still in their night-clothes, wandered dazed, not quite knowing what to do next or where to go. In the light of morning the full extent of the devastation could be seen and assessed. There was relief that, despite the speed of the deluge, there was only one fatality. It could so easily have been much worse. The noise of the thunder had given sufficient warning to save lives.

The fatal incident happened between Townholm and Kilmarnock. Alexander Pettigrew, William Campbell and James Bruce had been trying to get to a flooded stable to rescue two horses. The water there was already over three feet deep. Pettigrew held the stable door open against the floodwater. Campbell managed to get one of the horses out and Bruce was trying to rescue the other one. Bruce was having problems releasing the horse, so Pettigrew went to help him. As he did so the flood broke down a garden wall releasing a new torrent of water, which rushed in and swept Bruce away. His body was later found in Green Street.

Everywhere there was damage and destruction. Several bridges were gone. Some buildings had been demolished or seriously damaged. Trees had been uprooted and brushed away as if they had been saplings. Stones weighing several tons had been rolled along like pebbles. In some areas the bank of the river had collapsed. Kilmarnock had put up with floods before, but never on this scale. Many business properties were devastated. Shops were awash and stock ruined.

Stories circulated of rescues. Alex Geddes, the town jailer, was proclaimed a hero. The old jail was situated in the Townhouse in King Street, on the bridge over the river. Geddes went to the jail to bring out the twenty-one prisoners and he led them down King Street and along to the new Sheriff Court building in St Marnock Street. The rise in the floodwater was so rapid that this journey was extremely dangerous. Three of the prisoners were almost swept away. Near Waterloo Street one family had become trapped in a flooded room. They tried smashing their way into the neighbouring property by demolishing the wall at the back of a cupboard, and found that their neighbours were doing exactly the same in their attempts to escape.

The rain clouds that had missed Kilmarnock had settled over the moors near Fenwick and, in the space of an hour or so, had dropped an unprecedented quantity of water into a small area, swelling the burns that come together to form the Kilmarnock Water. At Alexander's carding and spinning mill, at what is now the village of

Waterside, a dam on the river was washed away. The water flooded the mill and shifted machinery weighing several tons. The water at the bridge, usually only a few inches, rose to an astonishing sixteen feet.

All along the course of the river towards Kilmarnock, fields were laid waste. At the Dean Castle, close to where the Fenwick Water and the Borland Water join to form the Kilmarnock Water, the old wooden Duke's Bridge vanished in the torrent. Not long afterwards, a more substantial stone one was built. It is still in use today. Close to the Dark Path, the river channel ended up several feet deeper than before the flood. The Bonnet Maker's Dam and the Foundry Dam were demolished. At Townholm a huge boiler weighing several tons was whisked away as if it had been an empty bottle.

Nearer the town the Townhead Bridge was demolished. As the torrent rushed on into the narrower confines of the town, the water was forced to find other channels and that is when it burst out into the streets, causing havoc and destroying many businesses. One man surveyed his losses and contemplated giving up and trying his luck in another country. He decided to stay and rebuild his grocery and whisky business. His name was Johnnie Walker.

Just below the Cross, the river tore down the wall of a house and burst into Bank Street. Further down the Sandbed the old Timmer Brig was smashed like matchwood and so was another wooden bridge at West Shaw Street.

Speculation mounted as to the cause of such a devastating flood. The most common explanation was that the reservoir had burst and poured millions of gallons into the river. But an inspection proved that nothing of the sort had happened. In the end, a consensus emerged: there was simply too much rain in a short period of time, over a small area. But it was agreed that other factors played a part. In previous years, rain had fallen on the countryside and been absorbed. By 1852 improvements in agriculture meant that more and more water was drained from the land and channelled into the rivers. In the town, the river course was narrow and often choked with weeds, bushes and rubbish. Therefore, from that time on, the Council took the decision to keep the river channels clear at all times; a policy our present-day authorities would do well to think about.

The shops soon had flood sales. Everywhere posters referred to 'The Deluge', 'The Great Flood', 'The Inundation'. A disaster relief fund was set up and more than £550 – a huge sum in those days – was collected. Much of it was distributed to the poorest families in the town who lost everything. It was estimated that 221 families sustained

The stone marked the 1852 flood but was destroyed during redevelopment.

some degree of loss. Included in that figure were ninety-nine families 'of the poorest class' who were unable to sustain such a blow.

The Council readily agreed that such a devastating flood should be marked in some way. It was agreed that, at selected properties, marks were to be chiselled to show the height of the water: six feet eleven inches at the railway bridge at Ladeside; six feet seven inches at the corner of Green Street; four feet three inches at the corner of Waterloo Street and the Cross and so on. A more permanent memorial was placed on the Fleshmarket Bridge, but it was destroyed when the town centre was rebuilt in the 1970s.

In several places the old river courses were considerably widened and deepened by the force of the flood and in some places the force of the water forged new channels for the river. Before long the cleaning up and the repair work were under way, but for an entire generation, there was something awesome about the night of the dry flood.

EIGHTEEN

THE MAN OF MANY TALENTS

DAVID LANDSBOROUGH WAS A remarkable man from a remarkable family. He lived in Victorian Kilmarnock and, like so many amateur scientists of his time, he could easily have been a top geologist, a leading naturalist, a first-class local historian or archaeologist, or a church minister capable of offering his congregation inspirational leadership. In fact, David Landsborough was all five. Geologists and naturalists still refer to his works and so do local historians. In the church, his legacy is that fine structure, the Henderson Church, in London Road.

He was born in 1826, one of seven children of David and Margaret Landsborough. His interests began with his father. David Landsborough, senior, became minister in Stevenston and was a prominent naturalist, discovering more than sixty new species of flora and fauna in Scotland. He wrote *A Natural History of Arran*, among various other publications, and his work won honours from various natural history societies in Edinburgh, Glasgow and London. He died of cholera in 1849, having been minister at Stevenston since 1811.

He had seven children including, of course, the subject of this sketch, David Landsborough junior, who was enthralled by the frequent field trips organised by his father. The young man inherited his father's intellect and his insatiable curiosity, along with a passion for all of nature. From the manse in Stevenston, the young lad walked the five and a half miles to and from Irvine Royal Academy every day and, when the time for a university education came, he walked to Glasgow.

Meanwhile his elder brothers, James and John, had gone to start a new life in Australia and tried their best to persuade him to join them. Another brother, William, became a prominent explorer in Australia – he and John McDowall Stuart were the first to cross the continent in 1862. His reward for this remarkable feat was about 2,000 acres of Queensland, which he named Lamerough. It was most probably William who sent seeds of Australian trees back to his brother in Kilmarnock.

David's interest in nature began with his father's trips to all sorts of places: quarries on fossil hunts; rivers and woodland in search of insects, butterflies, creepie crawlies and plants; the sea shore in search of new weeds. For holidays, there was the island of Arran, filled with searches for every kind of rock, plant and insect specimens.

Young David's interests were so varied and so deep that he was able to write booklets and papers. Like his father, David Landsborough junior wrote about the flora and fauna of Arran, works that for more than a generation were standard reference texts for those who wanted to study the island that is sometimes called 'Scotland in miniature'.

As a young man he made a particular study of molluscs and even had one named after him – *Eolin Landsboroughii*. For those interested, it's a species of sea slug. Presumably those who named the species of slug were paying the great man a compliment. He also had two fossils named after him.

His brothers in Australia were aware of his interests and sent him seeds of Australian plants. These David planted and carefully nurtured in pots at the Henderson Church manse in London Road. When the results had grown strong enough to be planted into the ground, David would take them to the manse at Corrie on Arran and plant them in the sheltered garden. Today, there are still tree ferns and eucalyptus trees growing there.

His passion for collecting fossils, plants and bugs was also well known to the members of his congregation, and he often had visitors at the London Road manse providing new specimens for him to identify or, perhaps, add to his extensive collection. A story is told that a parishioner arrived at the manse looking for the Reverend Landsborough, who was not at home, and so was met by the minister's wife. She was greeted by a young man with a broad smile who proclaimed, 'I've got another one'. Mrs Landsborough assumed the man was talking about his family's new baby, which was just about to be born. But he dipped into his pocket and produced a small cardboard box containing an unusual specimen of black beetle.

One of his major literary works was to rewrite and update his father's book, *Arran: Its Topography, Natural History, and Antiquities.* In this revised volume, he included a brief biography of his father. Landsborough also made an important contribution to local history in a series published in the *Kilmarnock Standard* and later collected in a book; *Contributions to Local History* contains much of value that was garnered from individuals in the town, as well as his own observations. It covers diverse subjects and includes details of everything from unusual plants and trees to accounts of long-lost customs.

His great passion found a focus, in a roundabout way, thanks to the *Kilmarnock Standard.* Early in its existence, the *Standard* published a series of articles by Archibald Adamson, based on his rambles around the area. The articles included much that related to local flora and fauna, and much that was based on the fact and the folklore of local history. Everyone loved them. Then, in 1872, the workers at the Glenfield works in Kilmarnock had a change in working arrangements and were able to take Saturday afternoons off. Inspired by the *Kilmarnock Standard* articles, many started going on afternoon rambles on Saturdays. This was all very informal until 1884, when the Glenfield Ramblers was formed and took an interest in natural and local history. David Landsborough readily accepted the position of honorary president and worked tirelessly in building up the society and contributing to its journal. He was also a frequent lecturer at the society's meetings.

After his death, in an appreciation of his contribution, an article in the *Annals of the Glenfield Ramblers* said:

> He knew every tree of note in the county of Ayr and far beyond it. He was conversant with all the varied forms of life along the western coast, and around his beloved Arran. There is not a quarry for many miles around Kilmarnock but has echoed to the sound of his hammer. There is not a rare plant among our hills and glens but he knew the spot where it grew.

But all this interest in nature and history was his hobby, his relaxation. His real work was the ministry and he devoted most of his time to God, the church and his people. Not long after he had completed his studies at the University of Glasgow, Landsborough became minister of the Henderson Church in Kilmarnock. He was just twenty-five and, at the time that he was elected, the kirk was a bleak building that had been constructed a generation before, in 1818. By the time the Reverend Landsborough arrived there in 1851 it still had no covered floor and the walls were made of bare stone. The new minister later commented that the congregation consisted of a handful of people who shivered in the pews. The church also had a serious debt problem. His passion and drive transformed the church. So much so that, in just a few years, it was well on the way to clearing its debt and had a rapidly growing congregation. He was to remain at Henderson for the next sixty years.

David Landsborough was a real inspiration to his congregation, even though he had a few beliefs that today would be thought of as rather eccentric. He believed that no work should be done on the Sabbath and even refused to allow milk to be delivered to the manse on a Sunday. There were eleven people in the household at the Kilmarnock manse; himself and his wife, seven children and two maids. They all had to be fed and, with no fridge in those days, a fresh daily supply of milk was essential. So an arrangement was made to ensure that, on Sundays, milk was surreptitiously delivered over the garden wall. Despite the ban on any work on the Sabbath, the whole household sat down to a meal on Sunday evening, prepared by the two maids, who presumably had a special dispensation from their master's strict rules.

He also resisted that most pagan of festivals, Christmas, declaring that the Bible teaches us to remember the death and resurrection of Christ and does not tell us to celebrate his birth. He often instructed his congregation that 'Christmas is an invention of the Roman Catholics and we should have nothing to do with it.'

But, for all that, he was a truly inspirational minister and there can be little doubt it was his leadership that enabled the magnificent Henderson Church to be built. The process had begun with the Earl of Glencairn appointing a new minister to the Laigh Kirk in 1764. There was so much resentment about this that one group started planning and raising money for a secession. This became the Gallowsknowe Church, which was built in 1773, a simple thatched building situated at the Gallowsknowe between what is now Fulton's Lane and Wellington Street. In 1814 there was another split over a new minister and some of the congregation went to the Spale Kirk in Back Street. A significant proportion of the congregation later established a church in Wellington Street and for the first time called it the Henderson Church.

It was to this church that the Reverend Landsborough came in 1851. By that time the congregation had dwindled in size and had a serious problem of debt. But Landsborough attracted a young and energetic congregation and built the church up to the extent that, by the time he retired, the building was too small and the search was on for bigger premises. In the end it was decided to raise money to build a new church in London Road. Various fundraising events were held, including a spectacular bazaar. The building was constructed in London Road and still serves the needs of the congregation.

David Landsborough died in 1912 and is buried in the St Andrew's Churchyard in Kilmarnock. In 1915 a memorial cairn topped with a metal plaque was erected by the Glenfield Ramblers on Craigie Hill. It pointed to all the key landmarks, and was very popular with walkers. But, in 1966, the memorial plate was removed and the perpetrators were never found. However, the Dick Institute held the original mould and eventually it was agreed that a slightly altered plate should be recast. Today that new memorial is in the Dick Institute along with many of the items that make up Dr

Reverend Dr David Landsborough: church minister, naturalist, geologist and historian.

Landsborough's important collections of shells, fossils, communion tokens and other material.

His wide and varied interests ensure that he is remembered today by national societies in a number of diverse fields. And, just as his father influenced and guided his interests, so the Kilmarnock minister influenced and guided his son, David Landsborough III, who became a doctor and missionary in Formosa. He founded the Changhua Christian Hospital. There, like his father half a world away, he worked tirelessly for his people. And he, too, instilled in his son the same qualities that had been evident in David Landsborough I.

In 1996, the lifetime's work of David Landsborough IV, then aged eighty-two, was recognised by his adopted country, Formosa. He was presented with the Order of the Brilliant Star with the Violet Grand Cordon, a rare honour in that far-off land. Indeed, it was such an important event that the award was made by the country's president.

NINETEEN

KILMARNOCK'S NOBEL PRIZE WINNERS

IN 1973 THE UNITED NATIONS opened a library specialising in food and nutrition literature. It was named in memory of Lord Boyd Orr, and was an appropriate gesture to the memory of the man who had been the first Director General of the UN's Food and Agricultural Organisation (FAO). Although it would have been a great achievement in its own right, he was much more than a nutritionist of world standing; he also won the Nobel Peace Prize. Today, the library consists of more than 2,000 books, 80 current periodicals and a vast collection of documents and publications of the Food and Nutrition Division of the FAO. The library has also built up a collection of the various works published by Lord Boyd Orr.

But who was this man? What was his background? John Boyd Orr was born in Kilmaurs on 23 September 1880. He grew up as one of seven children and he followed the normal practice of being educated in the village school, followed by a spell at an academy, in this case, Bellahouston Academy in Glasgow. After that he returned to Kilmaurs School, this time as a teacher. But he wanted to continue his education and, with the help of a scholarship, he took a teacher-training course and attended the University of Glasgow at the same time.

Years later when he wrote his autobiography, *As I Recall*, he noted that the years at university changed his life. It was not the work, nor the formal learning, which affected him most; it was the old slums of the city. Kilmaurs was, and still is, a charming rural village, but it is less than twenty miles from the city centre and the young student found it difficult to accept that there was so much squalor and poverty so close to his pleasant rural home. On Saturday nights he would tour the slum areas, examining how and why such deplorable conditions had come about.

Before long, he gave up the teacher-training course and concentrated on working for degrees in medicine and biological sciences at the university. He took his degrees in record time. Now he had to find work. At first he did a short stint as a ship's doctor, then he served as a locum, but he quickly realised that he did not want to practise medicine. He wanted to be at, in today's terms, the cutting edge of research.

Shortly thereafter, he won a two-year research fellowship in physiology from the Carnegie Trust. Then, in 1914, he took the post of director of the Institute of Animal Nutrition at Aberdeen University, but he was in for a shock when he got there. There was no such institute, and it was his task as director to create it. Within a few weeks he had his proposals ready, but they were too ambitious, too costly. He hammered out a compromise. He accepted that the main building he wanted could not be constructed immediately, but still insisted that the first wing should be hewn from local granite and not made from wood, as had been proposed by others. He wanted the building to last.

But, as Burns said, 'the best laid schemes of mice and men gang aft agley'. The world was plunged into the devastation of the First World War, and the institute at Aberdeen would have to wait. John Boyd Orr joined the Royal Army Medical Corps; later he served in the Royal Navy and, for a short time, he actually served in both services. He was seconded back to the army for research work into military dietetics. His military career was outstanding; he was mentioned in dispatches, and he won the Distinguished Service Order and the Military Cross.

After the war he returned to Aberdeen to make a start on the creation of the Institute of Animal Nutrition, but it was hard going and he had to spend a lot of his time raising money for its establishment. But he was successful and, following a substantial donation, the name of the facility became the Rowett Research Institute, and was dedicated in 1922. Then followed the Reid Library in 1923, the John Duthie Webster Farm in 1925 and Strathcona House, for research workers, in 1930. Then he launched and edited *Nutrition Abstracts and Review*. Boyd Orr continued to work on a number of research projects, mainly in animal nutrition, and his 1929 paper entitled 'Minerals in Pastures and their Relation to Animal Nutrition' was highly influential.

Despite his undoubted success, the memory of the Glasgow slums still haunted him and, in the 1930s, he started a research project into milk in the diet of mothers, children and the underprivileged. Extensive surveys of nutritional problems in many nations were carried out and he began campaigning for healthier diets and better education on health matters. One of the early results of this work was the publication in 1936 of his paper, 'Food, Health and Income'. It was a hard-hitting, no-nonsense report that severely criticised what he described as the 'appalling amount' of malnutrition in Britain regardless of income. The report became the basis for Britain's food rationing policy during the Second World War and John Boyd Orr found himself in the Cabinet Committee on Food Policy.

Although by the end of the war he was sixty-five, and retired from the Rowett Institute, his work was far from over. As well as a seat in the House of Commons, representing Scottish Universities, he spent three years as rector of the University of Glasgow. He also accepted the post of Director General of the Food and Agricultural Organisation of the United Nations. But he found this work very frustrating because of a constant lack of funds and lack of authority. Nevertheless, he enthusiastically pursued every avenue to increase food production and to ensure that it was distributed fairly.

The world was still in crisis in the years after the war and, in 1946, he set up an Emergency Food Council within the United Nations. It helped meet the immediate crisis of the postwar world. He wanted to see the establishment of a World Food Board and felt betrayed when Britain did not back him.

Soon, he decided to resign from the UN and go into business, but his efforts had not gone unnoticed by an appreciative world. In 1949 he was awarded the Nobel Prize for Peace. With typical generosity, he donated the money to the National Peace Council and the Movement for a World Federal Government, and began actively to campaign for a world government, a cause then fashionable among intellectuals.

His autobiography was written in 1966, a time when nuclear power and the Cold War cast a threatening shadow over the whole world. In the book, he argued that the principal questions facing humanity were whether it had attained sufficient wisdom for the nuclear age, and enough awareness to comprehend that we are one world in which all nations share the same fate.

John Boyd Orr died at his home in Scotland in June 1971, aged ninety, but the library set up in his memory continues his ideals. It supports the work of the Food and Nutrition Division of the FAO and helps researchers, field workers, institutions and governments with nutrition and related activities. In addition, it disseminates scientific and topical information on these subjects, particularly to the developing world.

*

Kilmarnock's other Nobel Prize winner also had a highly distinguished military record. Just as John Boyd Orr served in the Royal Army Medical Corps during the First World War, so too did Alexander Fleming. Like Orr, Fleming served with distinction and was 'mentioned in dispatches'. Before the war he had been researching bacterial infections, which gave him more than enough first-hand experience of what infection can do in wounds. At Boulogne in France he was faced with an endless flood of wounded soldiers; antiseptics were not working and, in some cases, they actually made things worse. Science knew how to kill people in increasing numbers, but not yet how to kill tiny bacteria. Fleming was the man destined to solve the problem and, for his efforts, he would win awards from across the world and a share of the Nobel Prize for Medicine.

But, first, what was his background? He was born in 1881 on the farm of Lochfield, four miles north of Darvel, on the bleak moorland close to the border between Ayrshire and Lanarkshire. His father was Hugh Fleming, who had four children by his first marriage, and married for a second time when he was sixty. His second wife also gave him four children, including Alex. Despite the age difference they were a close family, although the four younger children tended to play together. They would spend whatever time they could on the moor, watching the birds and making up their own games. When the weather forced them indoors, Alex would spend his time reading. Many respected commentators have argued that this isolation helped hone the qualities that were later a requirement for his work as a researcher – keen observation, and almost infinite patience.

As was, and still is, the custom in Scotland, primary education was conducted in the local school. In Alex's case this was followed by a period at Kilmarnock Academy. Then he moved with his brothers to London, where he worked as a shipping clerk for five years prior to attending medical school. Fleming qualified in two fields, as a physician and surgeon but, in 1906, his aptitude for research won him a post at St Mary's Hospital in Paddington, where he worked alongside the eminent bacteriologist, Sir Almroth Wright. He returned to St Mary's after service in the First World War, more determined than ever to tackle the problems associated with infection. What was required was a selective agent that would kill the infection, but leave the healthy tissue unharmed.

Fleming had the ideal personality for research. He was dogged, highly observant and tireless. He was also lucky with the women in his life. His mother Grace was devoted to Alex, reputedly her favourite child, and instilled great confidence and self-belief in him. He was equally lucky with his wife, Sarah (often called Sareen) McElroy, whom he married in 1915. Sareen, a nurse, selflessly sold her nursing home to give them a degree of financial security, enabling Fleming to concentrate on his research at St Mary's.

In 1921 Alexander Fleming made a startling observation, which could so easily have been missed. One day, he was suffering from a cold as he worked, and a drip from his nose fell on a plate of agar, in which colonies of contaminants were growing. A less meticulous researcher might have thrown the plate out and started again. Not Fleming. He never threw out anything until he was absolutely sure that nothing else could be learned from it. Something was learned from that plate. The drip from Fleming's nose had a profound impact on the contaminants. They were soon all killed. Fleming followed through the observation with typical thoroughness. He had discovered lysozyme. He later established it exists in saliva, tears, human milk, skin and nails, and also in various animals and plants. Useful in its own right, lysozyme would help pave the way for his discovery of penicillin. His research paper on the subject was a milestone in medical history, but was met with little interest at the time.

In 1928, a second lucky accident combined with Fleming's keen powers of observation, and has passed into scientific legend. Fleming was clearing out old cultures, which had moulds growing on them. He insisted on examining them before they were disposed of. One of the dishes was different. Fleming noticed that in every case, except one, the moulds co-existed with the staphylococci culture. In one case, the mould had destroyed the staphylococci close to it.

Fleming soon isolated the mould and grew more of it. He identified it. He knew that here at last we might have an antibiotic that could attack infection. He had discovered what he called penicillin but, once again, his research paper was greeted with little enthusiasm. The problem was now a more practical one; to find a way of mass-producing penicillin, and turn it into an effective medicine. If there is a criticism that could be made of Fleming, it is that he gave little thought to these commercial possibilities. In fact, very little progress was made in this direction for another ten years, and penicillin might have remained as purely a laboratory phenomenon were it not for the work of two pioneering biochemists at Oxford University – Ernst Chain and Howard Florey.

Over a period of several years in the early 1940s, the team headed by Chain and Florey worked tirelessly on solving the problems that would facilitate commercial exploitation. Their experiments initially on mice, and subsequently on humans, provided conclusive evidence that penicillin could destroy a wide range of lethal organisms, and they quickly devised ways of purifying it, thus laying the foundations for mass-production. The work undertaken by the Oxford team should not be underestimated. Although Fleming made the initial discovery, the painstaking research undertaken by Chain and Florey was crucial; without their considerable input, penicillin might have been little more than an interesting footnote in the history of science.

Therefore, by the time of the Second World War, medical science was on the verge of its biggest breakthrough in the battle against infection. Early in the war, penicillin was tried on soldiers with war wounds, but it was in desperately short supply. In August 1942, a man with meningitis was treated with penicillin, and it successfully beat off the disease. But thanks to the painstaking research work at Oxford a mass production capability was now in place in the United States. By 1943 there was enough to allow doses to be given to people injured in factory accidents. By June 1944, there were sufficient quantities to treat wounded soldiers on the D-Day landing grounds.

However, most of the credit went to Fleming, and rather ignored the work done at Oxford. There were several reasons for this. Fleming's life story was the stuff of legend – the story of the farm boy from rural Ayrshire who had walked to school in his bare feet, and made an earth-shattering discovery, captured the popular imagination. There was also a compelling need for good news stories in wartime Britain, and the government was keen for the media to promote the legend of the redoubtable Scotsman. Finally, Fleming had many influential friends in high places, including the newspaper baron, Lord Beaverbrook, and they helped to cultivate his legend.

Honours were showered on Fleming. In 1943 he was made a Fellow of the Royal Society, and he was knighted in 1944. In 1945, he shared the Nobel Prize for Medicine with Florey and Chain. Awards were made to him by Britain, the USA, France, Italy and by many other countries and institutions across the world. His portrait has been used on the postage stamps of more than half a dozen countries, including Mexico, Mali, Liberia and Mauritius but, disappointingly, not the United Kingdom.

The quiet scientist from Ayrshire had also become, in the terminology of today, a superstar. He undertook tours of Spain, Italy, France, India and Pakistan, and was given a rapturous reception in these countries. Perhaps the ultimate accolade to a life of painstaking research was his appearance on the front cover of the prestigious *Time* magazine in May 1944. The magazine described him as one of the great men of the twentieth century, and argued that his work was on a par with Galileo and Isaac Newton. He met kings, queens and presidents and, in 1949, was received in the Vatican by the Pope.

Sir Alexander Fleming with the then Queen Elizabeth (later the Queen Mother) in 1945.

But he still found the time to visit his ain folk and, in 1952, made what was to be his last visit to Darvel. Fleming died in 1955 and, following a cremation, his ashes were interred in St Paul's Cathedral in London. Thousands turned up to pay their last respects.

Fleming deserves his place in the history of science. As one of his biographers wrote, the discovery of penicillin was probably the greatest single medical advance of all time. *Time* magazine pointed out that 'his penicillin will save more lives than war can kill'. The work done by others should not be forgotten, but none of it would have been possible without the acute observational skills of the man from Kilmarnock. We must also say something about the man. Fleming shared another quality with Boyd Orr: a great nobility of spirit. Such was his character that, at a time when he was by no means wealthy, he refused to accept a gift of $100,000 from the American pharmaceutical industry, and donated the money to medical research. Nor did Fleming benefit financially from the mass-production of penicillin; because it is a natural substance, it could not be patented under British law. The financial return was not, of course, his main priority; service to humanity ranked far above material considerations.

TWENTY

ANDREW BARCLAY: GENIUS

NOW THAT WE INHABIT a global village, with everyone in instant communication with everyone else, it is hard to remember the time before communication satellites carried all our phone and television messages. Even in the 1950s, and into the early 1960s, people in Britain who wanted to phone someone in the USA or Canada were advised to book a time slot. The phone messages were carried by cable and the capacity of the cable was limited. Now, let's turn the clock back even further, to a time before the phone was invented.

It is surprising to many that the plan to lay an Atlantic cable predates the first phone. In 1840 Samuel Morse patented the telegraph. It quickly became the new means of sending messages and, within a decade, there was talk of laying an Atlantic telegraph cable. The problems this project posed occupied the finest brains in the country and, once again, it transpires that a Kilmarnock man was at the forefront of technical innovation.

In 1850, Matthew Maury (1806–73) started charting the Atlantic to find the best route for a cable. He discovered what he called the Telegraphic Plateau, which is known today as the mid-Atlantic Ridge. William Thomson, later Lord Kelvin (1824–1907), studied the capacity of a cable to carry a signal and invented ways of improving cables and galvanometers, without which the system would not have worked.

And then there was Andrew Barclay (1814–1900), a brilliant young engineer from Kilmarnock. In November 1858, Barclay was conducting promising experiments at Troon in relation to plans for the Atlantic telegraph cable and one press report noted that he had recently visited London for this reason. The project was financed largely by Cyrus West Field (1819–92) who had made his fortune in the paper industry. He withstood disaster upon disaster in his determined attempts to lay the cable. The first three attempts ended in failure, setbacks that would have caused many a lesser mortal to abandon the project. But the project was deemed to be too important and, at the fourth attempt, in 1866, the cable was laid . . . and it worked.

When one of the early cables stopped working, the general opinion was that parts of the insulation had worn away but Barclay proved, by laying a three-mile cable with no insulation, that a cable would carry a message with or without the insulation. He concluded that there was a break in the cable. Barclay also contributed various other important ideas for this project and was a pioneer of the use of alternating current.

At first, the idea of Barclay, the great railway engineer, getting involved in the Atlantic telegraph seems strange, but it was typical of the man. Barclay always wanted just one more mountain to climb. His engineering company took up any challenge. His inventive genius is recognised only at a local level, and yet he should be a national hero. But who was he? Who was this man who stands far above all the other local engineers?

Andrew Barclay was born in Dalry, Ayrshire. His father, John, was an engineer as were the uncles on his father's side. Barclay senior had the lease of Biggar's Mill in Dalry, where he made and maintained his own machines. About 1817, he sold machines to Gregory, Thomson & Co., a firm of carpet makers in Kilmarnock. It must have been a good deal for him, because he came to Kilmarnock to be the firm's millwright and engineer. It was a post he held for another forty years. The industrial revolution was gathering pace and Kilmarnock, with its great coal reserves and new railway to Troon, was in an ideal position to take advantage of the new opportunities.

Another local engineer, Thomas Morton, had invented the barrel carpet machine. This device was moved by a ratchet wheel, but old Mr Barclay invented a screw arrangement, which greatly improved the performance. He also invented a trap motion whereby the action of the barrel was reversed and this also helped carpet production, not only in Kilmarnock, but all over the country too. The most important of his various inventions allowed the production of three-ply carpets. To achieve this, Barclay fitted up a nine-inch loom in his workshop and made a piece of three-ply carpet, about nine inches square. His device totally transformed the carpet-making industry.

John Barclay had a large family. Andrew was his second son and, as a boy, he worked as a pike driver. This meant he had to deal with the pikes on the barrels that formed the pattern of the carpet. He was a constant understudy to his father, and soon learned to work the various machines and use his father's tools.

Before long he wanted to try his hand at making his own machines, and the result of his first attempt was a very fine musical clock. The young lad continually showed considerable talent as an engineer and craftsman. But he also showed his inventive flair early in life. Changing the pattern on a carpet often meant that the harness had to be retied, and this was a task that required a high degree of skill. One day a loom had to be retied, but the weaver was absent for some reason. Without asking or telling anyone, young Andrew set about the task. He had a yard of carpet worked on the new pattern by the time the weaver returned.

On another occasion the boy was set on an empty loom. The pattern drawer was not there, so Andrew went to his father, who quickly drew a design that was approved by the master. It was a particularly intricate pattern that required three different settings and tyings for the harness. And there was a flaw. Barclay senior had drawn the pattern just a little too broad. The overseer spotted it at once and smiled quietly to himself. Young Barclay went to work and soon discovered the error. Rather than ask for a change to the design, he reset the machine. And he was still just thirteen.

After a couple of years as a carpet weaver, Andrew Barclay became apprenticed to a Mr Lawson, a plumber, tinsmith and coppersmith who had his workshop in Portland Street, Kilmarnock. It was Andrew who made most of the water-closet mountings, heavy brass work, screw taps and dyes both for Mr Lawson and for Thomas McCulloch. At this time Barclay built a telescope, the first of several that he would make either for his own use, or for customers.

In 1840, at the age of twenty-five, Barclay left his employment with Mr Lawson to set up his own business in partnership with Thomas McCulloch. At the time the plan was to make shafting for mill works and machines for calico printers. The partnership lasted just two years and, from 1842, Andrew Barclay was on his own. At every turn, his inventive flair was obvious and his skills as an engineer were greatly admired. When he needed more power for his workshops, he designed and then built a 36-horsepower rotary steam engine. The castings for it came from the Caledonian Foundry in Commerce Street, Glasgow. Later Barclay would name his own works the Caledonia Works.

Other businesses in Kilmarnock were impressed and were soon asking him to build similar engines for them. Barclay built at least two others. Soon he was taking out patents on his various innovations. The first was concerned with gas-lighting equipment and was related to the suspension of gas lustres by a fuse and spring. Although an important invention, Andrew Barclay gained little from it. This was because of an accident that had nothing to do with gas, but which nearly killed him. He had been working with a rotary engine at St Marnock's Mill when the accident happened. His injuries were severe and Barclay was carried to a neighbouring house and laid out on a board. Those present thought he was dead, but the man who carried Barclay there stubbornly insisted that, dead or alive, his wounds were to be treated. That decision may well have saved Barclay's life.

But his recovery was slow and he could do no work for four months. With no other income, Barclay settled one of his accounts

A locomotive built at the Barclay works.

with the patent rights to the gas invention. They went to a firm called Laidlaw in Edinburgh, who went on to manufacture 36,000 of the patent gasoliers and made a fortune. By contrast, Barclay received only £150. His next invention also related to gasoliers and was sold for £500. On the strength of this the company moved out of the cramped buildings in Portland Street to more spacious accommodation in West Langlands Street. But there was another disaster just around the corner. The company that bought the patent went out of business and the money was never paid.

Despite this, the work on the new building went ahead. Barclay lived above the shop and even made part of it into his observatory. The loss of the expected £500 meant that savings had to be made. Barclay used his inventive genius wherever he could. He improvised with old equipment to ensure a supply of power. He even used an old grindstone for a flywheel, but he was back in business again. The first order when he was in the new premises came from the Reverend Dr Robert Stirling of Galston, another man of genius. He was as inventive as Barclay and today the principles laid down by Robert Stirling are being talked of as a possible answer to the world's energy problems. Stirling's sons, James and Patrick, went on to become leading locomotive designers.

It would be interesting to know to what extent, if any, the two of them discussed engineering problems. Stirling, however, made his first hot-air engine in 1815 when Barclay was still a toddler. One other engineer who certainly discussed engineering problems with Barclay was Thomas Kennedy.

By 1852 Thomas Kennedy, founder of Glenfield and Kennedy, had designed a water meter and was about to patent the invention. Kennedy's original design had a slit, a valve and registration mechanism. When he showed the design to Andrew Barclay, the astute Barclay tut-tutted and said he didn't think it would work. He suggested a design based on a piston, a cylinder and a butterfly valve. It is said by some this was the device that Kennedy patented shortly afterwards, one which was to prove a great commercial success.

But it was not always plain sailing for Barclay. A flamboyant entrepreneur with 'fiercely forked whiskers', his locomotive factory made him by 1870 the largest employer in Kilmarnock, with 420 in the workforce and annual sales of more than £70,000. But his ambition was all-consuming and, instead of sticking to a business he knew, Barclay invested heavily in the ironworks industry of the north of England. This so overstretched his finances that his companies went into receivership and he was only permitted to carry on under the strict supervision of his creditors. Despite his best efforts he was sequestrated on three subsequent occasions. His finances were not helped by the money soaked up in his attempts to build a giant telescope. Sadly, he died a virtual pauper in 1900, although the Barclay name was preserved in a new company.

He will be remembered for his great prowess as an engineer and inventor, in particular for the advances he made in the field of locomotive building. In the twentieth century the main products of the business he created related to the design and building of locomotives – steam, diesel and later electric, mostly for industrial use. One particular speciality of the company was the fireless steam engine. Such locomotives were designed to work in areas where fire was an unacceptable danger. The fireless engines took a charge of steam from another source, usually a stationary engine, and were then positioned in the danger area.

A large number of Barclay locomotives have been exported to distant lands, and many of them have found work in the equivalent of industrial retirement homes – the railway and industrial museums. As you would expect, a good number of the company's locomotives have been preserved at the Scottish Industrial Railway Centre, near Dalmellington in south-east Ayrshire, including a working example of a fireless steam locomotive.

TWENTY-ONE

THE 'UNCROWNED QUEEN OF SCOTLAND'

KIRSTY WARK IS WITHOUT doubt one of the most powerful women in Scotland. Although best known as an award-winning television presenter, she is also hugely influential behind the scenes as the co-owner of one of Scotland's biggest independent television-production companies. Her considerable professional success has ensured that she is now a leading figure in the Scottish Establishment, and her services are much sought after by charities, civic organisations and public bodies. Even the new Scottish Parliament building at Holyrood will bear her imprint; she was appointed to the panel responsible for selecting the project architect by the First Minister (the late Donald Dewar). It is perhaps little wonder that *The Scotsman* diarist described her, perhaps only half in jest, as the 'uncrowned Queen of Scotland'. Yet for all her undoubted achievements she retains a strong commitment to Scotland in general, and Kilmarnock in particular.

Kirsty Wark was born in Dumfries in February 1955 to James Wark, a solicitor, and Roberta Wark and lived until she was two in Castle Douglas. However, her formative years were spent in Kilmarnock where she attended Kilmarnock Grammar School on Dundonald Road (it has since been demolished and Kilmarnock Sheriff Court now occupies the site). It seems that her childhood was idyllic, and that the school was excellent. Wark remembered it with great affection in an interview with *The Guardian* in February 2000: 'The building was old-fashioned and austere with wood-panelling in the corridors', she recalled 'but it had a homely feel.' She gave much of the credit for Kilmarnock Grammar's high standards to two inspirational teachers – Miss Smith, the infants' teacher, and Mrs Kelly, the teacher responsible for Primaries 1 and 2.

For her secondary education, Wark's parents enrolled her at Wellington School, the exclusive private establishment next to the seafront in Ayr (and the *alma mater* of another famous Kirsty, the supermodel Kirsty Hume). A traditional school, with a strict policy on school uniforms, Wellington has an excellent academic record and sends many of its pupils onto higher education. But the young Kirsty did not lose touch with Kilmarnock. At weekends and during school holidays, she had a variety of part-time jobs in the town: these included waitressing in the Coffee Club in Bank Street, and a job in the china department of Lauder's Emporium in King Street.

After leaving Wellington, Wark won a place at Edinburgh University, where she took a degree in Scottish Studies. She joined BBC Scotland as a graduate researcher in 1976, where she worked for six years on radio programmes in the Current Affairs department and was quickly recognised as a potential high-flier. In 1982 Wark moved into television as a director and producer for BBC Scotland.

But her abilities in front of the cameras soon came to the fore. By the mid-1980s she was beginning to make a name for herself as the presenter of such heavyweight political and current affairs programmes as *Seven Days* and *Left Right and Centre*. She also fronted the BBC's flagship news programme, *Reporting Scotland*, and had a spell on *Breakfast Time* for BBC 1. Her trademark was rigorous preparation, and she often seemed to know more about policy matters than the politicians she was questioning. Wark was also happy in her personal life. She met a young researcher called Alan Clements, who was also working on *Left Right and Centre*, and they got married in 1990. Realising that there were significant opportunities for independent television-production companies, the couple set up their own business, Wark Clements, to make programmes for established broadcasters such as the BBC and Channel 4.

There was one interview in March 1990 that, more than any other, sealed her reputation. The interviewee was another strong, highly intelligent woman who had fought her way to the top – the then Prime Minister, Margaret Thatcher. Mrs Thatcher preferred to be interviewed by men and tried to have Wark replaced. But the BBC refused and the stage was set for one of the most combative encounters in Scottish political history. Wark asked Thatcher a number of highly penetrating questions about the poll tax, a highly unpopular system of local government finance that was introduced in Scotland before it saw the light of day in England. She even asked Thatcher if she considered herself a political liability because of her unpopularity in her own party and in Scotland. Thatcher tried to throw Wark off-balance on several occasions, but the Scot stuck gamely to her task and by the end of the interview had clearly rattled the Prime Minister. It was reported that Thatcher berated her inquisitor after they came off air, but Wark was even calmer than usual . . . and for a very good reason. She had just discovered that she was expecting her first child, Caitlin, and had made her mind up not to get stressed out. Nevertheless the interview – now often referred to as the 'legendary interview' – confirmed her status as a political journalist of the highest calibre.

Wark's on-screen career went from strength to strength in the early 1990s. She was the presenter of the Scottish current-affairs show *Up Front* from 1992 to 1993 and, pursuing her passion for the arts, she also fronted the prestigious *The Late Show*. Then came arguably the greatest accolade of all. In 1993 she joined *Newsnight* on BBC 2 as a main presenter alongside such heavyweights as Jeremy Paxman. Since then she has appeared in a wide variety of programmes, often as the main presenter, and her credits include *Rough Justice* and *One Foot in the Past*. Her work began to receive the recognition it deserved from her peers: Wark was named journalist of the year in 1993 by BAFTA Scotland, the first in a long line of awards that also included honorary degrees from several Scottish universities.

Her achievements as a programme maker have also been noteworthy. Wark Clements, the company she co-owns with her husband and which he runs on a day-to-day basis from its headquarters in Glasgow, has gone from strength to strength. It has produced a number of acclaimed programmes for the BBC, Channel 4 and others. These include *A Restless Nation*, *Playing Nintendo with God* and *Football, Faith and Flutes*. In December 2001 it was reported that the company had entered into a three-year, £3 million deal to make a range of programmes for the BBC. These will include *Great Scots*, a historical series for BBC Scotland. Then, of course, there is Wark's presenting deal with the BBC, reputed to be worth £250,000 per annum.

Further prestigious commissions followed: Channel 4 signed an agreement with Wark Clements to produce a major new documentary series on the First World War. Worth a reported £2$\frac{1}{2}$ million, it is said to be the biggest-ever contract awarded by Channel 4 to a company based outside London. Given the scale of the company's growth it is hardly surprising that there has been talk of floating it on the Stock Exchange, with one newspaper report suggesting it could be valued at up to £60 million. As Wark and her husband own sixty per cent of the shares this would make her a multi-millionaire overnight. There have also been unconfirmed reports that Wark Clements was poised to make a bid for the Scottish Media Group, owners of Scottish Television, *The Herald* and the *Evening Times*.

Yet despite these achievements Wark has, like many successful Scots, kept her feet firmly on the ground, helped no doubt by her upbringing and education in Kilmarnock. Colleagues testify to the fact that she has no side, and is an open and honest person. She is also devoted to her family, and has tried to minimise the impact of her work on her domestic life. It has often been reported how she

At the centre of power: Kirsty Wark with the leaders of Scotland's political parties before the 1999 elections for the Scottish Parliament. From left to right, the politicians are David McLetchie, Alex Salmond, the late Donald Dewar and Jim Wallace.

would travel down to London to present *Newsnight*, take the sleeper back to Glasgow and then rush back to her home in the west end of the city to prepare lunch boxes for her two children, Caitlin and James.

Although by any standards a household name, Wark is uncomfortable with some aspects of her celebrity. One source of irritation is the comparisons in certain sections of the media with other famous Scots called Kirsty. These include, of course, Kirsty Young the glamorous newsreader on Channel 5, and Kirsty Gallagher the equally attractive presenter from Sky Television. Indeed, even the venerable *Scotsman* ran an article entitled 'The rise and rise of the Kirstys' in April 2002. In a humorous vein, *The Scotsman* suggested that 'The three Kirstys, like the Three Graces, are the epitome of both beauty and goodness, and while their classical forebears were the handmaidens of Aphrodite the goddess of love, the Three Kirstys are the handmaidens of you, the viewer, captive on the sofa.'

It must also be rather galling for a serious journalist like Wark that many newspapers and magazines frequently focus on her looks, clothes, make-up and the juggling act she performs as a working mother. As Wark pointed out in one interview it is much more difficult for single, working mothers on a low income to balance work, family and money commitments. Wark is also well aware that salaries for successful media figures are somewhat disproportionate compared to people doing less high-profile, but vital, jobs in education and the National Health Service.

Kirsty Wark is one of that rare breed: a Scot who has made it big in England but prefers to live north of the border. It would no doubt have been much easier for her to relocate to London, the media capital of Britain. But she seems to have a genuine commitment to Scotland. She also retains a great deal of affection for Kilmarnock, and still sees it as 'home'. This is clear from an interview she gave to *The Scots Magazine*. Although acknowledging that she could no longer live in the town because of work commitments she went on to say that, 'I still feel I'm "coming home" as I drive over the Fenwick Moors from Glasgow . . . I'm always conscious of the fact that my roots are there . . . The town still has a great sense of community, and being brought up there taught me about industry: Massey Ferguson, BMK Carpets, Saxone, Glenfield and Kennedy, Johnnie Walker – these were familiar names, not just in the UK, but throughout the world.'

In fact Kilmarnock, in her view, was almost the perfect place to grow up and she listed the reasons:

There are a number of reasons why I think Kilmarnock's such a great place. Firstly, there's the size. A population of about 50,000 makes it not too big and not too small. When I was young, I knew it well, and this gave a great sense of freedom. I could get to grips with it.

It's unashamedly industrial, but isn't part of a conurbation, like some comparable Scottish towns. Though it's got all the usual amenities such as shops, entertainment, libraries, schools and so on, you're never far away from beautiful countryside, which surrounds it on all sides. I lived near the centre of town, and yet when I was young I used to cycle miles with friends, exploring the whole area. We got as far as Dundonald and Troon on occasions.

Of course there were the quiet country lanes, which criss-cross this part of Ayrshire, especially around Stewarton and Dunlop, an area I especially like. They were almost made for cyclists.

The town's public spaces also have much to commend them. John Finnie Street, one of the finest examples of planned Victorian architecture in Scotland is one of her favourite streets, as is Bank Street, 'a lovely wee street . . . one of the most attractive in the town'. Kilmarnock's parks are also close to her heart, as she explained: 'The parks are beautifully kept. I lived near the best one of the lot, Howard Park, and I used to play there with my friends all the time. Then there's the Kay Park, with the Burns Monument as its focal point, and the Dean Park on the Glasgow Road.'

Wark has a passion for architecture and finds much to admire in her home town. She regards both the Laigh Kirk and the High Kirk as gems, and the Dick Institute as 'one of the most impressive library and museum buildings in Scotland'. There is also the Dean Castle, the oldest building in Kilmarnock and home of the Boyd family, ancient lords of Kilmarnock. It is, she points out, 'a tremendous asset to the town and truly beautiful. It's got a lot of history attached to it, a bonus.' It was therefore fitting that, at Dean Castle in 1991, Kirsty Wark launched plans for celebrating the four hundredth anniversary of Kilmarnock's becoming a burgh. She did this by inserting the first stitches into what became the massive tapestry called the 'Threads of Kilmarnock'.

With the best interests of the town at heart Wark also made some rather scathing criticisms of more recent buildings, particularly those built after the redevelopment of Kilmarnock Cross in the 1970s, a move that she thinks tore the heart out of the town. One of the worst of the new structures, she argues, is the multi-storey car park at the top of the Foregate, which she believes should be pulled down. And, like many in Ayrshire, she takes the view that the A77 must be upgraded, preferably to motorway status, as soon as possible.

It seems clear that Kirsty Wark's star is very much in the ascendant and that she will have many more professional successes in the future. However, in common with many of the famous people from Kilmarnock covered in this book, like Sir Alexander Fleming and Andrew Fisher who also had to leave Kilmarnock to become successful, she has fond memories of the town and its honest, hard-working citizens. For them, it will always be home.

TWENTY-TWO

SPACEMEN OF KILMARNOCK

THE NIGHT SKY ABOVE Fenwick was darker than usual, but the air was cool and clear. Even the faintest of the stars seemed clear that night. The boy looked in wonder at the lights above: 'What are they?' he asked and he was told that they were stars. 'Yes,' he insisted, 'but what are they?'

The boy was John Fulton and his fascination with astronomy lasted for the rest of his life. Fulton was born at Spoutmouth, Fenwick in 1800. By the time he was thirteen, this son of the local shoemaker spent most of his time in the family business. He kept up his interest in the stars and planets. Now he wanted to build an orrery. An orrery is a mechanical model of the solar system. They cannot be built to scale, but they can show the relative motions of the planets and their moons.

The first thing Fulton had to do was to teach himself the complex mathematics involved in calculating planetary orbits. This he did, apparently with relative ease. His first orrery was made of wood, his second of brass. Both these machines appear to have been relatively crude. At the age of twenty-three, Fulton decided that he was going to build another orrery; not just any old orrery, but the best and most accurate one ever made.

It was not a passing whim. Having taught himself the maths involved, he now had to design the machine. The cogs and wheels he needed were not available, so he had to make his own. The equipment available to cut the teeth into the wheels was not of a high enough standard, so he designed and built his own equipment. All his spare time and all his spare money went into the great orrery and finally in 1833 it was finished. It had taken him ten years to build. Everyone in Fenwick wanted to see it, and for a time it was on free display in the kitchen of Fulton's tiny home. Could it pass the test of public approval? Would they appreciate its complexities?

Everyone who saw it marvelled at the wonderful machine. They had never seen anything like it and soon people were trekking from Kilmarnock and elsewhere for a look. After a few weeks, and quite a bit of persuasion, Fulton agreed to take the orrery on tour.

His machine was worked by clockwork. It had 175 wheels and more than 200 moving parts. It showed all the planets and all the moons that were known at the time of construction. It went on display in Fenwick, Kilmarnock, Glasgow, then all round the country. Lavish praise was heaped on Fulton, and the Society of Arts in Scotland declared that Fulton's orrery was indeed the most perfect orrery ever made. It displayed the planets and their moons, the tilts of the planets, the cause of the seasons and the tides and of eclipses.

Fulton soon found work as an instrument maker in London. He remained there for fifteen years but, when he took ill, he returned to Fenwick, where he died in 1853. He had never married and, on his death, the orrery passed to his brother, who cleaned, overhauled and then exhibited it. Around 1870, a nephew of the original John Fulton sold it to a group of businessmen for more than £200. They appear to have later given it to the Glasgow Industrial Museum. Today it is on display in the Transport Museum in Glasgow and, although the original clockwork drive has been replaced by an electric motor, the orrery is still used for demonstrations. In Fenwick, Fulton's legacy is the Fulton Memorial Hall, run by East Ayrshire Council and used for all sorts of village events.

*

It was Thomas Morton who took the local study of astronomy to new heights, literally. His father came from a long line of farmers, but decided on an alternative career as a brickmaker. His son, Thomas, the astronomer, was born in Mauchline in 1783 and three years later the family moved to Kilmarnock.

Even as a child, Morton's skills were clear when he made pocket-knives, whistles, toys and farmhouse goods. By the age of ten he was working with his father at Gargieston, and only attended school in winter when he was not required to help make bricks. In 1806 he set up his own business, making just about anything that was asked of him, including bagpipes. He even built a windmill to power his workshops. He invented a barrel weaving loom for the rapidly expanding carpet industry. His interest in science was obvious but his passion was astronomy and, in 1818, he completed work on his observatory at what is now Morton Place. He built two telescopes and a camera obscura for it. He also built telescopes for sale and devised new methods for simplifying the tedious task of grinding and polishing the mirrors and glasses for instruments.

The observatory at Dumfries still has telescopes made by Morton, and there is also one in the National Museum in Edinburgh. Their treasures include several telescopes, but the Morton one in the national collection is described as being 'technically interesting'.

It seems that other members of the Morton family were also interested in making telescopes. His son, Alexander Morton, made telescopes, but only one example is now known. It is in the United States. A report in the *Kilmarnock Standard* of 1 December 1866 says: 'We have just inspected a Newtonian telescope built by Mr Charles Morton of Morton Place.' This was four years after the death of Thomas Morton. Charles was probably another son of the illustrious Thomas.

It seems that Morton made his observatory available to others and there is no doubt that he was an inspiration to many. In particular, he was close to Thomas Lee, his son-in-law. When Morton died in 1862, the observatory passed to Lee, a teacher at Kilmarnock Academy. He had come to the school in 1843 as head of the commercial and mathematics department. Lee's interest and enthusiasm for astronomy were used to great effect in the school. Indeed, it was said that in the third quarter of the nineteenth century, the only school in Ayrshire in which science was taken seriously was Kilmarnock Academy.

Lee had married Morton's daughter, Agnes, who earned a reputation for writing hymns and poems. Thomas Lee made full use of the observatory for lectures and demonstrations to both students and the general public. The old observatory was later used by James Kilmurray for his weather forecasting work. It was demolished in 1957, the year that the space age dawned with the launch of Sputnik 1, the world's first artificial satellite.

*

Andrew Barclay was the most outstanding of the nineteenth-century engineers from Ayrshire and his career is chronicled in chapter twenty of this book. Like his contemporaries, he had a passion for science and for astronomy in particular. This interest was so great that he named one of his sons John Galileo Barclay, and another Archibald Newton Barclay. What they thought of this in later life does not appear to have been recorded.

Barclay's passion for astronomy started early in life and being the accomplished engineer that he was, he built his own telescopes. After a fire seriously damaged his workshops in 1876, Barclay had a large dormer window built into the attic at the west end of the building in Langlands Street. This served as his observatory window. At one stage when he was building a great telescope he was siphoning off so much of the company's resources that it was in serious danger of going bust.

One of Barclay's telescopes so impressed Sir John Ross that he proposed Barclay as a Fellow of the Royal Astronomical Society. Barclay carried out a lot of observations and, like any good scientist, kept meticulous notes. He sent papers to the *English Mechanic* magazine outlining his various discoveries, and there were many, or so it seemed. Among the various 'discoveries' claimed by Barclay, there were some dubious ones. He said he found mountains on Venus, Jupiter and even on the sun. In the *English Mechanic*, Barclay stated that on Saturn he could see a great valley round the planet; on Mars, to his credit, he could see no sign of 'canals'.

His findings were controversial and his telescope was inspected and found to be perfect. Barclay, it seemed, was just a poor observer. In one copy of the *English Mechanic* he gives the game away. He suggested that readers with telescopes should take a circular piece of plasterboard and put two smaller holes in it close to the edge. In this way, Barclay claimed, people would be able to see the planets in full relief.

Today it is easy to scoff at such ideas but, a hundred years ago, no one could have imagined that we would be able to send probes to the planets and have them fully mapped. Barclay was a brilliant engineer and one of his telescopes, having been restored at the observatory in Edinburgh, is now on display in the Dick Institute.

*

Another famous amateur astronomer from Ayrshire was Sir Thomas Brisbane, born at Brisbane House in Largs. He served in the army in North America in 1814, and was appointed Governor-General of New South Wales in 1821. He introduced vines, sugar cane and tobacco plants and encouraged horse breeding and land reclamation. He established an observatory and was the first to catalogue 7,385 stars of the Southern Hemisphere.

After he returned to Scotland in 1824, the observatory was given little official support and it closed in 1847. However, in his short time in Australia, Thomas Brisbane had made a significant contribution to astronomy. In 1978 the city of Brisbane opened a new planetarium and observatory, calling it the Sir Thomas Brisbane Planetarium in honour of the pioneer of Southern Hemisphere astronomy and today there is also a moon crater named after him.

Then there was Professor R. Kalley Miller from Kilmarnock. In 1873, he was appointed to the Chair of Mathematics at the Royal Naval College at Greenwich and was the author of a book on astronomy. He tried to popularise the science that, until his time, had largely been the preserve of professional scientists. The success of his book suggests that he had begun to popularise a complex science, but one that relies heavily on the work of amateurs.

James Blackwood was another man who was a typical scientist of the Victorian era. He was very good at some sciences and brilliant at others. His main passion was for geology and to pursue this interest he built his own microscopes. He is also known to have made telescopes.

James Walker was a man of many talents, among which were his regular contributions to the press, notably the *Kilmarnock Standard*. His book *Old Kilmarnock* is full of folksy local history. Another of his interests was astronomy. One evening he had given a lecture on astronomy, but next day he was taken down a peg or two by one of the students who found it difficult to believe the distance from earth to moon could be measured.

He challenged Mr Walker: 'Did onybody ever get up and staun on the min wi' a lang string in his haun, and some ither body staun doon here wi' the ither end o' it, an' then measure it wi' a yardstick or a fit rule after him? Naw, naw, you'll no' dae. Ye needna try tae swall oor heids wi' yon sort o' stuff.'

The Reverend Hector Macpherson of Newmilns was another eminent amateur astronomer. Between 1917 and 1922 he was a regular speaker on astronomy to the members of the Kilmarnock Glenfield Ramblers. His topics encompassed the sun, the moon, the stars and the planet Mars. On 5 December 1918, he spoke about Mars and asked the pertinent question: is it inhabited? It is a question that is still unanswered by our space probes, but one that serves to illustrate the timeless quest for knowledge about the other planets, and the need to answer one of the fundamental questions of our time, 'Are we alone in the universe?'

TWENTY-THREE

THE LONG AND WINDING ROAD

BEFORE THERE WERE ANY built roads, there were rough tracks which usually followed hard ground, and served as tenuous lines of trade between neighbouring communities or linked inland settlements with major rivers or the coast. No one knows just when the first track between Kilmarnock and Glasgow was in regular use. It is not even known for certain whether or not the Romans used a road directly between the two communities, but as time went on a regular track did emerge.

In the days before coaches began to ply their trade, it was only pedestrians and horses that used the long and winding road from Kilmarnock to Glasgow. To be more precise, it was a road from Ayr to Glasgow, with Riccarton and Kilmarnock on the route. In the earliest days it could hardly have been called a road. It must have been little more than a track, with traffic moving at a leisurely walking pace. Then, in 1669, Scotland's parliament passed a law saying that all highways had to be at least twenty feet wide. It was the beginning of road regulations but, even so, there was very little trade between Kilmarnock and Glasgow. Indeed, in 1763 all trade between Kilmarnock and Glasgow was carried by a train of just twelve packhorses. The route through the Fenwick Moor was, of course, difficult and, wherever possible, it followed rocky ground as it had done for centuries.

Before the great businessman and inventor, John Loudon McAdam (1756–1836), began his career as a road builder in 1815, roads were either rough tracks, or had clay surfaces. Either way, they were vulnerable to bad weather that, at times, made them impassable; not the sort of thing we expect in the twenty-first century. And yet, even as recently as February 2001, this road between Kilmarnock and Glasgow was closed because of heavy snow.

But let's return to the middle of the eighteenth century. There was little incentive to improve the road between Kilmarnock and Glasgow, or any other road for that matter. Things began to change. Starting in 1751, Parliament in London began passing various Turnpike Acts, allowing turnpike trusts to improve or construct roads and then to levy a toll at the turnpikes.

The first of the Ayrshire Turnpike Acts came in 1767. Another followed in 1774. Together they allowed many of the old tracks to be widened and otherwise improved. Of course, tolls were set up at various places and some local place names still reflect this, such as

Bogend Toll, just south of Kilmarnock. By 1787, the roads in general had improved so much that the Royal Mail decided to send mail from Carlisle to Glasgow by coach. Kilmarnock magistrates and business-men immediately started to lobby the Post Office to persuade it that the route through Lockerbie and Dumfries, then on to Kilmarnock was a better option than the less populated route through Lanarkshire. The Royal Mail agreed and the mail coach came through Kilmarnock.

Ayrshire roads were of a very high standard and praise was heaped on them by local and national surveys. This was good for trade and good for new businesses. The roads were of such high quality that farmers started to buy wheeled carts, produced by local craftsmen, to take produce to market. Carriers' businesses were also soon established. However, not all the roads were maintained to a high standard. Around 1820 the road from Kilmarnock to Glasgow sometimes became so deeply rutted in places that it caused serious problems. It was well known as a poorly maintained road, and one local anecdote tells of a coach driver coming across a man digging by the side of the road.

'I'm glad tae see some repairs here at last,' the driver called to the man repairing the road.

'Ach repairs, naething,' the workman called back, 'I'm jist howking fur ma horse an' cairt.'

In those days there were no bypasses either of Kilmarnock or Fenwick. With coaches travelling at the speed of a horse, the journey was often broken for a refreshment, sometimes at Fenwick, but more often than not at the Kingswell Inn, which was situated next to the turning that now takes traffic to Eaglesham. In those days the route from Kilmarnock to Glasgow swung round Drumboy Hill to the east, rather than west, as it does now. The inn was fairly isolated, but as traffic on the route to Glasgow increased it was a popular place to break the journey.

The Kingswell Inn was also the scene of a trick that for many years plagued the quiet life of Jamie Finnikim. Jamie was a weaver, and also beadle at the King Street Church. He was small and pot bellied and his lower jaw and lip hung down a little. It may have been his unusual appearance, or his very trusting nature, which made him a target for pranksters. One day he was asked if he could go to Glasgow on church business. The coach was expensive, so Jamie started asking around to see if any local carrier was heading to Glasgow. Soon Jamie had found someone who was planning to travel to Glasgow. And so at about ten o'clock at night Jamie and his fellow traveller set off into the darkness.

When they reached Kingswell, they stopped to feed and rest the horse and refresh themselves. And so, 'the night drave on wi' sangs and clatter'. While they were engrossed inside the inn, someone turned their horse and cart. By the time Jamie and his by now bosom buddy came out of the inn, they had no thought of which direction the horse was facing. They trundled through the two Fenwicks and in the grey light of pre-dawn, Jamie suddenly realised that he did not know where he was. It was certainly not Pollokshaws. He confided in his companion that he thought they must have come off the road somewhere in the darkness. Dawn was breaking when they passed a castle, one that reminded him of the Dean Castle back home, but one that he had never seen before on the approach to Glasgow. A little further on, the intrepid twosome concluded they were now thoroughly lost.

Then Jamie spotted a woman. He jumped off the cart and approached her: 'Whit toon is this?' he asked politely enough. 'We wir gaun tae Glesca, but I doot we've lost the road'.

The woman eyed him suspiciously. Then she scorned him: 'Jamie Finnikim, I aye kent ye was silly, but I never thocht that ye wis so daft as tae no ken yer ain toon.' The hapless duo were, of course, back in Kilmarnock.

*

All through the Victorian period, most road building materials came from small quarries close to where it was needed, and there are still signs of quarrying work alongside the present route of the A77. The system served the route to Glasgow well for most of the nineteenth century. Traffic on the road grew slowly, mostly because it was usually more convenient to use the train. But a revolution was coming; a revolution caused by the invention of the internal combustion engine. The rapid growth of the use of cars, buses and lorries in the early twentieth century soon made the old road to Glasgow completely inadequate for the new needs.

In dry weather the heavy vehicles kicked up a lot of dust, so much so, that nearly every bus in the country was nicknamed 'Stoorie Aggie'. The solution was to spray the surface of the road with tar, a process that produced hard-surfaced roads, suitable for motorised vehicles. However, scant attention was paid to the layout of junctions, lighting or sign posting and there were no bypasses, which at times caused congestion in villages such as Fenwick.

These problems were all recognised and a major reconstruction of the Kilmarnock to Glasgow road was undertaken in the 1930s. Improving transport, however, was not the major priority here; rather, it was creating employment. It was at this time that the Fenwick bypass was created, and upgraded to a four-lane highway. While it did not have a central reservation, it did at least have lane markings.

There was very little traffic, and the cars and lorries that were on the roads in the 1930s were all much slower than today's vehicles. In the 1930s, people could, and did, walk on what is now the A77. But, from time to time, young bucks came to Ayrshire from all over the country to try out their cars on the road. They knew that they could get speed up. The road was treated as a racetrack, and many of these unskilled drivers soon discovered to their cost that they could not control their vehicles at speed. Several paid with their lives.

In the years immediately after the Second World War, car owner-ship began to grow rapidly, and traffic from Ayr to Glasgow contin-ued to pour through Kilmarnock. A western bypass was started but never completed. Today it is Western Road. By the early 1950s the need for a bypass was widely acknowledged, and a route from Spittalhill in the south to Meiklewood in the north was agreed, but a considerable period elapsed before the bypass was opened. When it was finally built, the A77 bypass was far in advance of anything that could have been imagined in the days of Jamie Finnikim. It required the excavation of 1.7 million cubic yards of material and no less than twenty-two bridges, not all of them obvious to the motorist. The road was a dual carriageway – in effect two separate roads, with a central reservation, and two lanes to each carriageway.

When the bypass was opened, it was linked to the recently built dual carriageway to Prestwick and Ayr, and optimistic statements suggested that the road from Kilmarnock to Glasgow would soon be made dual carriageway as well. It was indeed an optimistic forecast. Time went on without major improvements, but traffic volumes rose sharply and so did vehicle speeds. Soon the road from Kilmarnock to Glasgow was wholly inadequate. Some improvements were made, but it had become clear that what was required was not simply a dual carriageway, but a motorway.

Despite various improvements, accidents were frequent and the road has attracted an unwanted reputation as one of the most hazardous in Scotland. Between 1985 and 1990, seventeen accidents resulted in the deaths of twenty-one people. By the early 1990s, the case for a motor-way was overwhelming and was approved by the Scottish Office, with work scheduled to start in 1995. Work, however, did not start in 1995, nor in 1996, nor even in 1997. By 1998, the *Kilmarnock Standard* was running a vigorous campaign for a motorway and so were local resi-dents, exasperated by the wholly inadequate standards. Eventually, plans were approved to build a new motorway alongside the A77, leaving the existing road for local and farm traffic, walkers, cyclists and horses. Although this plan has also been the subject of delays, the Scottish Executive has approved funding for the project and, by the spring of 2003, preliminary work will have started.

It can not come a moment too soon. The hazards posed by the A77 were graphically illustrated yet again in June 2002 when Troon resident, Chief Inspector Hugh Davidson of Strathclyde Police, and Jason Muir of Kilmarnock, were killed instantly when their cars collided head-on just south of the Fenwick moor turn-off. This brought the death toll in the twenty years from 1982 to 2002 to 153, with nearly 800 injured in the same period. We can only hope that the new road will spell the end of such tragic accidents.

TWENTY-FOUR

REBELS WITH A CAUSE

DEMOCRACY IS A RELATIVELY new concept in Britain. We take our right to vote for granted, and yet it was a hard battle to win that right and many suffered in the long and, at times, bitter struggle. Kilmarnock men were at the forefront of that battle in the nineteenth century, and women played their part in the twentieth century.

Before the dawn of the nineteenth century not much attention was paid by the ruling classes to the needs and desires of the masses of ordinary hard working people who created the wealth of the nation. Those who dared stand up to their masters could be transported to the colonies or even hanged as traitors. A few brave souls tried to make the system work against itself. There is no doubt that Robert Burns was a revolutionary, and he went as far as he could with the poems that carried his own name. Indeed, some works with a radical tone were published anonymously and are now thought to have come from his pen. Perhaps understandably, he did not put his name to them because open support for the French Revolution, or for democracy in Britain, could have led straight to the gallows.

But a growing number of people did think that things should change. In December 1792 a group of men met in the Angel Inn in Kilmarnock. This was the very building that Burns referred to in his poem, 'The Ordination', though at that time, the place was known as Begbie's. It was brave of them to attend the meeting. The men represented nine societies and they advocated the dangerous concept of democracy. The British Establishment was so terrified of change that the men at this meeting could have been arrested; they could have been transported to the colonies; they could have been hanged by the neck until they were dead. They were cautious, perhaps too cautious. They passed resolutions praising liberally minded Members of Parliament, and reaffirmed their support for peaceful change and good order in society. It was, perhaps, not surprising that none of this had any effect. The Establishment ignored them. The years rolled on with no democracy and no free speech.

In the early nineteenth century, there was war in Europe and war with America and, with these wars, came sharp increases in taxes to pay for them. This tended to fan the flames of protest and increase the demand for the reform of a voting system that excluded the vast majority of the population.

By 1816 the few lone voices were coming together in organised agitation. On 7 December 1816 a protest meeting was held in Kilmarnock. Despite the bitter winter wind and frequent showers of snow and hail, more than 5,000 gathered to support the case for reform. One of the ringleaders, an Alexander McLaren, told the crowd that the narrow-minded policies of the country's rulers were causing poverty throughout the country.

James Johnston told the meeting that poverty was a result of the lack of proper representation in Parliament. He said that only 156 people in Ayrshire were entitled to vote, and even they did not vote freely. He argued that the system meant that the ordinary hard-working people of the country had no more representation in Parliament than the cattle on the hills. Archibald Craig spoke eloquently of the consequences of the war. That cold winter's day, the meeting passed sixteen resolutions declaring that the representation of Scotland in Parliament in London was unreasonable, unconstitutional and unjust.

The meeting broke up in high spirits. Those who had attended had hopes that at last things would begin to change and all those who worked and paid taxes would get some voting rights. It was also decided that for the benefit of those who had not been able, or had been too afraid, to attend the mass meeting, the main speeches would be widely disseminated. In Kilmarnock, Thomas Baird saw to the printing and distribution of the leaflets.

But still the forces of the Establishment were determined to keep things as they were. They moved against the organisers of the meeting, and against McLaren and Baird in particular. They were arrested in February 1817, and accused of sedition; that is, inciting people to rebel against the government. They faced trial in Edinburgh the following month.

The two men were well known and well respected in Kilmarnock. They were not seen as rebels; they were folk heroes. Despite the testimony of various witnesses as to their character, and notwithstanding the efforts of an able defence lawyer, the men were found guilty and jailed in Edinburgh. It had been nothing more than a show trial, part of the determined effort of the Establishment to nip the democracy nonsense in the bud.

It was not the end of the quest for reform. By 1819, the tide of opinion was rising again. On 18 September another mass meeting was held in Kilmarnock, this time at open ground near Morton Place. This time it was not just a meeting for Kilmarnock folk.

People marched from neighbouring towns and villages, with

seven thousand, maybe more, in attendance. The meeting advocated universal suffrage – votes for all. It was agreed to send a petition to the Prince Regent seeking substantial changes to electoral law. Another mass rally followed on 20 November at the same place. This time 16,000 people attended . . . more petitions; more protest and still no action on parliamentary reform.

To some it seemed that the idea of peaceful petitions and resolutions was a waste of time, and some folk started talking of rebellion and armed revolution. The tensions across the country came close to breaking point: 1 April 1820 was fixed as the date for the armed rebellion to start. Communications were difficult and, in consequence, there was no possibility of organising in secret. Posters proclaiming the coming revolution were displayed and weapons were stashed. The motto of the rebels was 'Liberty or Death'. The placards proclaimed that the organisers were not lawless rebels, but brave, generous people determined to be free.

In Kilmarnock the signal that the rebellion had already started was to be the non-arrival of the mail coach. The first of April dawned, but there were no banners or flags for the new era. No demonstration or show of strength. There were no weapons on display. It was, to the casual observer, just an ordinary day. There was, however, a widespread feeling of apprehension. Everyone wanted something to happen, but everyone wanted someone else to make that 'something' happen. Then, right on time, the mail coach arrived in Kilmarnock, to the dismay of a few but to the great relief of many.

The day passed without incident, but once again the forces of reaction were preparing to hit back at those who dared challenge the established order of things. Two weeks after the day that nothing happened, the army turned up in Kilmarnock with a heavy gun, which was placed at the Cross. It was a show of strength. It was a threat to the people. Roads leading in and out of the town were closed. Kilmarnock was sealed off. The army had a list of those it considered to be the ringleaders of the mischief, and they wanted to take them away.

The soldiers patrolled the streets. People were told to stay in their homes that day. Most of those who might have had something to fear from the army were well hidden by friends, but a few of the townspeople were arrested and thrown into an overcrowded county jail. The army was in other towns apart from Kilmarnock that day.

Archibald Craig spent four months in prison. Yet he was never found guilty of anything. He was so disgusted with the political

The Reformer's Monument in the Kay Park, complete with the liberty statue which was blown off in 1936.

oppression in this country that he left for the United States, where he became a preacher. He was not the only one. Many others left Scotland forever.

The show of strength by the army did nothing to slow the momentum for change. More protests, more demonstrations, more petitions. In Kilmarnock, one petition was signed by 3,000 people in just three days. Another mass meeting, this time near Kilmarnock House, probably on land now occupied by Howard Park, attracted a crowd estimated at 17,000. They later marched through the town, this time displaying something like 120 flags.

Eventually, the Establishment could ignore the demands no more and proposals for reform went through Parliament. The Reform Act of 1832 was the start of the long road to democracy in Britain. It was widely welcomed and the celebrations were long and sincere, but the Act fell far short of the universal franchise that some had hoped for.

Further improvements were required and there came demands for more radical legislation. There gradually came a series of changes, principally in 1867 and 1884, which extended the franchise until, in 1918, a Bill was passed guaranteeing the vote to all men aged twenty-one and over. By this time, the heroic effort of the pioneers was recognised, and a monument was built on a hill in the Kay Park. Originally it consisted of a column, with a statue on top to represent liberty, but the statue was blown down during a storm in 1936, and has never been replaced.

*

As the twentieth century dawned, there was no longer the danger of being transported to the colonies or hanged for advocating change. Yet, even so, Britain had a long way to go to reach the goal of a system that was all-inclusive and fair; it was still far from a democratic society. A growing number considered that women should also be entitled to vote. The British Establishment resisted for as long as they could. Then, during the First World War, women did the men's work while the men were dying on the killing fields. They did the work as well as, and sometimes better than, the men. Their reward was long-overdue democratic rights, and in 1918 women aged thirty and over were granted the vote. The process was rather belatedly completed when women aged over twenty-one were granted the vote in 1928.

And still there was a demand for greater democracy. After all, adults over the age of twenty-one and, from 1970, over eighteen, had the right to vote. Demands grew for a Scottish Parliament. Predictably, the British Establishment resisted for as long as it was able but, in the end, a Scottish Parliament, with restricted powers, was established and the first elections were held for the new body in 1999.

We have a monument in Kilmarnock to the pioneers of democracy. We do not have a monument in Kilmarnock to the heroic women who campaigned for their right to vote, nor to those who stood up to the Establishment to win a Scottish Parliament. We still have rebels today, advocating further change in the way that the country is governed, but the Establishment continues sternly to resist any change.

We have free speech now and anyone who looks through the political columns of our newspapers will see that there is a healthy debate on a wide variety of political topics. These are simply not comparable to the debates of 200 years ago, and go far beyond what the people of that time would have thought possible. Today some ask if Scotland should be independent; others argue that Britain should rid itself of the royal family and become a republic; some advocate that we should have a written constitution. Many advocate that we should join the European currency, abolish the House of Lords, or have proportional representation for Westminster. We can debate these matters today without the fear of transportation, or of being executed, only because of the brave men and women, many from Kilmarnock, who stood up for their beliefs. They will not be forgotten.

TWENTY-FIVE

WORDS IN *GUID BLACK PRENT*

NO ENTHUSIAST OF THE life and works of Robert Burns can study the poet for long without coming across details of Kilmarnock. Although Kilmarnock cannot claim to be the birthplace of Burns, nor the place where he lived or died, the town and its people played a unique role in the young poet's life.

Several people in Kilmarnock became his firm friends and others gave him inspiration for some of his best-loved works. His poems, songs and private correspondence all combine to give a unique view of Kilmarnock in the closing years of the eighteenth century. Today very little remains in the town of the buildings which were associated with Burns and his contemporaries, but Kilmarnock's associations with him are of paramount importance in the story of his life.

After the death of his father, Robert moved from Alloway to Mossgiel Farm near Mauchline as a farmer in his own right. Kilmarnock at the time was little more than a large village, but it was the market town serving the Mauchline area, and so it was to Kilmarnock that Burns came to buy his seed, grain and other supplies. It was to Kilmarnock that he looked for customers on market days to sell his produce, just as the family had looked to Ayr on market days when they were living at Alloway.

Perhaps of even greater importance, in Kilmarnock he found a ready audience for his work, and he met influential people who encouraged him to publish a collection of his poems and songs. And, as things turned out, when Burns decided to go ahead with producing a book of poems, written chiefly in the Scottish dialect, it was to John Wilson in Kilmarnock that he looked for the printing and bookbinding.

The Kilmarnock of the late eighteenth century was very different to the place we know today. The town was crowded and compact with poorly lit, narrow and twisting streets and lanes compacted around the Cross and the kirk. The boundary to the south was about the Netherton. Riccarton was quite separate, and few of the weavers and cobblers at the Netherton considered themselves to be part of Kilmarnock, even though by the time of Burns, a long wide, straight road had been built from Kilmarnock to Riccarton right through the Netherton. The boundary on the east was not far beyond Tam Samson's house in London Road, probably about where the Dick Institute is now. The western boundary was around the line of Grange

Street. And, to the north, there wasn't much beyond the High Kirk, at least not until you came to the little clachan of Beansburn, but, of course, that wasn't really part of Kilmarnock either.

Burns was what today we would probably call a charmer. When he started making regular trips to Kilmarnock to buy grain or sell his goods, he made an immediate impression on the good people of the town. He charmed them with his wit, he delighted them with his intellect, and he shocked them with his political vision of an international brotherhood and of democracy. These were dangerous concepts to support. Burns also quietly hinted at support for the republican revolution in France. Open support for this cause would have invited charges of sedition and possibly even the death penalty. Burns was a rebel, but he was smart enough to know how far he could go, at least in public. He was also young and handsome, charming, intelligent and witty. Everything the young girls of Ayrshire dreamed about.

Burns quickly attracted the attention of the leading citizens of the town. He met them while making business transactions, but he was soon invited into their social circle. They met for drinks at various inns and pubs, but the favourite was the Bowling Green House. As the name suggests, this was an inn close to the town's bowling green. The town's bowling club had been founded in 1740, almost twenty years before Robert Burns was born.

This club still exists, and today is the oldest continuously run bowling club in Scotland. At the time that Robert Burns frequented the inn, the club and the adjacent inn were at the top of what became Portland Street. It was in the Bowling Green House that Burns met and socialised with people who would not only encourage him to produce a book of poems, but would also actively promote the book and sponsor its production.

Burns probably enjoyed a few games of bowling on the green next to this inn but it was in the Bowling Green House that he would drink 'divine libation' with people like John Goldie, a theologian and businessman and also a man of considerable intuition and intellect. He was impressed by the poet's work and was one of the leading Kilmarnock men who put cash up front to convince John Wilson that printing the farmer's poems really was a good idea.

There was also Tam Samson and his brother, John. Tam ran a seed business which had been founded in Kilmarnock in 1759, the year Burns was born. The business lasted in Kilmarnock until 1984. In the late eighteenth century the business served the needs of local farmers, like Burns. There was the town clerk, William Paterson, who was another leading businessman in the town. Robert Muir, a wine merchant, was there. Another regular at the Bowling Green House was Tom Greenshields, who ran a brewery in Grange Street. Other important Kilmarnock men who played a part in the life story of Robert Burns included Dr William Mure and William Parker, a banker and wealthy local landowner from Assloss. Sandy Patrick was nearly always there as he was the owner of the Bowling Green House. He married Tam Samson's daughter. These men might have considered themselves to be friends of the eccentric farmer that some called Rab the Rhymer. Many found immortality through his writings.

If Burns had any doubts about his own abilities as a maker of rhymes, then this group of influential folk did not. They clearly recognised that, in this well-educated local farmer, there was literary genius and they not only encouraged him to push ahead with a book, but also ordered advance copies, ensuring a successful publication. Robert Muir, the wine merchant, bought 72 copies out of the total production run of just 612.

One man who seemed to be missing from this important circle of individuals was another local businessman, John Wilson. He ran a printing business in a side street off the Cross and had a bookshop facing the Cross. It was John Wilson that Burns asked to do the printing work in July 1786. Wilson was the same age as the poet, and also took a keen interest in local affairs. He was a magistrate in the days before elections were open to the public, and he was keen to produce works that would help to educate the ordinary man. It was this John Wilson who established the first Ayrshire newspaper. He is central to the story of Robert Burns and his Kilmarnock connections, and today his statue stands alongside Robert Burns at Kilmarnock Cross.

But the personal life of the poet-farmer was complicated. He had fallen for Jean Armour, the daughter of a master mason from Mauchline and, shocking for the time, she became pregnant before they were married. At the time that Wilson was finishing the production of the book of poems, Jean Armour's father took out a warrant to force Burns to contribute towards the upkeep of the baby Jean was carrying. As it turned out, she gave birth to twins. Burns went into hiding at Old Rome near Kilmarnock with his mother's half-sister, Jean Broun, who had married James Allan, a carpenter on the Fairlie estate. This was the same Allan family who later founded the Allan Shipping Line, which grew to become the world's biggest privately owned shipping line.

The family already had shipping connections and Burns planned to use any money he made from the sale of his book to go to Jamaica where he would leave his troubles behind and start a new life. He changed his mind when he realised the book that has become known as the Kilmarnock Edition was an immediate success, not just locally among his friends, but also nationally. The book was universally admired and an adoring public demanded more of his poems. Burns hoped that he could now make enough money in Scotland to look after Jean and the twins.

Following the publication of the Kilmarnock Edition, Burns was immediately lionised by the leading citizens, not just of Kilmarnock but also throughout Scotland. He was an instant national celebrity and, wherever he went, he charmed people with his wit and good humour. Several of his poems have a Kilmarnock theme. 'Tam Samson's Elegy' is about the Kilmarnock seed merchant, and refers to the narrow and confined roads in Kilmarnock as 'streets and neuks'.

Burns loved to satirise the pompous nature of the Establishment and in the Church he found a great deal of inspiration. Kilmarnock ministers feature in a number of his works, including 'The Ordination', which tells of the disruption in the Laigh Kirk follow-ing the ordination of an unpopular minister against the wishes of the congregation. This poem also refers to Begbie's, an inn that later became the Angel Hotel. This building was demolished in the 1970s.

He referred to several ministers in various poems including James Mackinlay of the Laigh Kirk, John Robertson, John Murtrie, John Russell, John Robertson and James Oliphant. He also mentioned one of the Masonic clubs in Kilmarnock, as well as areas around the town such as Riccarton and the Netherton.

It is therefore a matter of great regret that Kilmarnock has virtu-ally nothing to show tourists interested in Burns. There is a monument and statue in the Kay Park; a statue of Burns and Wilson at the Cross, and a few scattered plaques marking some of the sites associated with Burns. There are some gravestones of interest. The Laigh Kirk has stones to the Reverend Mackinlay, Tam Samson and the Reverend John Robertson, and the High Kirk has stones or plaques to John Wilson and the Tannock brothers who painted his portrait, but that is all the tourist can see. There is no longer a museum room in the Kay Park monument, and there are only occasional exhibitions in Kilmarnock related to Burns.

The enthusiast has to go to Ayr, Alloway and Irvine, where the civic leaders seem to be more in tune with the needs of tourists and those local people who make a living from tourism. Kilmarnock, however, is home to the World Burns Federation and the No. 0 Burns Club. Kilmarnock is important to the story of Burns, just as Burns is important to the history of Kilmarnock. He immortalised the town and many of its most notable citizens. Anyone who studies local history can learn much about Kilmarnock and its people in the closing years of the eighteenth century by reading the poems and other writings of Rab the Rhymer.

TWENTY-SIX

JUST FOR A BET

THE SMALL GROUP WHO sat by the fire in Pie Reid's pub were all regular customers and they were all friends. This night they seemed to be having something of an argument. It was not an aggressive argument, more a heated debate, for these friends would not fall out over a minor disagreement about, of all things, walking.

Among the company that night in the 1920s was Sandy Mackie. He supped on his pint, put the glass down gently and declared emphatically: 'Ye ken naething aboot it at a'. I bet I could still walk tae Edinburgh as fast as anyone.' His companions didn't really doubt it. Sandy was not as young as he once was, but he had been a good and powerful athlete. Seeing that his pals did not seem to be all that impressed, he added, 'Backwards', and he paused to see what effect that had on the company before adding, 'Tied tae a pram.'

The others rose to the bait. They wanted to make sure that he was not kidding. He was not. Sandy was emphatic that if challenged to do so then he would walk from Kilmarnock to Edinburgh and, yes, he repeated he really would walk backwards, tied to a pram.

Perhaps they had all had just a little bit too much ale or whisky that night and one of his pals told him not to be so daft, and to let the matter drop. Sandy would not let the matter drop. His reputation was at stake and, of equal importance, bets had been laid. Things had gone too far to pull out of it now. Next morning, after the effects of the demon alcohol had worn off, far from seeking out his friends to cancel the bets, Sandy started making preparations for the epic journey to Scotland's capital city.

If any man could walk for more than sixty miles backwards while tied to an old pram, it was Sandy Mackie. He had been an outstanding athlete in his youth. In the days when runs were timed with a hand-held stopwatch, Sandy could run 100 yards in a little more than ten seconds. He was just as proficient at the longer distance of 440 yards.

He had been brought up in Kilmaurs and had gone to work in the mines at the age of eleven. His abilities outside the mine were varied. Apart from his athletics and his boxing, he was a fine drummer and an expert piper. When the miners at Ballochmyle were on strike for a decent wage, Sandy kept his comrades entertained with pipe music. And when soldiers guarded the Ballochmyle Viaduct during the First World War, he kept them entertained too, also with rousing pipe music. His outstanding skill on the athletics field brought him fame and attention from all over Ayrshire and beyond, and he won many medals and trophies. At all the events he took one special person: his trainer, coach, and medical adviser – his mother. Ann Mackie was a remarkable lady, who helped Sandy along every step of the way.

Although by the 1920s he was no longer competing against the young men of the county, he knew that he was still fit, hence the argument in Pie Reid's pub that night. Sandy's plans were refined and approved by his friends. He found an old pram, and it was converted to a sort of cart to carry the provisions and other things that he would need on the journey. In the interests of safety, he was allowed take a friend along with him. He chose Tucker McCluckie, who was permitted to walk forward. The pram was fitted with a locking mechanism, so that Sandy could only get out of the contraption if someone else freed him.

Soon, everything was ready and on a Saturday morning, cheered on by a great crowd, Sandy and Tucker set off for the other side of Scotland. Sandy was fit and he was determined, and he managed to reach Edinburgh without difficulty. Amazingly, he had won his bet. Later, he walked an even greater distance to London, this time looking where he was going!

*

Another very odd bet concerned a Riccarton man who was known throughout Ayrshire as a fine musician. The group that gathered at the foot of the new Riccarton Church didn't quite know what to think. A few muttered that the whole thing was just an odd rumour that had got out of hand, but when a hush swept over them, they realised that the man being led towards the church was indeed Sandy McCrone. The mood changed instantly from one of amusement and expectation, to one of apprehension.

Sandy McCrone was one of the best fiddlers in town. He entertained at all the important weddings and other social events. At one of them he had rather rashly said that he could climb the scaffolding that surrounded the new kirk at Riccarton and stick a potato on the beak of the weathercock. And when he had been rebuked for being daft, he had insisted. Bets had been laid and now Sandy was about to perform the task . . . and not only that, he would do it at night.

Some made a last-minute attempt to reason with him. They warned Sandy that he would surely fall to his death. But the fiddler would not listen. He reiterated that he could, and would, stick the

Riccarton Church: When it was being built, a blind man climbed the scaffold to put a potato on the beak of the weathercock.

tattie on the beak of the bird. Knowledge of the bet was confined to a small group, for if word had got out the authorities would surely have put a stop to it. Nevertheless interest was intense among those in the know, and it was heightened because Sandy was blind. How could a blind man possibly perform such a thing?

Sandy had become blind as the result of having smallpox as a child. But he had grown up blind and had made the most of his situation. His blindness gave him an acute sense of hearing. On one of his walks he led a sighted man to a lark's nest, which Sandy was able to locate by sound alone. He had a good musical ear and, unlike many other musicians around, could play to perfection. He was first choice at all the society events and, what's more, he could find his way to and from the houses for miles around his native Riccarton.

As far as his famous exploit was concerned, for him it was a simple matter of climbing until there was no scaffolding left, then feeling for the beak of the weathercock. After he had been up the scaffolding and come safely back down, someone made a remark about adding to the danger by doing the climb at night. With a wry smile, the bold Sandy declared that as far as he was concerned darkness and light were all the same. That night Sandy won his bet, and a place in local folklore.

*

Betting can, of course, get out of control, as it did for Rab Crooks. Now, no one in Kilmarnock would have said that Rab Crooks was a wicked man. He was just a bit of a rogue who was a little too fond of games of chance. Some time around the start of the nineteenth century, Rab started a shoe business in Kilmarnock, but the enterprise did not last long, because Rab preferred to spend his time and his money drinking and gambling. He soon acquired a well-earned reputation for borrowing and being a bit slow to repay his debts.

His friends did what they could to get him to break the habit, but in the end Rab met his match when he tried to outwit an old lady. He met the old widow woman one day at the head of New Street and, knowing that she was fond of a wee gamble, Rab asked her if she wanted a game. She agreed. Lady Luck was not with Rab that day at all, and soon he owed her the grand sum of thirty shillings. Now Rab knew well that the old lady could neither read nor write and he decided to exploit this to his advantage.

When Rab said that he would have to go, the old lady said: 'Ah weel, pay me an' gang awa' when ye like.'

'Pay ye!' Rab exclaimed. 'I'm sure I'm no awn ye onything ava.'

The two argued for a while and Rab parted saying that he would only pay the debt if he were made to but, as she kept no books, that wouldn't happen. The old lady had a lot more determination than Rab had realised. She went to the town bailies and they called Rab up before them to answer the claim of an unpaid debt.

'I'm sure I'm no awn her a bawbee', Rab said, 'But if she'll bring in her buik an bring onything agin me, I'm willing to pay.' Rab smiled confidently to himself. The old lady could not read or write. How could she possibly keep books?

The old lady explained to the court that she could neither read nor write and Rab's smile broadened a little. 'But', the old lady continued, and Rab for the first time began to doubt his decision to take her on, 'I hae a' things merkit doon on the bakeboard yon'er, and I can fetch it in three minutes.'

The court pondered this unusual state of affairs for only a moment before granting the old lady permission to go and get her bakeboard. It was, after all, evidence.

Off she went to get her version of an account book and there was considerable amusement when she returned with it. She explained the system she had developed for her own use. There was a short scratch for a bawbee, and a longer one for a penny; a wee circle for a sixpence and progressively larger ones for a shilling and a half-crown and a crown. She could read her own books and give day and date for every one of her transactions, including Rab's debt. She explained it all clearly and concisely. Rab was mortified. He hung his head in shame and had nothing more to say in his own defence. The result was not in doubt. Rab was ordered to pay the thirty shillings and, as the decision was announced, the court burst into loud cheers and roars of laughter.

*

Gambling, of course, was not always what might be called an entirely legal pursuit. But even at the time when it was illegal, it went on and it was fairly extensive.

James Kilmurray, the man who earned a reputation as a weather prophet, at one time had a job as an insurance man. The job very nearly landed him in trouble with the gambling laws. A Highland policeman, new to the Kilmarnock area, had been out on patrol when he noticed a suspicious looking man flitting from house to house. He seemed to be taking money at each door and noting something in a book.

Using his experience of the Scottish Highlands, the policeman concluded that the suspect – James Kilmurray – was probably at the head of an illegal gambling racket. But the situation was cleared up before any real embarrassment could be caused.

TWENTY-SEVEN

SETTING THE STANDARD

THOMAS STEVENSON WAS AN ambitious man. He served an apprenticeship in the Kilmarnock printing works of James McKie, but he wanted to do more. In his spare time he taught himself the art of shorthand. He had ambitions to become a reporter, and he achieved that goal by joining the staff of the town's leading newspaper, the *Kilmarnock Weekly Post*. In his position as a reporter, he won the respect of many people of influence in the town. Then Stevenson decided to start his own business selling books and taking commercial printing work. His business flourished and yet he still hankered after the idea of being a reporter again.

His opportunity came not long after stamp duty on newspapers was abolished. This was a time of wider education and cheaper newspapers, and the time was right for a new newspaper in Kilmarnock. In 1863 Thomas Stevenson decided to launch a new newspaper, his newspaper, one which he could not only write for but also own. At this time the *Weekly Post* was still being produced by his old boss, Mr McKie. But his paper cost tuppence – two pennies – quite a lot of money for a working man. Stevenson wanted to sell his newspaper for half that price, just one penny – but could it find enough support to make it viable at that price?

Stevenson issued a prospectus that promised his newspaper would carry local news, and 'take a lively interest in every question affecting the well-being of the community and be of fair value for the price asked'. People and businesses in the local community agreed to back the project and Mr Stevenson went ahead with his new newspaper, which he named the *Kilmarnock Standard*. But what to put in it? As things turned out, that very first issue of the *Kilmarnock Standard* in June 1863 came out with a cracking good local story. True, the other papers had it too, but the discovery of a huge hoard of ancient silver coins was the talk of the town.

So the *Standard* was launched with more of a bang than could possibly have been imagined. *The Kilmarnock Standard* was very much Mr Stevenson's baby, as he was its founder and editor. The early editions carried mostly formal local news reports from the Town Council, in which just about every cough and wheeze was reported, and reports from Presbytery appeared almost verbatim. There were few of the human interest stories that are the meat and drink of most newspapers today.

The early copies of the *Kilmarnock Standard* also carried national and international news, because newspapers at that time were the only reliable source of information about what was happening in the world, and few people could afford to buy one every day. Some working men's clubs would pool their funds and buy a daily paper, which was then shared. Sometimes the men met at a public place, such as the Holm Square, now Glencairn Square, and they would discuss the politics and issues of the day, usually advocating a further extension of the franchise or better conditions for the working man. At the Holm Square such meetings became known as the Holm Parliament.

Stevenson found just the right balance of local and national news and, at that time, the *Standard* reported on events in most of the towns and villages in Ayrshire. Sales rose quickly and, by the early 1870s, the *Kilmarnock Standard* was selling more copies than any of its rivals. Soon new daily newspapers were coming on the market offering a reliable and cheap source of national and international news. In consequence, the *Kilmarnock Standard* dropped its reporting of national events and concentrated on purely local affairs. It was a wise decision; business continued to flourish and sales rose steadily.

But in 1878 there was a crisis. After an illness lasting four months, Thomas Stevenson died in Gardener's Cottage in Park Lane. He left a widow and a young family, but no obvious successor to run the business. It could easily have been wound up, but on the staff was another remarkable man, George Dunlop. He was adamant that the *Kilmarnock Standard* was the right newspaper for the people of the Kilmarnock area, and he was equally determined that the business would not die with its founder.

George Dunlop was born in the Gas Brae, the youngest of eight remarkable sons and the only one of them who did not make a name for himself in either the ministry or medicine. He was educated at Kilmarnock Academy, where after completing his studies he became a teacher, but he didn't care for this profession and soon joined the printing firm in King Street run by a Mr Brown. He later worked for James McKie, and it was with him that he first took to journalism. For several years he was the Kilmarnock correspondent of the *Ayr Advertiser*, Ayrshire's first newspaper. It had been established in the county town by John Wilson of Kilmarnock, the man who first published the works of Robert Burns.

Towards the close of the 1860s George Dunlop was offered, and accepted, a full-time post with the *Kilmarnock Standard*, and was soon assisting Stevenson in the production of the paper. On the death of Thomas Stevenson, Dunlop was alert to the danger that the paper could simply be closed. What he needed urgently was a business partner to help him take over the *Standard*. He thought he had found one in James Rose, but Rose pulled out of the venture at the last minute, leaving an even deeper crisis. But just as quickly, a new partner appeared on the scene in the shape of William Drennan. He had previously been involved with the printing and bookselling business of his stepfather, that same Mr McKie who had so influenced both Thomas Stevenson and George Dunlop. It seemed like an ideal partnership, and it was.

Dunlop and Drennan soon flourished, with George Dunlop as editor of the *Kilmarnock Standard*, running the newspaper, and William Drennan looking after the printing works. Business continued to grow. In the 1890s, the *Standard* printing works was moved to new premises in Grange Place, a custom-built printing works, which today is a listed building. In 1892, Matthew Osborne joined the firm to develop the commercial arm of the business.

George Dunlop was a superb journalist. He would frequently write reports himself, but from others contributing to the paper he insisted on the highest possible standards of accuracy and integrity, thus helping to enhance the reputation of the *Kilmarnock Standard*. He had a fine private library, which included a number of original manuscripts and he was very knowledgeable about the works of Robert Burns. He was President of the Kilmarnock Burns Club, and was one of the founders of the International Burns Federation and a key campaigner for the erection of the Burns Monument in the Kay Park. He was keen to commemorate the reformers who campaigned for changes to the way the country was run and helped get a monument erected in their honour, which can also be found in the Kay Park.

George Dunlop was editor for just over thirty years. He died of pneumonia in 1909, leaving the *Standard* looking for someone to emulate his excellent stewardship of the paper. Such was the impact he made that, by the time of his death, the business was well established and there was no doubt about its future.

The third editor of the *Standard* was John P. Dickson. He had been on the editorial staff of the *Standard* since 1892 and for seventeen years had been chief reporter, working closely with George Dunlop. He had cut his journalistic teeth on the *Ardrossan and Saltcoats Herald* under the paper's founder, Arthur Guthrie. He seemed a natural choice to lead the paper in the new century. Like his two predecessors, he was a long-serving editor, taking the paper through the tur-

Printing apprentices at the *Kilmarnock Standard* almost 100 years ago.

bulent years of the First World War and up to 1939. During his time at the *Standard* the circulation continued to rise, and new methods of production were introduced to improve efficiency.

The fourth editor was again chosen from the staff. He was Tom Lyon and, although a native of Kilmarnock, he had left the town for a new life in Canada. However, he returned to Scotland and joined the staff at Kilmarnock in 1911. For many years he was assistant editor. He took a break from the *Kilmarnock Standard* during the First World War and was wounded on active service in France. While in the army he continued to write for the paper, sending home a series of contributions noting the lighter side of army life. They were published under the pen-name of Leo, and were later collected in two books.

After Tom Lyon came Willie Scott, editor for the nine years from 1951 to 1960. Willie Scott started his working life as a message boy on the *Dunfermline Press*. He joined the *Standard* staff in 1925. He had a genuine interest in the well-being of journalists and was a founder-member and the first chairman of the Ayrshire branch of the National Union of Journalists. A keen Burnsian, he was for a time vice-president of the Burns Federation. He retired from the *Standard* in 1960.

It was the *Standard's* sixth editor, John MacLennan, who was at the helm for the paper's centenary, and during his tenure in office a period of rapid innovation began. During the first hundred years, there had been little change in the technology of newspaper production. The news was set in metal type and the appearance of the paper remained much the same, with intimations and other adverts on the front page. It was John MacLennan who put news on the front page for the first time in 1965 and it was he who changed the size of the paper from its large broadsheet pages to a handier tabloid size in 1971.

The last quarter of the twentieth century saw the whole of the news-paper industry change beyond all recognition. Computer technology allowed greatly increased news and advertising content. In 1978 the printing of the *Standard* was switched from the traditional hot-metal system to web offset, allowing more pages and the use of colour pictures. The previously labour-intensive industry gradually became one employing only a fraction of what was once required.

The march of technology has been relentless and today a selection of the news and features from the paper is posted on the internet every week. Kilmarnock ex-pats, no matter where they are in the world, do not have to wait a week or more for the postman to bring the *Standard* to them.

It must be something of a record that, as the *Standard* is about to enter its one hundred and fortieth year, there have only been eight editors, each one bringing his own individual flair to the paper, and each one keen to see the paper and the town flourish.

The trend towards globalisation also brought changes in owner-ship. In the 1960s Dunlop and Drennan sold out to George Outram, a company with newspaper interests across Scotland. By the 1970s, the *Standard* was part of Lonrho, a multinational group with a wide range of businesses in many countries, then headed by the legendary entrepreneur 'Tiny' Rowland. Today it is part of Scottish and Universal Newspapers, one of several companies in the Trinity Mirror family. Trinity Mirror is Britain's biggest newspaper publisher.

The very first *Kilmarnock Standard* in 1863 had just four pages. Today, it often runs to 128 pages a week, and sometimes more. Yet for all that, the *Kilmarnock Standard* remains what Thomas Stevenson intended it to be – a newspaper that gives the people of the Kilmarnock area a reliable source of fair and accurate information on local matters.

TWENTY-EIGHT

RETROSPECTIVE ON AN ARTIST

THE YOUNG MAN WHO walked into Kilmarnock from near Symington had a mission. He was searching for work. The first cobbler's shop he came to was that of Jamie Sellars. He looked in, hopeful that he would at least get a trial; a pair of boots to make, or a pair of shoes, perhaps. This determined young man was John Kelso Hunter. He was born on 15 December 1802 at Gillhead Cottage on the Dankeith estate between Symington and Dundonald, the home of the Kelso family. The estate is an ancient one, which used to extend around Symington. The Dundonald kirk records refer to a Lady Dankeyth as early as 1628.

At the start of the nineteenth century the grounds were still extensive and rambling and, at the tender age of eight, John had started to earn his keep by working as a herd boy, keeping the sheep and poultry out of the corn. As a youngster he had often visited Symington and there he met Jock McPherson, the local cobbler. John loved the smell of fresh leather and he loved the advice that he got from Jock – be independent.

One day the boy was stopped by Colonel Kelso from the Big House. He told John that he had a position for him as boy to Mr Fleming of Barrochan, but John stood his ground. With as much respect as he could muster he said he would be his own master. He would go to Jock McPherson and learn shoemaking. Kelso's brutal response to this 'impertinence' was to crack his whip across the boy's shoulder. Immediately, John headed for Jock in Symington, where he was treated with sympathy and respect. Jock could not provide work, but said he would speak to Mr Rowat in Dundonald, who agreed to take John on as an apprentice. As for Jock, well, he lived to a ripe old age and if you want to see his likeness, look at the statue by Thom in the Burns Monument at Alloway. The model for Souter Johnnie was Jock McPherson.

So, young John Kelso Hunter tramped to Dundonald to learn the art of shoemaking. But when he had completed his apprenticeship, times were hard. War had brought high taxes. There was an economic slump. Demand for all sorts of products was falling and Mr Rowat, who had taught John his trade now had to tell him that he did not have enough work for the two of them.

Still, Dundonald was not a big place. There were bigger towns, such as Kilmarnock. There were plenty of shoemakers in Kilmarnock, and John was determined to find work at one of them. He called at every shoemaker's establishment, large and small, on the front street, and in the back streets. He asked the same question in every shop and in every place he got the same demoralising answer. There was no work.

The next day he retraced his steps. He visited the same shops and he asked the same question. He was given the same answer at every single shop. There was no work. He was persistent and went back for a third day. He repeated the exercise and got the same answer in every shop as he had the day before and the day before that.

On the fourth day he called in at John Borland's in Portland Street and was greeted rather gruffly by the man at the cutting board: 'Ye were here yesterday, an' I telt ye then we had nae work for ye.'

'Weel,' said John, 'That's true, but if I dinna get work ony place else the day, I'll be back again the morn.'

Impressed by his determination, Mr Borland gave him work there and then. This little incident in itself might have been enough to preserve John Kelso Hunter in the annals of Ayrshire folklore, but he went on to much better things, not as a cobbler, but as an artist of some note. Despite having no formal training in art, John took easily to painting and rapidly made a name for himself as a fine portrait painter. Soon he was in demand, painting the portraits of the wealthy and well-connected. There were no cameras in those days to make instant portraits for posterity.

In 1831 John was one of about a dozen or so local artists who helped to establish the Kilmarnock Drawing Academy; Hunter was one of its leading lights and an inspiration to the others. Some of the other people who joined the society later became well known. They included Thomas Barclay, who later went on to earn a name for himself as a carpet designer of repute; and James Douglas, who became a portrait painter in Edinburgh. The society rented a room in a building in Cheapside Street for exhibitions and as a place where they could study other paintings.

The Kilmarnock newspaper of the day was the *Kilmarnock Chronicle*. Ayrshire journalist, James Paterson, who helped establish and run the *Chronicle* later wrote his life story under the title of *Autobiographical Reminiscences*. He recalled sitting for John Kelso Hunter, apparently at the request of the artist. But this portrait was never completed because James left Kilmarnock.

Paterson recalled in his autobiography that 'One of the earliest duties of the *Chronicle* was to record the formation of an association of artists, whose works were considered so good as to lead to a local exhibition.' Several exhibitions were mounted. The *Chronicle* was there to promote and comment on the displays. During one of the Kilmarnock exhibitions, the paper reported: 'Visit the Academy during the daylight and you will find the shoemaker a devoted student of Titian; and at night go to his dwelling, and you will find him the hard working son of Crispin; instead of delineating with a pencil the divine features of the human face, he is beating out the soles of a pair of shoes with his hammer.'

At another exhibition where there were forty-five paintings by various artists on display, no less than sixteen were the work of the cobbler-artist, John Kelso Hunter. Life was indeed a continuous struggle for Hunter. He had a wife and no fewer than eight children to support and when he was not painting, he was making and repairing shoes. After he had given up shoemaking, he took up writing as well as painting.

The society borrowed fine works to study and to copy in order to learn their craft. They became ambitious: they wanted to take over the ruin of the old Kilmarnock gunpowder store, put a roof on and use it as their academy of art. But not long after the society had been founded, Kilmarnock, along with the rest of the country, was hit by a serious outbreak of cholera. Hundreds died and the country could think of nothing else. Meetings and exhibitions were abandoned and the Drawing Academy soon folded.

But John Kelso Hunter continued to find relief from the tedious work of shoemaking through his art. He had a reputation for working quickly and producing striking likenesses. In 1834, he found some work through the Irvine Burns Club. He painted portraits for hundreds of customers, and eventually decided that the best way ahead was to give up shoemaking and become a full-time artist. And by now, for the man from Dankeith who had learned his trade in Dundonald, even Kilmarnock was too small.

So, in 1838, he moved to Glasgow to work as a professional portrait painter. In the city, he faced much greater competition, but his works were frequently put on display in the city's top institutions such as the McLellan Galleries. His self-portrait, now kept in the Dick Institute's collection in Kilmarnock, was put on exhibition in the Royal Academy in London in 1847, and his works were often on display at the Royal Scottish Academy between 1849 and 1872.

Even in Glasgow, he continued to take a keen interest in the affairs of Ayrshire in general, and Kilmarnock in particular. He joined other Kilmarnock men in helping to form and run the Glasgow Kilmarnock

Benevolent Society, which raised money to help those folk from Kilmarnock who had fallen on hard times in the city.

Many of the fine portraits that John Kelso Hunter produced are today retained in museums and art collections and many are in private hands. Given his prowess in this field, it is perhaps surprising this John Kelso Hunter is best remembered not for his art, but for yet another talent. He was an accomplished writer. While books such as *Memorials of West Countrymen, Manners of the Past Half Century* and *Life Studies of Character*, are now all but forgotten, it is his autobiography that is treasured by students of local history.

The Retrospect of an Artist's Life (cited in some references as *The Retrospective of an Artist's Life*) was an immediate success when it was first published in 1868. It is not just the story of John Kelso Hunter's struggle through the first half of the nineteenth century; it is about life in general in Ayrshire at a time of rapid change. It dwells on the dying days of smuggling and provides a racy account of the trial of the first steam locomotive ever brought to Scotland in 1816. The style is colourful and it is peppered with his sharp wit and comment. The book is especially strong on the characters he encountered in Ayrshire. Those who bought the book when it was published must have known many of the people mentioned, and those who read it today for the first time are given a vivid impression of what life was like in an era long gone.

John Kelso Hunter died in Glasgow on 3 February 1873 and was brought back to Symington where he was buried in the local church-yard. His son of the same name had a son who was also named John Kelso Hunter. He in turn had a son whom he named John Kelso Hunter. This one was born in Greenock in 1921 and when he was about two or three years old, the family moved to the USA, settling in New Jersey. By the time he died in 1970, he had named his son John Kelso Hunter and in turn this John Kelso Hunter named his son John Kelso Hunter. Six generations; six John Kelso Hunters.

John Kelso Hunter, the original one, is still something of an enigmatic character who flits through the pages of Ayrshire's local history. Hardly a subject relating to early nineteenth-century Ayrshire is mentioned without a reference to *The Retrospect of an Artist's Life*, and yet, there is little recorded about the man himself. However, he continues to fascinate us. As recently as 1985, more than a hundred years after his death, the Dick Institute hosted an exhibition on the man and his work as part of Ayrshire Heritage Week.

Like John Kelso Hunter, the estate of Dankeith flits in and out of

Ayrshire history. It must have changed little throughout his life. Then the old property was rebuilt in 1893. A stone with the date of reconstruction is above the door. At the rear of the property, part of the original building was retained. At one time the crescent-shaped estate almost enclosed Symington. The crest of the Kelso family was a wheatsheaf and this was the name chosen for the popular pub in Symington.

At the end of the nineteenth century, Dankeith passed from the Kelso family to the Mann-Thomsons, the last family to live in the property. When the Second World War broke out, the building at Dankeith was requisitioned by the RAF and because of its relative seclusion was an ideal venue for high-level and top-secret gatherings. It was here that several meetings were held to plan details for the allied landings in North Africa and for D-Day. At the end of the war the estate, along with that of the neighbouring estate of Coodham, passed to the ownership of the Passionate Fathers, who used it as a training centre for Catholic priests. They stayed there for twenty years, from about 1948 to 1968, at which time Dankeith became a caravan park with the main building being used as offices.

TWENTY-NINE

LET US ENTERTAIN YOU

THE OLD LADY HAD just finished preparing the sheep's head and had put it in a pot. She turned to do something else when something astonishing happened. The disembodied sheep's head began to bleat. But this old lady was wise to the world and, as she looked out of the open window, she saw a young lad who was obviously quite pleased with himself. She recognised him, of course, for Kilmarnock was not a big place in the early nineteenth century.

She leaned out of her window and, in a half-hearted attempt at mock anger, shouted after the lad: 'Duncan McMillan, ye wee rascal. I'll tell yer mither on ye.' But then she smiled quietly to herself. Young Duncan's joke had been a good one. She could have sworn the bleating came from the sheep's head.

Duncan McMillan was something of a marvel around the Holm area of Kilmarnock. He had a real talent; a magic voice. He could make a voice come out of a pouch or a pot; he could make a cow talk or a sheep's head bleat. Folk in the Holm and around Kilmarnock were getting used to his tricks.

He was what Kilmarnock folk called a Holm Callan: that is, he was born in the area of the holm between Kilmarnock's two rivers, in 1817. His parents were not wealthy and could only afford to give him a fairly basic education before he became an apprentice to one of the many local weavers. At the time, weaving was a thriving industry in Kilmarnock and seemed the best prospect for a young lad. However, when he was very young a touring ventriloquist visited Kilmarnock and Duncan was captivated. Somehow he managed to get involved, and from the travelling showman he learned the basics of the talent that would change his life. He learned the art of ventriloquism.

Today we tend to think of a ventriloquist as someone who manipulates a dummy and persuades an audience that it has its own personality and character. In Duncan's day a ventriloquist could throw his voice and make you think that the voice was coming from somewhere else . . . a sheep's head, for example. Duncan polished the art. In addition to such tricks, he soon learned how to mimic others, he taught himself to sing and later he learned the even more mysterious art of hypnotism.

All these talents became clear while Duncan was still at school. He often had his classmates in fits of laughter by accurately imitating the teachers' voices. It wasn't just the teachers he mimicked. Like modern-day impressionists, he mimicked anyone and everyone. One elderly lady was moaning to her friend about how cheeky Duncan had been in imitating her voice, but she got no sympathy from her friend. Just a comment: 'Aye, he's an unco callan, Duncan, but ye needna complain, for he acts us a'.'

His reputation began to spread. He played so many tricks on so many people that, by the age of fourteen, he was known throughout Ayrshire and his talents were widely acknowledged. Soon he was in demand to put on private shows for local dignitaries. It wasn't long before he was giving public performances on the professional stage.

Duncan may have been proud of his abilities, but not everyone in his family was. His grandmother did not approve at all. She had a deep-rooted aversion to anything theatrical, and she made it clear to Duncan that his funeral would cause her less grief than his going on the stage. After thinking long and hard about this, Duncan chose to go on the stage anyway.

He was a huge success and after his first public performance the young man went home with several pounds in his pocket. Even this did not soften the attitude of his grandmother. She would look after the money for him all right, but she threw the coins into the corner of a drawer and would not even let the 'Devil's money' touch the other coins in the house, which had been honestly earned by hard work.

One of the earliest of his public performances was held in the Turf Inn Assembly Room in Kilmarnock. This was the premier venue in Kilmarnock at the time and, to ensure that the hall was well filled, a brass band toured the streets of the town drumming up interest.

For some time the ventriloquism was simply a hobby. Duncan kept to his day job, working long hours at the loom. But all his spare time was taken up practising what he could do with that voice, polishing his shows, for a little extra money and for the sake of doing something that he loved. He also studied the history of ventriloquism and built that into his act. Soon he had devised a format for his performances. He would start by telling his audience a little of the origins of the art. One evening, early on in his career, he was performing in Ayr. These were troubled times. Radical forces were at work demanding political change. The army was on high alert. But, on this particular night, there was no sign of trouble and the audience at the show included a large contingent of cavalrymen.

Duncan came on stage and all went quiet. 'Ladies and gentlemen,' he greeted them, 'the art, or gift, of which I confess to being in complete possession, is of very ancient origins . . .'

But he got no further than that. One of the soldiers stood up. 'It's a' blethers', shouted the soldier. 'I ken him brawley. He's frae the Holm in Kilmarnock and kens nocht aboot it ava – nae mair than me an that's precious little.'

The audience laughed. The soldier sat down and Duncan carried on. Just as the laughter died down a faint sound drifted into the room from somewhere far off. Then it was heard again; no mistaking it this time. It was the shrill call of a trumpet note: a call to arms. The cavalrymen hurriedly left the hall and rushed back to their quarters to report for duty. But when they got there, all was quiet. There was no emergency and no call out. The men realised that they had been tricked. There never had been a trumpet call, only the magic voice of Duncan McMillan. They rushed back to the hall to catch the rest of the show and when they arrived, they were treated to hoots of laughter and a round of applause. They settled down to watch the rest of the performance with a new respect for the man on the stage and his unusual talents. The soldier who had made the original interruption was later reported to have said: 'It was well worth the price o' a coo tae hear him.'

Another of Duncan's very early performances was for a group of miners near Ayr. This show was held in a school. Close to the end of his act he hypnotised a few of the miners, instructing them that they were to talk to their comrades about the show. One described a man 'wi an iron thrapple', another said the performer had 'leather lungs' and another said he was a man 'wi' a wean in his pouch'.

Then something happened that was to have a profound impact on Duncan's life. The weavers of Glasgow embraced the new technology being offered by steam engines. This so enhanced the efficiency of the industry in Glasgow that Kilmarnock suffered badly, and Duncan found it increasingly difficult to earn enough from weaving. And so, at the age of twenty-seven, he decided to leave weaving behind and become a full-time entertainer.

He was already well known across Ayrshire and in some neighbouring areas. Now it was time to tour England. At each place he visited, he first noted local variations of the dialect and he built this into his act, thus giving each performance something of a local flavour. His hope was this would help attract a local audience and maintain interest in the show. It did. He was an immediate success. And wherever he went he was not just a performer; he always took a bit of that rascal who had tried to scare the old lady with the sheep's head trick. He just could not resist playing practical jokes.

Duncan McMillan: the man with the magic voice.

On one occasion his tour took him to Lincoln, where Duncan was keen to see the town's impressive cathedral. He followed the verger up seemingly endless stairs until they reached the top of the building. Duncan asked the verger if he could see the building's famous bell, but the verger said that that was impossible, because it was the other verger who took visitors to see the bell. Just before they started down again a voice drifted down from the bell-tower: 'Hello, down there. I'm to be kept here till doomsday, I suppose.'

The surprised verger tried to find out more. 'How long have you been there?'

'About six hours,' came the voice from the bell-tower. And so the verger had to go into the bell-tower and make a search and, as he did, Duncan quietly looked around and got an excellent view of the bell.

The verger couldn't find anyone. 'Where are you?' he demanded, and the voice came back, 'I'm here below the roof.'

By the time Duncan left the building a search party had been formed and was making its way up the stairs. It was only when posters appeared all over the city advertising the ventriloquist's show that the verger realised that he had been tricked.

Duncan's reputation just grew and grew. Instead of small local venues he was now playing to capacity audiences in major theatres across Scotland, England and Ireland. In Scotland he filled halls in Glasgow, Aberdeen and Dundee. In England it was the same story in London, Manchester, Hull, Bath and Durham. His tours were often long but he never forgot his home town and his humble beginnings. When he did return to Kilmarnock, he put on free shows to entertain the patients in homes and asylums. Indeed, one of his last ever performances was on 11 September 1865 in the Corn Exchange in Kilmarnock.

But suddenly, in January 1866, Duncan McMillan died at his home in Bentinck Street. He was just forty-nine and, as the *Kilmarnock Standard* said, 'in the very zenith of his fame'. Many fulsome tributes were penned by his admirers. The *Kilmarnock Standard* obituary noted that Duncan McMillan had been 'possessed of a large fund of humour, to which he gave full scope, yet such was the natural kindness of his disposition that it never was exerted offensively against anyone.' And the *Ayr Advertiser* also wrote in glowing terms, saying that Duncan McMillan 'had few, if any, equals in his walk of life.'

No doubt if Duncan McMillan had been born 150 years later he would have had a top-rated television show. And yet, television has irrevocably changed the art of the ventriloquist from its traditional one of making a voice appear to come from somewhere else. McMillan was a man who made a big impact on the lives of many people and yet he is largely forgotten, except by dedicated local historians. From these old newspaper reports, we can piece together something of the talents of the man, but we can only guess at the wonder of the audience as they listened to voices and sounds from the ether, made not by electronic wizardry, but by the man with the magic voice.

THIRTY

KILLIE'S GLORY YEAR

IT IS NO EXAGGERATION to say that, in season 1964/65, Kilmarnock Football Club achieved more than any other provincial club in the history of Scottish football has ever done. Killie were not only crowned champions, but also produced one of Scotland's greatest-ever results in European football. Given the apparently endless dominance of Rangers and Celtic in the modern era, these achievements are unlikely ever to be equalled.

It was a team with an abundance of highly talented players, many of whom have become club legends. The two Scotland international goalkeepers, Campbell Forsyth and Bobby Ferguson, who was later transferred in 1967 to West Ham United for a then record fee of £65,000. The ever-dependable Matt Watson at left back. The inspirational skipper Frank Beattie (no relation to the author) who signed for the club as a nineteen year-old in 1953. The wily veterans Bertie Black and Davie Sneddon. Leading goalscorer Ronnie Hamilton, who subsequently became a Kilmarnock director. Hamilton's strike partner Jackie McInally, the father of Alan McInally, who himself became a top goalscorer with Celtic, Aston Villa and Bayern Munich. Local boy Jim McFadzean, one of the most versatile players in Scotland. Nor should we forget a seventeen year-old right winger who was beginning to carve out a massive reputation for himself – one Tommy McLean – who would achieve great things with Rangers and Scotland later in his career. The team was also lucky with the man at the helm; Willie Waddell, appointed manager in 1957, had been one of the giants of the Scottish game as a player and would go on to even greater heights as Rangers boss.

There had been signs in the recent past that the team had outstanding ability; in the four seasons from 1959/60 to 1962/63 Killie had been runners-up in the league championship on three occasions. The team achieved this feat again in 1963/64, recording a number of famous victories along the way, including a 4–0 win against Celtic and a spectacular demolition of a hapless Falkirk side by nine goals to two. It was the same story in cup competitions: Kilmarnock had lost two Scottish Cup finals in the previous eight years; in 1956/57 to Falkirk after a replay and in 1960 against Rangers (which meant that Kilmarnock finished the 1959/60 campaign as runners-up in the two major domestic competitions). There were also two League Cup final disappointments: the first of which was a defeat at the hands of Rangers in 1960. The second, in 1962, was especially disappointing: the team put together a tremendous run that included a thrilling 3–2 win over Rangers in the semi-final, a game that some thought the greatest ever in the history of the tournament. Sadly Killie fell again at the last hurdle as Hearts beat them 1–0 in the final. After so many second places, Killie were surely overdue a trophy.

Kilmarnock started that fateful season of 1964/65 with a new formation of 4–2–4 and, at first, the team struggled to adapt. The initial rounds of the League Cup were played in a sectional format during the month of August, and Killie had been drawn in a formidable group that also included Celtic, Hearts and Partick Thistle. Following two draws and a 4–1 defeat at the hands of Celtic, the team grew in confidence and, although it was not enough to qualify for the next stage, won its last three games. The good form carried over into the championship; the first six games of the campaign were all won as Killie surged to the top of the league.

However, all of this was completely overshadowed by a spectacular result in the Inter-Cities Fairs Cup, the equivalent of today's UEFA Cup. Kilmarnock had been drawn against one of the most powerful sides in Europe, the mighty Eintracht Frankfurt, the team that had played Real Madrid in the greatest-ever European Cup final at Hampden Park in 1960. Although the Germans were beaten 7–3 it is generally acknowledged that the Spanish maestros were the best club side of all time and gave a football masterclass that night. Many of the players who had faced Madrid were still in the Frankfurt team in 1964. It seemed that Killie were in for a tough time.

The first leg in Germany on 2 September 1964 confirmed Kilmarnock's worst fears. Despite gradually establishing dominance, Killie were stunned by an early goal from the home team. This was followed by two further counters from the Germans, who ran out comprehensive winners by 3–0. Despite the heavy defeat, Waddell was still confident of overcoming the deficit at Rugby Park. He gave two reasons for this optimism: the 4–2–4 formation adopted in Frankfurt would be ditched, despite its success in domestic football; and, of equal importance, the passion of the Kilmarnock supporters would be like an extra man.

In the run up to the second leg on 22 September, Killie's league form was excellent; three straight wins and not one goal conceded, with Messrs Hamilton and McInally in cracking form. By contrast, the Germans were experiencing major problems and were forced to make six changes to the team that had run out in Frankfurt. Among the absentees were their influential captain Hofer and the centre forward, Landerer, who had broken his leg in the first match. There might be a glimmer of hope for Killie after all.

An expectant crowd of 14,930 rolled up to Rugby Park and saw the following team take the field: Forsyth, King, McFadzean, Murray, McGrory, Beattie, McLean, McInally, Hamilton, Sneddon and McIlroy. But their hopes of a good start were cruelly dashed when a powerful thirty-yard drive from inside left Huberts smashed into the Killie net. The deficit was now four goals and Killie's cause seemed hopeless.

But this was a Kilmarnock team composed of eleven fighters. Inspired by an exuberant home support, the team mounted wave after wave of attacks and pinned the Eintracht team into its penalty box. The breakthrough came after thirteen minutes when the wily Davie Sneddon sent Ronnie Hamilton through on the Eintracht goal. Hamilton netted and only four minutes later McIlroy grabbed Killie's second. Stunned by their opponents' never-say-die attitude, the visitors then showed why they were rated as one of the best teams in Europe and stormed into attack. The pressure almost paid dividends as Campbell Forsyth was forced to make a wonder save from Schamer to keep Killie in the tie.

The keeper's exploits seemed to rouse the Scots to even greater heights and, in the fifty-second minute, Kilmarnock scored the goal of the game to make it 4–3 on aggregate. Jim McFadzean, who had been performing heroics in an attacking full-back role, leapt to connect with a McGrory free kick and sent an unstoppable header past the German keeper. The crowd was now in raptures, and it seemed that the impossible might actually happen.

Kilmarnock grew in strength and confidence, and continued to besiege the opposition goal. The valiant Germans resisted manfully and it seemed that the richly deserved equaliser would never come. But with only eight minutes left the crowd's prayers were answered. A wonderful cross from McIlroy was met by McInally, his header flashed into the net and the tie was all-square. Unable to contain themselves the delirious Killie fans invaded the pitch to acclaim their heroes. But the best was still to come. Following outstanding wing play from Tommy McLean an Eintracht defender was forced to bring him down. With only two minutes to go, Sneddon took a short free kick and Ronnie Hamilton scored with the aid of a deflection. Incredibly, it was 5–4 Killie and the fans showed their joy with another pitch invasion.

The scenes at time up were truly remarkable: the final whistle prompted the third pitch invasion of the night as the ecstatic Killie fans mobbed their heroes. The players had shown they were a match for Europe's finest and there would be no stopping the celebrations. With almost 15,000 happy people on the field the police had a hard job shepherding the players into the relative calm of the dressing room. The newspapers, so often full of stories about the Old Firm, were full of praise: the story of Kilmarnock's triumph was the lead story on the front page of the morning edition of the *Daily Record* under the headline 'Town's Night of Triumph'. The *Record* went on to describe the result as a 'soccer miracle'.

Although Kilmarnock would go down to a powerful Everton side in the next round, the team, in its first venture into Europe, had shown it could compete at that level, and there would be many more glory nights in the seasons ahead. Back on the domestic front Killie came out with all guns blazing and were to remain undefeated in the league until mid-December. The run of results included a memorable 5–2 thrashing of Celtic at Rugby Park in which both McInally and the ultra-dependable McFadzean grabbed a brace of goals. The team may have been galvanised into action by the shock announcement that Waddell intended to retire from football management at the end of the season to go back to journalism. There could be no greater incentive for winning the league title than the realisation that it was to be the great man's final season in charge.

Perhaps the only cloud on the horizon was the size of the crowds at Rugby Park. Excellent gates were achieved at the big games: 32,021 for a league match with Rangers on 14 November, which ended with honours even at 1–1; 23,561 for the clash with Everton; 19,122 for the Celtic game; 18,285 for a league clash with Hearts. Yet for a team challenging strongly for the league title some of the gates were disappointing, a point made frequently by the *Daily Record* and other papers throughout the season. Even during the run-in to one of the most exciting championships in Scottish football history, only 5,193 turned up at Rugby Park for a vital game with Aberdeen on 27 March 1965. This was followed by an equally disappointing attendance of 5,816 the following Saturday for a match against Clyde.

However, on the field things were decidedly rosy. Despite a 5–1 defeat away to Morton on 12 December 1964, Killie went into 1965 joint top of the First Division with Hearts, whom they had defeated by three goals to one at Rugby Park the week after the setback against Morton. The New Year started brightly; St Mirren were

Soccer sensation: the *Daily Record* reporting Killie's amazing triumph over Eintracht Frankfurt.

trounced 4–0 at Rugby Park on 1 January with goals from Sneddon and Murray, and two from the prolific Hamilton. Then, inexplicably, the team's form slumped badly. Of the four remaining league games in January – none of them against top opposition – three were lost and one was drawn. February was just as bad – despite wins in the Scottish Cup against Cowdenbeath and East Fife, Killie lost two out of three in the league. This was certainly not championship winning form. The month of March was to be an entirely different story – perhaps inspired by an epic Scottish Cup quarter-final tie away to Celtic which the home team won by the odd goal in five. Killie roared back to form with a 4–2 home win over Dundee United. This result was the catalyst for a great run of six wins and one draw that took the Ayrshiremen to second place in the table with only one game left to play. That game, of course, was against the team at the top of the table: Heart of Midlothian, who had fifty points to Killie's forty-eight. The simple fact was that Kilmarnock had to beat Hearts at Tynecastle by two goals to take the league championship on goal average. The scene was set for what the *Daily Record* called, with some justification, 'the most dramatic league game of all time'.

Prior to the game Hearts were considered strong favourites by the national press, although the legendary sports journalist of the *Daily Record*, Hugh Taylor, tipped Killie. On the great day, Saturday 24 April 1965, thousands of fans travelled from Ayrshire in the hope of witnessing a famous victory. Willie Waddell sent out the following eleven: Ferguson, King, Watson, Murray, McGrory, Beattie, McLean, McInally, Black, Sneddon, McIlroy. There was no place either for leading goalscorer Ronnie Hamilton, whose form had shaded in the title run-in, or for the versatile Jim McFadzean. The manager had opted for experience and Killie would rely heavily on veterans such as Frank Beattie, Bertie Black and Davie Sneddon in the cauldron of Tynecastle.

In front of a crowd of 36,348, Hearts started strongly and forced the visitors on to the back foot. After only six minutes Jensen, an import from Norway, outpaced the Killie defence and unleashed a tremendous shot. Fortunately his effort crashed against the post and the Killie support could breathe again. This seemed to spur Hearts to even greater efforts as they launched wave after wave of attacks. But the Killie defence was solid, particularly the ever-dependable half-back line of Murray, McGrory and Beattie as they dealt confidently with everything Hearts threw at them.

With the defence secure, Kilmarnock began to feature as an attacking force and midway through the half sensationally took the

Just champion! Jubilant Kilmarnock manager Willie Waddell leads his team back out at Tynecastle after clinching the 1964/65 league title.

lead. Good work from McInally was followed by an inch-perfect cross from Tommy McLean to Davie Sneddon, whose accurate header gave the Hearts keeper, Cruickshank, no chance. Only three minutes later Brian McIlroy scored the most important goal in Kilmarnock's history. A great run from Bertie Black enabled him to release McIlroy and the forward coolly despatched the ball into the net. It was 2–0 Killie and the dream was on.

In the second half, Hearts again came out with all guns blazing and immediately put the visitors' goal under siege. But, with keeper Bobby Ferguson outstanding, the Kilmarnock defence held firm. As the minutes ticked away, Kilmarnock's travelling support grew in confidence and gave the team fantastic encouragement. Yet, there was another scare to come; deep into injury time, the away supporters had to hold their breath as Hearts striker Alan Gordon was put through with only the keeper to beat. Gordon struck a fierce, accurate drive to the right hand side of Ferguson's goal. The massed ranks of the away support could scarcely bear to watch, but the keeper pulled off a magnificent save and pushed the ball away to safety. The resultant corner was cleared and almost immediately the referee blew for time up. Killie had won the title . . . by 0.04 of a goal! The scenes were unprecedented as joyous players and supporters acclaimed Kilmarnock's magnificent achievement. Willie Waddell ran on to the Tynecastle pitch to hug his eleven heroes and was promptly joined by thousands of fans bedecked in blue and white favours. At home, Killie supporters, listening anxiously to the radio commentary on the BBC erupted in a mixture of relief and ecstasy. The celebrations would continue long into the night.

The reaction from the Scottish media was praiseworthy, if some-what condescending. Despite the fact that the decider had been played on the same day as the Scottish Cup final between Celtic and Dunfermline, the *Daily Record* found space for a two-part special on Killie's year of years. In the articles, Hugh Taylor extolled Kilmarnock's virtues and pointed out that season 1964/65 had been the 'greatest success story ever in Scottish provincial football'. Yet Taylor could not resist a rather patronising conclusion – in winning the League, he argued, Killie had shed the image of 'stuffy provincials . . . the team was symbolic of the industry and traditions of the town itself. Indeed you could call Kilmarnock the practical realists of Scottish soccer.' It is doubtful if the same tone would have been adopted if either half of the Old Firm had won the league that season.

It is a measure of Kilmarnock's achievement that only two other provincial teams managed to win the league championship in the twentieth century: Third Lanark in 1903/04, and Motherwell in 1931/32. Without any of the financial advantages enjoyed by the Old Firm, or indeed the clubs from Scotland's other three cities, Kilmarnock's successes in 1964/65 must be regarded as the greatest ever in the history of Scottish football. Nor was the fairy-tale over; there was the small matter of the European Cup and a trip to face the mighty Real Madrid in the Bernabeu Stadium. But that is another story!

THIRTY-ONE

A TALE OF TWO MINERS

THE TWO MINERS HAD common roots, but they made their marks at opposite ends of the world, and history remembers them for very different reasons.

Coal had been worked for centuries in Ayrshire, but only on a small scale. Then, with the advent of the Industrial Revolution, demand grew sharply. To meet the needs of industry, the coalfields around Kilmarnock were developed by the Marquis of Titchfield who was the leading local figure in the industry. From the harsh world of mine working in the Kilmarnock area, there emerged two men who, in their own ways, changed the way two emerging nations developed. Robert Dunsmuir went to British Columbia, Canada, while Andrew Fisher journeyed to Australia. They were a whole world apart and, as things turned out, they were also worlds apart in their philosophy.

Robert Dunsmuir (1825–89) was born at Barleith, near Hurlford, the son and the grandson of coalmasters. He was educated in Hurlford and at Kilmarnock Academy. Not much is known about his family history. The young Robert Dunsmuir was brought up by his uncle, Boyd Gilmour, and his mother's sister, Jean. Just what family circumstances brought this about are not known for certain. His father, also named Robert, was the owner of a coalmine at Skerrington, not far from Barleith. When his school education was complete, young Robert went to work in his father's mine. Robert married Joanna Oliver White, the daughter of a Kilmarnock couple, Alexander White, a miner, and Agnes Crooks.

When Dunsmuir was a young man Canada had not yet become a nation-state, but the Hudson's Bay Company was eager to exploit coal reserves on Vancouver Island on Canada's west coast. In 1848 the first group of miners arrived from Ayrshire. They were John Muir and his wife, Anne; their daughter, Marion, and her two sons; the Muirs' nephews, Archibald Muir and John McGregor, along with John's wife, Mary and their three sons; and John and Marion Smith and their sons. They settled at Fort Rupert and set about exploiting its coal reserves for the company.

The Hudson's Bay Company must have been pleased with the Ayrshire folk. Two years later they looked to Ayrshire again to hire an oversman for their Fort Rupert operation. They hired Boyd Gilmour. He went along with three other men: Arthur Quigley, Archibald

French and Robert Dunsmuir. It was Dunsmuir who was to make the biggest impact on Vancouver Island.

Life at Fort Rupert was harsh. The settlement consisted of a defensive wooden surround in the traditional wild-west style, and single-room log cabins with a central stone fireplace and bunk beds set against the wall. Water was drawn from a communal well; communal ovens were used for cooking. The settlers had a good relationship with the local Indians, who were allowed free access to the fort.

The coal they found at Fort Rupert was poor and so, in 1853, the Dunsmuirs moved 200 miles south to Nanaimo, a small port which was based on the fur trade and fishing. It was here that a local Indian told the settlers where they could find stones that burn. And so, for nothing more than a bottle of rum, the coal industry at Nanaimo was established. It is still central to the economy of Vancouver Island.

Dunsmuir worked his way up from miner to oversman, but he was now in his forties and restless. He wanted to do more. He wanted to do something on his own account, and he frequently went searching for an outcrop of coal that he could develop for himself. In 1869 he went on a fishing trip. At a small lake called Divers Lake, his miner's instincts told him the area was rich in coal.

Dunsmuir secured the right to exploit it on his own. Soon, he began to accumulate wealth. But he always wanted more. He secured a huge land grant from the Canadian government in return for building a railway linking Nanaimo and Victoria. The deal gave him twenty per cent of the island, along with coal, coal oil and other minerals. As his fortune mounted he was soon the leading businessman in British Columbia. Although he owned a series of impressive houses, he was determined to keep a promise made to his wife – to build her a castle. He lavished a fortune on the new property, and it was built in a style that would not have been out of place in his native Scotland. Even the granite used in its construction came from Aberdeen. And he gave it a Scottish-sounding name – Craigdarroch Castle, a magnificent and opulent mansion. It was the family home until the death of his wife, Joanna, in 1908. Today it is a tourist attraction.

But the wealth came at a price. Dunsmuir was a ruthless master. His treatment of workers was shameful, and his answer to strikes was to sack the workers and employ others at lower wages. His great personal wealth was built on the exploitation of thousands of workers who were left bitter and resentful. One strike vividly illustrates his ruthless nature. In 1877, Dunsmuir cut his miners' wages by thirty per cent. Despite the workers' willingness to negotiate, Dunsmuir would have none of it. A strike was inevitable and, when it came, it was bitter and violent. Dunsmuir used every trick in the book to get his own way, including evicting miners and their families from company-owned houses. After six months the men still refused to give in, and Dunsmuir called in the local militia; many bloody confrontations ensued. Eventually, starving and worn down, the men had no option but to return to work.

Yet, despite his often ruthless methods, there can be no doubting the man's commercial acumen. In the years that followed, he built a huge business empire encompassing railways, sawmills, quarries and a shipping line. When he died in 1889, he was a multi-millionaire, although few of the people who worked for him mourned his passing. He left his entire fortune, including control of his businesses, to his wife Joanna. This decision greatly dismayed his sons, who had been managing the businesses for some time and, inevitably, a family feud and protracted litigation ensued. Such was the bitterness it engendered that Joanna Dunsmuir and her eldest son, James, were not on speaking terms for the last eighteen years of her life.

Eventually, the businesses were sold. James Dunsmuir went into politics and became the Prime Minister of British Columbia and later its Lieutenant-Governor. But the family's reputation among ordinary people was a wholly negative one. Robert Dunsmuir's treatment of his workers saw to that.

*

The Kilmarnock man on the other side of the world, and on the other side of the social and political divide, was Andrew Fisher (1852–1928). His father, Robert, was also a miner. Life in the Ayrshire mines in the 1860s was tough. The hours were long. The work was hard. Pay was poor. Housing conditions were appalling and, because of the health hazards, miners had a short life expectancy. But Ayrshire miners were a tough and resourceful group of people.

Robert was determined to improve the lot of his fellow miners and make things better for the next generation. He married Jane Garven, the daughter of a travelling grocer. It was probably her influence that encouraged Robert and a few other miners to scrape together £15 to launch a business venture. In March 1863, when Andrew was only five months old, Robert and his comrades founded the Crosshouse Co-operative Society. It was not for glory or wealth, but was simply a self-help, non-profit-making venture aimed mostly at breaking the truck system, through which mine owners paid workers in tokens that had to be spent in the company shop.

Robert and Jane had a big family: John, Andrew, Robert, Jean, Janet, David and William. His father's hard work, honesty and unlimited willingness to work for a common cause, were all-important influences on Andrew. So was the Church of Scotland. Andrew Fisher had his education in the schools at Dreghorn and Crosshouse. But his schooling was interrupted by a disaster at home. His father became ill with pneumoconiosis, a dreadful coughing disease that the miners called 'black lung', caused by an excess of coal dust in the lungs. Robert was no longer able to work. John and Andrew became the breadwinners, working as long and as hard as any man down the pit. And Andrew was still just ten years old.

Despite this, Andrew did much to improve his own education. When time and money allowed, he took evening classes in Kilmarnock. Many people from a working-class background realised that no one was going to help them. They had to do it for themselves, and they recognised the crucial importance of education as a way out of poverty and to improve their prospects. The local Co-op that had been founded by Robert Fisher had by now provided a library, and Andrew Fisher made full use of it whenever he could. He was influenced by men such as Keir Hardie, the radical trade unionist and socialist politician, and he longed for the time when working men would have the political power to make mines safer and their living conditions so much better.

But he was astute enough to realise that this could only be done through working men being organised, and so at the age of just seventeen he found himself elected to the post of secretary of the Ayrshire Miners' Union. By nature he was not always a radical, and usually looked for compromise rather than for confrontation. However, he soon found that the mine owners did not care for compromise. Sometimes, it seemed, they manipulated a situation to provoke a strike, and then would hand-pick the miners they would take back. It was no great surprise when, after leading a strike in 1881, Andrew Fisher was blacklisted.

His interest in politics was also developing in tandem with his trade union activities. In 1884, Britain's unelected House of Lords blocked moves for a further extension of the franchise. Andrew Fisher chaired the Crosshouse meeting that was opposed to this latest attempt to stop democracy from flourishing in Britain. The following year, after yet another strike, Andrew was blacklisted again. Now, he had no job and little prospect of finding one. Andrew had the idea of going to Queensland, Australia, but was reluctant because of his sense of duty to his brothers and sisters. But they were growing up. They were no longer dependent on him, and it was they who encouraged him to go.

Like so many others, Fisher left behind the political restrictions of Britain to find something more democratic and socially just. He had escaped the hardships of the mines in Scotland but, ironically, he discovered that the only work he could get in Queensland was in the mines. A new socialist movement was developing in Queensland and Fisher was keen to be involved. By the election of 1890 the socialist party was advocating such radical ideas as compulsory education paid for by the state, pensions for the elderly and an eight-hour day.

Fisher settled at Gympie and it was here that he started to work relentlessly for the socialist cause. His sincerity and reliability made him an ideal candidate. He was elected to Parliament, and great things beckoned. The colonies were eager to form an independent federation. The first federal election went well for Fisher's group, as the Labour Party held the balance of power, and the largest Labour group was from Queensland. Fisher soon became its leading spokesman.

By now his path was clear, and he became the second Labour Prime Minister of Australia in 1908, a post he accepted with a degree of reluctance, but one that he would hold on three occasions. No Prime Minister in a democracy can expect to govern unopposed, but history regards Fisher with more affection than most because of his obvious sincerity. Today the house he lived in at Gympie is a museum, his portrait has been featured on a postage stamp and he is widely recognised as a good Prime Minister and an honest man.

And, back home, Fisher was, and still is remembered with affection. In 1916, he became High Commissioner for Australia, based in London. In that year he returned to Crosshouse to visit friends and family, and stayed with a cousin called 'Skipper' Fulton who escorted him around the area. The two had been colleagues in the mines together. It is a nice twist that, during this 1916 trip, 'Skipper' Fulton invited Andrew to stay with him in his home . . . the Crosshouse Co-op building.

And even now, Fisher is remembered in Crosshouse with a cairn and a memorial garden. In February 2001, the Community Council of Crosshouse sent the people of Australia a commemorative scroll marking the career of Andrew Fisher and the centenary of Australia. Not surprisingly, no such affection lingers for the miner from Barleith who was on the other side of the social divide in Canada.

THIRTY-TWO

CAPTURE THE EAGLE!

TWO GREAT ARMIES FACED each other and the battle-hardened soldiers knew that the future of Europe rested on the result of the looming battle. Every man knew this might be his last day on earth. It was a Sunday, and as men on both sides prepared for what they knew would be a long and bloody conflict, many of them prayed for God's protection. The armies had gathered near a small town in central Belgium. Few had heard of it before arriving at the scene, but soon everyone in Europe would know the name of Waterloo. It would pass not only into the history books, but also into the language as a byword for a total and crushing defeat.

On one side of the battlefield that June weekend in 1815 there were the forces of the British, Dutch, Belgian and the Prussians under the command of the Duke of Wellington. On the other, the French under the command of Napoleon. He had escaped from Elba and was once again threatening the peace of Europe. This was the final showdown. This was the battle that would finally end Napoleon's domination of Europe . . . or see the collapse of opposition to his ambitions.

Among the British there were many Scots, and among them, a strong contingent from Ayrshire. Many were with the Greys who had been recruiting extensively in Ayrshire not long before the battle. The leading recruitment officer was a Corporal Wyllie, a Kilmarnock man, who is said to have had a 'soft persuasive tongue'. The Greys were first raised in 1681 under the name of the Royal Regiment of Scotch Dragoons and in 1751 they became the 2nd Royal North British Dragoons. They took the name 'the Greys' not from their uniforms but from the colour of their horses.

The war against France had been going on for years in one form or another and many young men were keen to join up and do their bit 'for king and country'. Among the Ayrshire men who were at Waterloo there was William Merry from the Strand in Kilmarnock, James Smith from Symington, John Dunn, Robert Reid, James Montgomerie, John Gibson, Matthew Anderson and William Fleming. They all survived the battle to become labourers, carpet weavers and the like in civilian life.

Some were new to battle. Some were veterans. One of the most experienced of the soldiers from Ayrshire was Sergeant Charles Ewart. He was a Kilmarnock man with considerable battle experience. He was born in 1769 and joined the 2nd Royal North British Dragoons – Royal Scots Greys – in 1789. He was a big man, certainly several inches more than six feet tall and, according to at least one report, nearly seven feet tall.

Before joining the army it is said he trained as a barber, but he didn't care much for the trade. James Ramsay in *Gleamings of the Gloamin'* (1876) quoted him as having said: 'The shaving didna suit me at a'. I stood ower heigh aboon the folks' heids.' He was an expert swordsman. At the time of the Battle of Waterloo, he was already forty-six but at least as strong as many of the other soldiers who were in their teens or early twenties. Ewart's background is something of a mystery, for researchers have been unable to say just where he was born. Ewart himself told at least one writer that he was born at Waterside, Kilmarnock. But does this mean what we now know as Waterside Street? Could it mean the hamlet of Waterside, near Fenwick? Or even the farm of Waterside, near Galston?

There are other claims. One researcher expressed the opinion that Ewart was not even born in Ayrshire, but at Biddles Farm near Elvanfoot close to the border between Lanarkshire and Peebleshire, and yet another claim is that he was born near Beattock Summit. It is reminiscent of the debate over Sir William Wallace's place of birth, but it does not matter much where the man was born, but what he did with his life. And this man, this Ayrshire man, influenced the battle with an incident that has etched itself in the history of Scotland and Europe.

The Greys had been largely inactive for the best part of twenty years. Now they were needed. Mobilisation orders came on 6 April 1815 and they started the long journey to meet the enemy. April and May were spent waiting, and training.

The battle had been raging for an hour or so when the Royal Scots Greys – the Royal North British Dragoons – were ordered into the action. Ewart's name lives on as the man who captured the French Imperial Standard with its symbolic eagle. Not only did he seize this icon of the French army, but he took it from the French 45th Regiment of the Line, who called themselves, with Gallic arrogance, The Invincibles.

The heroic fight for the Standard is legendary but who better to tell the tale than the man himself. Not long after the battle, Charles Ewart wrote to his father describing the day's incident:

> It was in the first charge, about eleven o'clock, I took the Eagle from the enemy. He and I had a hard contest for it. He thrust for my groin, I parried it off and cut him through the head, after which I was attacked by one of their Lancers, who

PROUD KILMARNOCK: STORIES OF A TOWN

threw his lance at me, but missed the mark by my throwing it off by my sword at my right side; then I cut him from the chin upwards, which went through his teeth. Next I was attacked by a foot-soldier, who after firing at me charged me with his bayonet, but he very soon lost the combat, for I parried it and cut him down through the head, so that finished the contest for the Eagle.

It sounds bloody, but it is a purely matter-of-fact description, and was not intended for an audience wider than his immediate family.

An incident shortly before Ewart took the French Standard was just as bloodthirsty, but as a matter of honour, it was one of which Ewart was prouder than his legendary capture of the Eagle. Engaged in fierce hand-to-hand fighting with a French soldier, Ewart disarmed his enemy and would have slain him but for the timely intervention of his troop officer, Cornet Francis Kinchant. Hearing the Frenchman's plea for mercy, Kinchant urged Ewart to spare his life and make him a prisoner. The French soldier was grateful and surrendered his sword to Kinchant who, in French, told his enemy to retreat to the rear.

The incident over, Ewart turned to rejoin the charge. But he heard a sharp pistol report. He turned in time to see Kinchant fall from his horse and the Frenchman he had spared tuck a pistol into his coat. Enraged by such ignoble conduct, Ewart moved in and, deaf to a second round of pleading for mercy, decapitated the French soldier with a single swing of his sword.

The same Francis Kinchant had written a letter before the battle about the men in his regiment. In his missive, he noted that nearly all the privates were Scotsmen, but only three of the officers, who, he said, were a 'fine gentlemanly set of fellows'. He said there wasn't a private under five feet eleven inches and, as far as he was concerned, his regiment 'is without doubt the best disciplined and most crack cavalry corps in the Service'.

Having taken the French Standard, Ewart's problem was what to do with it. It was more than a symbol. It was the French rallying point and, without it, there was just that bit more confusion. Ewart had given at least some of the British side a tactical advantage. His first thought was to rejoin his comrades, Eagle and all, but his commanding officer – Major-General William Ponsonby – who would later perish in the thick of the battle, ordered him to take the trophy to the rear.

It distressed Ewart greatly when he took time to survey the battle. He reported later: 'I retired to a height that gave a general view of the field. I cannot express the horror I felt – the bodies of my brave comrades, horses innumerable, so thick upon the field it was scarcely possible to pass.' Ewart did not know the casualty figures at that

188

time. At the start of the battle the Greys had 391 men. By the time the sun had gone down 102 were dead, and 98 wounded.

After a while Ewart did rejoin the battle, but news of his capture of the French Eagle had spread, even beyond the battlefield. Two French Eagles were captured that day and, as symbols of French nationhood, their loss was demoralising.

The battle won, the war won, the troops were warmly welcomed across Europe. On his triumphant entry into Brussels after the conflict, Charles Ewart was met by his wife, Margaret. She, of course, was delighted that her husband had survived the fight when so many had died. She threw her arms around the horse's neck in a gesture of welcome. Her husband was not impressed and is reported to have exclaimed, with a powerful expletive: 'It seems Maggie, that ye think mair o' the horse than ye do o' me.'

As with Ewart's place of birth, there is also a little bit of mystery over his wife. They were married on 31 January 1812. But Margaret's own name is sometimes given as Geddes and sometimes as Snape. In Scots law a woman retains her own name after marriage and so her maiden name and her married name should both appear on legal documents. Perhaps Margaret was married to a Mr Snape before she married Charles Ewart.

In the immediate aftermath of the battle, Sergeant Ewart was promoted to Lieutenant. Later still, when he was with the 5th Royal Veterans Battalion, he accepted the title of Ensign. He was also presented with a Waterloo Medal, something that set the trend for future campaigns when men of all ranks received a campaign medal. His regiment redesigned its badge to honour the capture of the French Eagle.

Ewart, like old soldiers everywhere, began to fade away. He moved to Davyhulme near Manchester, perhaps because his wife came from Stockport. For a time he taught swordsmanship and each year for most of the rest of his life he returned to Ayrshire. He was often asked about his part in the battle but shied away from such questions, saying he would rather fight the battle again than make a speech about it.

He died in 1846 and was buried in a churchyard at Salford and there he should have rested, but his story doesn't quite end there. Eventually the church closed. A factory came and the old grave was covered over. A new century came; millions died in a new and horrible conflict. But Ewart was not forgotten. In 1938 further changes were being made at the site of that old church and Ewart's grave was rediscovered. Now was a chance to honour the man properly. His body was exhumed and taken to Edinburgh. It was reburied at Edinburgh Castle with full military honours, where a granite memorial marks the site of Ewart's resting-place. A museum in the Castle has several reminders of the man, including his Waterloo medal, his coat, a watch and, of course, the Eagle he took from the French that sunny Sunday morning in 1815.

Strange to say, that was not quite the end of Sergeant Ewart's posthumous moves. In 1967 repair work was required at his burial place and his remains had to be exhumed once more, but only temporarily. He was soon reburied, again with military honours. And not far from the castle entrance, visitors can call in to a pub named in honour of the Waterloo hero. In the Ensign Ewart, thirsty customers can see a magnificent painting showing the moment when Sergeant Ewart, the shy yet formidable soldier from Kilmarnock, captured the very symbol of an enemy's power and invincibility.

THIRTY-THREE

KILMARNOCK AT WAR

IT WAS A BALMY SUNDAY evening in August 1914 and Kilmarnock Cross should have been quiet. But on this particular Sunday evening, it was crowded. Most of the folk who had gathered there had heard rumours – rumours of war. Rumours always travel faster than truth. The crowd was excited and the tension mounted as they waited for the cars to bring the special newspapers from Glasgow. Newspapers on a Sunday night – this news must be important.

Most of the folk in the crowd had been at church that day, praying for peace. All the churches had been crowded. People pray more in times of crisis, and most of them knew in their hearts that peace was unlikely. War was in the air. A new rumour: the cars were on their way. They had passed Fenwick. No, they were already in the town. And they were, too. As soon as they stopped the crowds surged forward. Special editions, printed on Sunday night. What news was so important that it could not wait for Monday morning?

The headlines told the good people of Kilmarnock all they needed to know. Germany was already at war with Russia and with France. There was no doubt now. Britain would stand by France, and the country would soon be at war. Less than forty-eight hours later the Territorial Army was assembling in halls in John Finnie Street, and the 4th Royal Scottish Fusiliers had assembled at the Agricultural Hall, now the Grand Hall. The Yeomanry met at the building on the corner of Titchfield Street and Old Cast Lane, and Rugby Park was commandeered for the inspection of horses. The army needed horses as well as men and every stable in the town was asked to, and did, contribute horses for the war effort.

In that last week of peace no one could possibly guess what lay ahead for their family, the country, the world. For some folk, the whole thing was exciting; for others, particularly the women, it was a time of dread. Panic buying set in and prices soared. Some goods were soon selling for three times their usual price. But the local shopkeepers were quick to impose a system of rationing to help stabilise the situation. Things soon settled down and returned to as near normal as could be expected.

Young men joined up, many believing the propaganda that it would all be over by Christmas. They didn't want to miss the adventure. One brave Kilmarnock man who joined up was George Barr. In

March 1972, nearly sixty years later, he gave a vivid account to the *Kilmarnock Standard* of the excitement and the fear of those first few days of war; and of how the adventure turned into a nightmare.

Young men flooded into Kilmarnock from other towns and villages; from Irvine and Largs, from the Valley towns and from the coastal communities. Schools, churches and other public halls were taken over. George and his comrades were trained at the Grammar School and later in the Grand Hall. George recalled how the young lads from Kilmarnock and from across north Ayrshire proudly marched through the streets of Kilmarnock every day on their way to the Howard Park, which was used as their parade ground. The boys wore Baden-Powell headgear or Glengarries and many of them carried weapons – rifles left over from the Boer campaign; another war, another era.

Hours and hours they spent being drilled, then they would proudly march back into the town with a piper at the head of their parade. Two hours to themselves at the YMCA for free cups of tea and cake and then they were back to the billet for lights out at 9.30. Bed was a humble affair made up from two trestles, three boards and a bag of straw. The men had to be guarded, just for show, of course, so there was a rota: two hours on; four hours off. Training was hard, but the pay was a shilling a day.

Then, all of a sudden, the easy bit was over. The men, although in truth many were little more than boys, were on the move. On 19 May 1915, George and his comrades of 155 Brigade, 4th and 5th Royal Scottish Fusiliers and the 5th King's Own Scottish Borderers, set off by train for Liverpool. The 'adventure' had begun. The lads were heading for Liverpool to join a ship that would take them to the war. They were to sail on the *Mauritania*, sister ship of the *Lusitania*, which had been sunk by the Germans a few days before with heavy loss of life.

It was all they could think of as their train steamed over the border and into England. In the next few days, two more troop trains followed them with more soldiers. The last train in this trio never made it to England. On 22 May, at Quintinshill, close to the border, a signalman intent on catching up on paperwork lost track of the train positions. The troop train smashed into a stationary one, and a minute later an express ploughed through the wreckage. The result was devastating: 227 dead, more than 200 seriously injured. The war was claiming casualties before the men were even out of the country.

Ten days on the ship . . . a few scares with U-boats, and the men disembarked on the Greek island of Mudros and from there they moved on in destroyers and trawlers, heading for a place that George had never heard of before – Gallipoli. They came under heavy fire immediately and suffered their first combat casualties. Friends were killed. The adventure was turning sour.

They had nine months at the Dardanelles, and George recalled the horror of that time:

> The mangled bodies of the dead were unburied, half buried and partially dug up by the high explosive shells. Under the fierce heat, the loathsome clouds of flies could only be got rid of by burning the bodies; everywhere disease was making its ravages felt. There was dysentery, jaundice and worse.
>
> Then came December, and the evacuation. The division, by this time, had lost more than half its strength by such diseases and by shot and shell. How glad we were to leave such a graveyard, but it was with sad thoughts for those comrades we were leaving behind us, who had given their all, lying in graves on the beaches at the foot of Achi Baba.

Of course, back home, the general public was not aware of the full horrors of the battles and of life in the trenches. They were, however, aware of the mounting casualty list. Week by week, the flower of the country's youth was being taken to the killing fields. Many never returned.

As the numbers of injured men soared, the country's hospitals filled up and, all across Britain, public buildings were commandeered for use as auxiliary hospitals. One such building was the Dick Institute in Kilmarnock, which the Red Cross took over, having been promised that it would be available for the duration of the war.

Injured and recuperating soldiers were hailed as heroes by local people. In Kilmarnock this meant that some luxuries that others had to pay for were given to the soldiers for free. They could travel on Kilmarnock's trams free, and on Wednesdays and Saturdays they could go to the theatre or the cinema, again free. Football was a favourite and again the wounded soldiers, who had given so much for king and country, could look forward to complimentary front row seats. No one grudged the men these perks.

For most Kilmarnock folk it was about as close as they got to the war. Newspaper reports adopted a positive tone and played down the horrible conditions and the appalling death toll. And yet, week by week, more and more families lost a loved one. There were occasional times when long lists of dead, missing and injured were published and the public knew that another major push had been launched. As always, families in communities looked after each other.

By the onset of the winter of 1918, there was no longer any excitement about the war, just a growing number of casualties. And still the young of the country joined up as soon as they were of age.

After the First World War this peace tree was planted in the Howard Park.

Hardly a family in the country was left without a loss. Children aged eight could not remember life in a time of peace; children like Jim McBurnie. One cool dry day in November 1918, this eight-year-old walked from his home to Bentinck School as usual. It seemed like any other day. But in the wider world great things were already happening. There was an air of expectancy, excitement, even. In the *Kilmarnock Standard* office the phone rang. The editor answered it. He asked for confirmation of what had just been said to him. He asked if it was official. He replaced the receiver quietly, smiled a gentle smile and wiped the start of a tear from his eye.

'It's over,' he said softly to anyone within earshot. 'The war is over'.

The *Standard* staff put a huge poster in the window. This was news that could not wait for a newspaper.

Back at Bentinck School, work was following its usual disciplined routine, when the boys and girls in the class heard something unusual. Somewhere outside there was the sound of men shouting. Some of the children strained to make out what the cries were. It seemed more like a chant. Suddenly the air was pierced by a shrill whistle from the Saxone shoe factory. Odd, it was too early for lunch. Another whistle – Glenfield and Kennedy this time; and another, Barr Thomson. The children knew every whistle and the time they should be sounded. What on earth was going on?

The chanting men were getting closer to the school now. The factory whistles continued. The bells on St Andrew's Church began ringing. The children were too excited for class work. Something was going on, something important, something exciting.

At Duke Street, an unusually large crowd gathered outside the *Standard* office, reading the poster over and over again. The crowd at the Cross was also growing, and everyone asked the same question: 'Is it true? Is it really true?' Many had tears in their eyes . . . the years of slaughter had ended.

The chanting men burst into the playground at Bentinck School. They climbed on to the wall that separated the girls' playground from the boys'. They chapped on the windows of the classroom where Jim and his friends were still supposed to be working. Suddenly, the children all realised what was going on . . . and just in case there was any doubt, the men had a new chant:

The war's over . . . send the weans hame

The war's over . . . send the weans hame

The war's over . . . send the weans hame.

The war . . . the war that had carried off fathers, uncles and brothers had ended. The men pulled up the windows and climbed in. Jim noticed that they still had dirt on their faces and hands. He guessed they were engineers, probably from the foundry at Glenfield and Kennedy.

Now there was more noise and confusion. The men shooed the children out of the classroom with a great deal of shouting and arm waving. Soon the whole building was in uproar and the teachers were powerless to stop the men. Within a few minutes the school had been emptied. Later that day all the schools and most of the work places in Kilmarnock were closed to celebrate the peace. It was not a peace that would last forever, as we now know, but at that priceless moment, the world believed that war – not just the war – was over.

THIRTY-FOUR

DEATH FROM THE SKY

WHEN THE SIREN SCREECHED its hideous warning in the early hours of Tuesday 6 May 1941, the people of Kilmarnock knew exactly what to do and where to go. They included children like Irene Gibson of Witchknowe Avenue, Kilmarnock. Startled from her sleep, she and her six brothers and sisters took shelter in a cupboard. They huddled into their father who had specially enlarged the cupboard for use as an air-raid shelter. The children had gone through this same procedure on several other occasions when the Luftwaffe had flown over Kilmarnock.

A few weeks before, on the night of March 13/14, and again on the night of March 14/15, German bombers had pounded Glasgow, Clydebank and other Clydeside towns, trying to destroy the ship-building industry. Clydebank had been particularly badly affected. The Gibson family did not know the full details of those two terrible nights, but they had heard stories of many people killed and injured, including some from the Kilmarnock area who had been in Clydebank with friends. Later it would emerge that 1,083 people died in Clydebank, another 1,063 were seriously injured and, of the town's 12,000 houses, only eight remained undamaged.

Irene began to think about what was going on. It seemed that the planes had been attacking the Glasgow area again. It was too late for them to be going there, so they must be returning to base. That was a relief; at least she and the rest of the family only had to wait till the planes had flown over, then they would hear the all clear and be able to get back to their beds. Irene's train of sleepy thought was suddenly shattered by a dull thud and then another, and another. Bombs were dropping and exploding somewhere outside . . . but where?

Closer to the epicentre of the falling bombs, young Alexander Wilson was also sheltering with his family and listening intently. His father was the superintendent of the Kilmarnock cemetery. The family lived in the cemetery lodge in Grassyards Road. There was a Royal Observer Corps post not far from the lodge and, in common with many other boys of his age, Alexander had taken a keen interest in aircraft, both allied and enemy. Now he used those silent, worrying moments of shelter to listen to the enemy aircraft flying overhead. He was trying to identify the types of aircraft from the engine noise when the explosions shook the cemetery lodge.

Explosions! The Luftwaffe was dropping its deadly ordnance on Kilmarnock. His town. And the bombs were falling very close to his house; too close for comfort.

As the attack began, Air Raid Protection (ARP) warden Bill Muirhead was close to the cemetery lodge and took refuge there, sheltering with the Wilson family, wondering what horrors he might have to face up to when the raid was over. Across the town many other families like the Gibsons and the Wilsons were also sheltering, listening and, in some cases, praying.

For others, there was work to be done. David Miller was also with the ARP, but was not in such immediate danger as Bill Muirhead. It was the responsibility of the ARP to determine the extent of the damage caused by the bombs and to allocate resources to where they were needed most. David had already seen the horrors of the aftermath of bombs falling from the sky. He had been in Clydebank to help the ARP and the Home Guard in the rescue efforts after the great blitz in March. Now the bombs were falling much closer to home. At first no one knew if this was a full-scale air raid on Kilmarnock or just a few stray aircraft, perhaps jettisoning their loads before heading for home.

First reports were confused, but it soon became clear that urgent help was required in Culzean Crescent. It seemed that a block of flats had been hit. People were injured. Some were possibly trapped. The rescue squad arrived quickly. Neighbours were already on the scene. Half of the block of four flats was gone; turned in a few moments from two homes into one pile of rubble.

One of the rescue workers looked closely at the buildings in the street. He was astonished to see that several windows in the block that had been hit remained intact, and not a single pane of glass was broken in the buildings on either side of the one that been hit. On the other side of the street, however, several windows were shattered. But the rescue workers had no time to ponder such odd occurrences.

David knew instinctively that there must be casualties. But the first priority was to get to the living, establish what injuries had been sustained and get them to the infirmary for treatment as quickly as possible. From the part of the building that was left standing, rescue workers helped lead two women and two young children to the safety of the street. The planes had gone, and the all clear had sounded.

The two ladies were a Mrs Robertson and a Mrs Cree. The names and ages of the two young children do not appear to have been recorded in the reports of the day. Moments later, Mr Robertson was also accounted for. He had been at the back door of the house when the bomb fell and he had thrown himself full-length close to the gable of the building. It astonished the rescue party that none of the five of them had the slightest scratch or injury.

But it was quickly established that four other people from the two demolished flats were still not accounted for. They were a Mrs McGeachie, an elderly woman, her middle-aged daughter, Alice, John Bissett and his housekeeper, Dorothy Armour. To add to the complications of the rescue, neighbours told the ARP men that Mr Bissett was a deaf mute. If he had survived the blast, he would be unable to shout for help; nor would he hear the rescuers calling to him.

Rescue workers tore at the pile of rubble. Soon they found one body, then another. Two more bodies were found several hours later when demolition squads were removing the debris. Before the day was out, the survivors had all been rehoused by the Council and work had started on clearing the site. Today, if you walk along Culzean Crescent, you can easily pick out the site where a replacement building was later constructed in a different architectural style.

As the rescue in Culzean Crescent was still going on, frantic efforts were being made to account for all the bombs that might have been dropped. The first two that had fallen came down near the Dark Path. One of them had failed to explode, and had to be dealt with as quickly as possible. The next two fell on open ground, now occupied by St Joseph's Academy. Five fell on the cemetery. One fell just south of the cemetery on land between McGregor Drive and the railway line. The penultimate bomb to fall on the town hit the houses of Culzean Crescent. One last bomb fell harmlessly into Riccarton Moss. As the reports came in and were checked, there was great relief. Of the twelve bombs that fell over the town area, only one had caused fatalities. It could easily have been so much worse.

Thoughts quickly turned to why the town had been hit. Did the Germans know that a carpet factory was now turning out shells? Did they know how important the town's engineering plants were to the war effort, or that Glenfield and Kennedy had already provided floodgates to allow the underground railway system in London to be used as air-raid shelters? Or had the raiders just dropped bombs that they had been unable to unload on their main target? In short, had Kilmarnock just been unlucky or had the town been targeted? Would the Luftwaffe be back?

One theory was that the plane had indeed been over the Glasgow area and had jettisoned a spare load of bombs after seeing the fire from a steam locomotive. There are two versions of this story. One is that a locomotive had been at Kilmarnock station, but the crew had difficulty closing the fire door when the alarm was sounded. So the crew pulled the engine out of the station. Another version is that there was a locomotive driven by Sandy Woods, stopped at signals close to McGregor Drive, where one of the bombs fell. This engine appears to have been on its way into Kilmarnock from the Riccarton loop line and, as the planes were returning from their raid, the spare bombs were jettisoned at the first place where they might have done some harm.

At some of the places where the bombs fell on open ground, the harmless craters were left for a while and local children found a new and exciting place to play. In the cemetery, several graves had been hit and workers had the harrowing task of 'tidying up'. In short, this meant finding bits of long-dead corpses and arranging for their reinterment. Some were fairly old, but at least one was a recent burial.

Of course, everyone in Kilmarnock was well aware that bombs had fallen on the town. Everyone knew that four people had been killed. But there were restrictions on reporting such matters and, on the Saturday after that air raid, the *Kilmarnock Standard* was able to report only some of the details. It was not permitted to say that the town hit in the raid was Kilmarnock. The names of the dead were reported, but the extent of damage in the cemetery was not. The paper could only report that several headstones had been 'disturbed'.

Much of the true damage in the cemetery only came to light half a century later when Francisco Haro of Stewarton began to research the family tree of his wife's niece. Several graves were destroyed or damaged that night, including that of a popular local policeman, William Fraser, better known to folk in the town as 'Fifty Waistcoats'.

There's a comic side to one of the episodes associated with the night the Luftwaffe bombed Kilmarnock. James Sloan was a teenager on Home Guard duty outside the George Cinema, with others from his platoon. Luftwaffe planes flew overhead, presumably on their way to bomb Clydeside towns that night. But soon the men of Dad's Army could hear the sounds of machine guns being fired, and anti-aircraft guns shooting back at the Luftwaffe. They could hear the changing sound of aircraft engines as they peeled off from the flight. Having at first assumed that the raiders were on their way to attack Glasgow, the Home Guard men grew increasingly concerned as the unseen battle raged somewhere in the darkness above them.

'They're very close tonight' was the general opinion. And, because of the darkness of the night, and the tricks that sound can play when it is carried in the wind, the men could not be certain where the battle was. Frantic efforts were made to find out and it turned out to be a lot closer than any of the Dad's Army men had imagined. It was inside the cinema, which was showing a war film with the sound turned up just a little higher than usual!

The days following the raid on Kilmarnock were anxious ones. The great fear was that the raiders would be back. Thankfully, they did not return.

Alexander Wilson, the young lad from the Cemetery Lodge, was keen to see the *Kilmarnock Standard* on the Saturday after the raid. On the day that he read about the raid, something quite dramatic happened. Late that Saturday night, Alexander saw a German plane fly overhead. It was odd. A single German plane, and not one that would be expected in this area. But the plane had a very special pilot – Rudolf Hess, Hitler's deputy. But that, of course, is another story.

THIRTY-FIVE

MIGHTY JOE

IT WAS THE BIGGEST military operation in history. The preparations had taken years. The build-up had taken months. It involved countless men and women, not just front-line troops, but also planners and all manner of civilian support. Everything was ready, but now at the last minute there was a hitch. Something had gone wrong. Joe MacGregor was told that the whole operation was now on hold for twenty-four hours. The part he was to play was dangerous – perhaps even suicidal – but he didn't mind. He knew it was vital. He was annoyed by the delay, as every minute that passed threatened the security of the project, and exposed the men to greater danger.

As a Lieutenant with the Screaming Eagles of the 533 Eighth Street Paratroopers, Joe MacGregor was to lead the pathfinders and make preparations for other airborne troops. Joe didn't know the full details of the invasion plan, but he knew that hundreds of aircraft and thousands of ships would follow him. The full might of the United Kingdom, the United States, Canada and other nations was about to be thrown against Nazi Germany's fortress Europe. This was to be a day that would change history forever.

Joe had been ordered to rest, but he found sleep difficult. He found himself using this waiting time to think about his new bride, Rachel, back in New York, and her parents whom he still referred to respect-fully as Mr and Mrs Copeland. His mind drifted back to childhood . . .

Joe MacGregor was born in Kilmarnock and brought up in Lawson Street, the son of Alexander MacGregor, who worked for Young's Oil Company. Joe was one of seven children; he had a brother, Archibald, and five sisters, Ann, Marge, Agnes, Helen and Elizabeth. Before going to the United States, Joe had attended Bentinck Primary School. He had fond memories of the school and of playing football. Joe's father was a soccer referee and Joe inherited this love of football, so much so, that he managed to become a ball boy at Rugby Park on Saturday afternoons. He remembered the Laigh Kirk Boys' Brigade, and he remembered being so proud of being the first boy ever to have his name inscribed on the new Lymburner Shield, the highest accolade a boy could win in that BB group.

But then, in 1930, when he was fourteen, Joe's parents decided to leave Scotland for a new life in the United States. They settled in New York. Joe took his love of football with him and for some years

Mighty Joe. This photograph of Bentinck School was taken sometime in the 1920s. Joe MacGregor is fifth from the left in the back row.

played for a variety of New York teams. After completing his education, Joe went into banking. He joined the legal transfer department of the New York Bank and Trust Company, where he distinguished himself. When the American Institute of Bankers introduced a tough new banking exam, it was Joe MacGregor, the lad from Kilmarnock, Scotland, who was the first person to pass and have his name entered on the Roll of Fame.

Joe thought deeply about the Second World War and the issues involved. Listening to the grim news from Europe. Listening to the arguments about whether or not America should join the British. And he remembered that day of infamy when the Japanese attacked American ships and American sailors at Pearl Harbor. It was that attack that made Joe decide he was going to do his bit. He joined up immediately afterwards and, as he had done in the sedate world of banking, he quickly proved that he was a capable soldier and a reliable leader.

Now the training was over. Joe did not know much of the invasion plan, but he knew his part in it and he knew that the Allies were determined to free Europe from Nazi tyranny. As it turned out, there were to be five invasion beaches: Gold, Sword and Juno were the responsibility of the British and Canadians; Omaha and Utah were the responsibility of the Americans. The invasion was to be supported by more than 1,000 aircraft and 5,000 ships. Five divisions, consisting of more than 45,000 men, were to be landed on the beaches, and there to support them would be three divisions dropped behind the enemy lines by parachute.

But their way had to be prepared, and so the pathfinders were to be dropped some hours before the invasion started . . . and that's where Mighty Joe came in. Joe's team was to land behind Utah beach and help guide the paratroopers in. The plan was that the men in his unit, part of the 101 Airborne Division, would link up with the other paratroopers who had landed behind Omaha.

All was ready. Every ship was in its place. Every aircraft was primed. Every man was as ready as he ever would be . . . and now, a delay; not because of any human failing, but because of the worst Channel storms that anyone could remember. All too soon, the twenty-four hours were over and Joe and his comrades were back on the aircraft. There was a brief lull in the dreadful weather. The storm was still threatening to gather strength again, but there would be no more delays. This was D-Day. This was what one leader had already said would be 'The Longest Day'. This was the day that would determine the whole future of Europe, the world, of civilisation.

Everything was in place. Secret signals had been sent to resistance groups across Europe. A massive deception, the most complex and sustained in history, had been building over the years to mislead and confuse the military might of Germany. At dawn the massive invasion force would start coming ashore. Before that, the paratroopers had to land and secure the causeways and the dry land; before that, the pathfinders had to land to help guide in the paratroopers. Joe was one of the pathfinders, one of the Screaming Eagles.

Just after midnight, ninety minutes before the main body of para-troopers, Lieutenant MacGregor jumped from his aircraft with a handful of comrades and silently floated to the ground – to Nazi-occupied France. History would record that it was Lieutenant Joe MacGregor who was the first American to land in France on D-Day.

Things did not go well for the pathfinders. They came under heavy fire as soon as they were out of the aircraft. Several were killed or captured. Lieutenant MacGregor landed on the ground with his parachute in flames but he managed to evade the searching German troops and soon made contact with a few of the other survivors. The hope was that he would meet the paratroopers, but as things turned out the men of the 101 were scattered over a wide area, too wide. For a short while they were not an effective fighting force.

Hopes that the invasion force would find Joe and his comrades proved over-optimistic, too. As it turned out, for six days, Joe and his companions were on their own, living off their wits and what they could scavenge. They had no food and precious little water. Despite these setbacks, they did what they could to slow the German counter-attack. The handful of pathfinders were an outstanding success, and they attacked a range of German installations. Joe had been briefed about a key target. He knew that at a village just south of Carentan, the Germans had converted three houses into heavily fortified redoubts. There was only Joe and four comrades but, despite being greatly outnumbered, they decided to attack anyway.

The five of them launched a fierce offensive at the German posi-tions with hand grenades and tommy guns, killing about two dozen enemy soldiers. The rest of the German soldiers were unsure how strong the American force was and retreated from the village. Victory was bittersweet, as Joe was the sole survivor of the attack group and the village was left in his hands. At last he was able to eat, drink water and get cleaned up. Soon he was off to locate the men of the main invasion force. When he did find them he stayed with them for another month.

For his outstanding bravery in those six days Lieutenant Joe MacGregor was awarded the Bronze Star, the Oak Leaf Cluster, a Presidential Citation and special leave. He chose to spend it in his native Kilmarnock. He stayed with his sister in the Learmont Building at the head of Titchfield Street and took time to visit friends and relatives. This hero was a modest man and details of his exploits had to be teased out of him. He admitted only that the six days behind enemy lines had been 'pretty tough'.

Soon the leave was over, and Lieutenant MacGregor was off to war again. Before the end of the year the Germans had chosen their battle lines, and counter-attacked in a desperate attempt to push the Allies back into the sea. Lieutenant MacGregor was with a group parachuted into the Netherlands. By this time he was a First Lieutenant with the Parachute Infantry. On 18 September 1944, he was near Vechel. His company's position had come under heavy attack and Joe was ordered to withdraw his men. He took up a position at an exposed road junction and used his sub-machine gun against the enemy to give his men a little extra time. He was seriously wounded and taken prisoner, but not for long. Next day he was rescued by the advancing Allies and hospitalised. One of the duty officers at the hospital was Robert Templeton from Stewarton. It was his job to speak to all the wounded soldiers and get their name, rank, serial number and details of next-of-kin. Most of the soldiers were American, and Robert was delighted to have a fellow Ayrshireman to talk to.

Soon Joe was well enough to go back to the fighting, and he did. He was parachuted into Belgium and wounded for a second time on 30 December. Next day he was back in the thick of the fighting, for an epic confrontation that has come to be known as the Battle of the Bulge. He was based with other Americans at Bastogne, the centre of the counter-attack. The fighting at Bastogne was fierce and it raged from mid-December 1944 to mid-January 1945. The Germans saw it as their last chance to stop the Allies. If the Allies took Bastogne, German resistance might crumble and the allies would march into the heartland of Germany itself.

At first it looked as if the Germans had the upper hand. They were able to surround Bastogne and pounded it mercilessly. There were heavy American casualties, including Joe MacGregor, who was killed on 9 January 1945. Lieutenant Joe MacGregor is not forgotten. His bravery was an inspiration to many others at a time when Europe stood at a crossroads. Today his gravestone pays silent tribute to Mighty Joe. It is situated in the Henri-Chapelle American Cemetery on the highway between Liège in Belgium and Aachen in Germany, along with thousands of others who gave their lives at that time.

There is an interesting footnote to Mighty Joe's story. Long after the peace had been won, and the Cold War had come and gone, Joe's brother, Archie, was at his home in Clearwater, Florida. He was reading a book, which stated that his brother had won both the Bronze and Silver Star, and yet the family had only ever received the Bronze award. He made enquiries and soon it emerged that the Silver Star was awarded for Joe's bravery in the Netherlands, in helping his men escape. However, due to a clerical error, it had never been sent to his family. It was 1982, almost forty years on, but when the oversight was pointed out, Washington was determined that the great man should be honoured. And so, the Silver Star won by Joe MacGregor from Kilmarnock, was taken from Washington by courier to Clearwater in Florida and presented to his proud brother.

THIRTY-SIX

DAYS OF DISASTER

THE CHILLY OCTOBER WIND didn't bother George Guthrie as he made his way to church that Sunday afternoon. Unusually George, whose father owned Mount House and its estate on the edge of town, was not going to the High Kirk, his usual place of worship. Instead, he was going to the Laigh Kirk, for the charge at the High Kirk was vacant and George had decided, like many others, to join the worshippers in the Laigh Kirk. It was a rare chance to hear the almost legendary Reverend James Mackinlay. Mackinlay was at the very zenith of his fame as a preacher and was a popular man throughout the district.

The church was crowded. It had been built about fifty years before, at a time when the population of the area was still quite small and largely rural. On this particular Sunday, 18 October 1801, many people from more than one other church in the area had come to hear the great man preach and, of course, they were warmly welcomed by the congregation. Despite the crowd, George Guthrie settled in. No one could have suspected that before long George and many other worshippers would be dead.

Many people in Kilmarnock had long suspected that the building was rather unsound and an uneasy comment that the building might one day fall down had grown to the proportions of a prophecy. On this particular Sunday, that prophecy may have been far from the minds of the visitors, although they were certainly aware of the notion. The Reverend Mackinlay was just about to enter the church and the congregation grew quiet. Then something happened at that afternoon service, minor in itself, but tragic in its consequences. Some say a piece of wood snapped with a loud sharp crack; others say that some plaster fell from the ceiling. Someone screamed that the building was falling down. Panic flashed through the worshippers, each one believing that the building really was falling down about them, and each one desperate to get out before it did.

The first of those who reached the doors did get out of the building, but the place had not been built with rapid evacuation in mind. The corridors were few in number and extremely narrow; the stairs were steep and narrow. The church was so crowded that afternoon that some people were actually seated in the passages. There were too few exits and, on the ones that did exist, the doors opened inwards against the flow of people struggling to get out. It all added up to a major disaster.

The Laigh Kirk, Kilmarnock pictured at the close of the nineteenth century. Part of the tower is said to date from 1410.

As those in the gallery rushed to escape, the pressure of the crowd became too much for a railing, which gave way. Several people fell on to the congregation below.

The crush of people caused an immovable jam and their combined movement pushed the doors shut. They could not be opened against the onrush of those trying to escape. Some were suffocated in the crushing crowd; others were horribly trampled. It had all happened in a few sickening moments, and still the panic was there. The majority still believed that the building was coming down. Some made their escape through the windows, but two or three of the more rational among them went to the pulpit and tried to appeal for calm; but to no avail.

Within minutes, and while many were still in the building, word spread from one end of the town to the other, gathering lurid details as it went from mouth to mouth . . . an accident at the kirk . . . the steeple fell on the people . . . the roof collapsed as they prayed. As fast as they could people anxious for news about their loved ones were soon arriving at the kirk, adding to the confusion.

There was no police force in Kilmarnock then. There was no fire brigade, no paramedics, but the Royal Kilmarnock Volunteers were called in. This was not what they had been formed for. The Volunteers were a military force, set up by the authorities to crush the fledging movement then campaigning for democracy.

The doors were jammed. Ladders were called for, but the rescuers, untrained for anything of this nature, were uncertain about the stability of the building and thus reluctant to put the ladders against the walls, lest they hastened the collapse of the church. Eventually, a few brave souls did climb up the ladders and entered the building through the windows.

They were faced with a scene of carnage. Bodies of the dead and injured were piled up at the foot of each stair. Gradually each of the victims was pulled free and taken out to the churchyard, which soon took on the appearance of a battlefield after the fighting had ended. In all, twenty-nine people had died in the church and about eighty were injured. One of the injured died not long after the accident.

The building was never again used for worship. Not long after the disaster, it was decided to pull down the old church and build a new one on the same site. Only the old steeple remained and the new building addressed many of the factors that had contributed to the accident. The new building had wider corridors and stairs, stronger banisters, more seating, more exits and the doors opened outwards. There was even one exit direct from the pulpit to Bank Street and, although not used today, the stair from that exit can still be seen in Bank Street.

*

The disaster in the Laigh Kirk was unexpected and it happened in a few moments. In 1832 another disaster swept through the town, but this time people knew it was coming. They just didn't know what to do to stop it. Cholera was like a plague of old. It swept in. It killed. It went away.

Early in 1832 cholera had been rampaging across Europe and in the spring of that year it appeared in Britain. It leapt from town to town, devastating cities and villages. In many areas it killed one in five of the population. In July it hit Kilmarnock. The first victim was a carrier, who probably caught the disease in Paisley. Soon those who had close contact with him, including his doctor, were showing signs of cholera.

Fear stalked the streets as case after case was reported and death after death occurred. In some cases death came swiftly, within twenty-four hours of the first sign of illness. Some locked themselves away, refusing to meet anyone else; some moved to other areas. A temporary hospital was quickly prepared at Wards Park, now part of the Howard Park, to care for the poorer people of the town. Daily the death toll mounted and, by October, when the disease burned itself out, 250 of the town's citizens were dead. They were buried in the Wards Park and today a simple stone memorial marks the mass grave in what is now the Howard Park. A less virulent form of cholera hit the town in 1849, and this time 130 people died. In this instance an unused printworks in Welbeck Street was quickly converted to a temporary hospital.

Precautions began to be taken and in 1853 a cholera hospital was built on the banks of the River Irvine not far from the town centre.

But it was never used. The last appearance of cholera in Kilmarnock was in 1854 when it killed thirty-four people.

*

Disaster comes in many forms and one type of disaster still common is fire. Today at the first sign of a fire, we call on the help of the fire brigade, but 200 years ago, there was no such band of dedicated and well-trained firefighters.

Saturday 26 April 1800 began like any other as the people of Kilmarnock started to busy themselves with their affairs, but a disaster was looming. At that time Glencairn Square, also known as the Holm Square, was becoming increasingly important as traffic on the road between Kilmarnock and Riccarton grew.

At lunchtime a malt kiln in a shop on the east side of the square overheated and started a small fire. It should have remained a small fire. It should have been put out quickly, but there was no fire brigade in Kilmarnock then and no one had any training in how to keep a fire under control. To add to the problems, it had hardly rained for weeks and the thatch on the houses was tinder-dry; and, of course, the houses were all closely packed together. On this particular dry April day a strong wind was blowing. The scene was set for a catastrophe. The flames from the small fire spread rapidly. They leapt from roof to roof, pushed on by that strong wind. The building next to the one where the fire started was the Holm School, a new building, but it quickly succumbed to the flames. Flames soon leapt across the street. As soon as it became known there was a fire, able-bodied men, and many women too, turned up to help. Although chains of people could quickly pass buckets of water to put out the flames, it was no use; the fire had a strong hold on houses and shops. Choking smoke swept down Low Glencairn Street. People in its path recognised the danger to their own properties, but few had time to save any belongings, for the flames were still being fanned by a strong wind. The smoke was so dense that even the mail coach could not get through the street.

The efforts of the fire-fighters made no impression and so it was decided to make a firebreak by cutting the thatch from the houses ahead of the flames. The plan worked and soon the fire burned itself out. But in just ninety minutes, the Square had been turned from a busy commercial market into a scene of desolation and despair.

In all, thirty-two houses and the Holm School had been destroyed; seventy-six families, involving more than three hundred people, were suddenly without a home. A national disaster appeal was launched to assist the victims and this proved highly beneficial. Soon the authorities were insisting that new buildings should have roofs of slate; even so, it would be more than a hundred years before the last thatched house in Kilmarnock had its roof slated.

*

Coal was once an important industry in Kilmarnock and it is therefore not surprising that there have been several fatal accidents in Kilmarnock coal pits. In 1900, an explosion in the Nursery Pit killed three miners; four men were killed in the same pit in 1908 following another explosion. Five men died after an explosion in the Kirkstyle Pit in 1925.

The worst mine disaster in Kilmarnock was not the result of fire or collapse, but of flooding. In November 1909 heavy rain caused flooding which burst into Caprington No. 41 pit killing ten of the sixteen miners in the pit at the time.

The Caprington Mine Rescue Brigade: men from Ayrshire and Lanarkshire came to Kilmarnock for rescue training.

But, as always, man's response to disaster was to fight back. In the early days of mining, accidents were accepted as an occupational hazard. By the twentieth century this was no longer enough. An Act of Parliament of 1911 compelled mine owners to set up rescue stations. The coal proprietors of Ayrshire and Dumfries set up a regional mine rescue station at Bonnyton in Kilmarnock and men from pits across the two counties came to Kilmarnock for training in rescue techniques. The men who volunteered for mine rescue work were given two weeks of training at Bonnyton, then further training at their own pit and at Bonnyton. There is no doubt that they saved the lives of many miners. The Bonnyton Mine Rescue Station served until the demise of the coal industry in Ayrshire.

THIRTY-SEVEN

DEAD END

A BITTER WINTER WIND swept through the narrow streets of Kilmarnock, tugging at the shutters and trying to infiltrate the buildings by getting below the thatch. Inside the pub, the men huddled a little closer to the big log fire. They supped on their tankards of ale and listened. Robert Laurie was telling one of his stories.

Robert had once been a soldier. He had fought at the great battle of Waterloo and had often enthralled listeners with tales of his adventures. Although a storyteller, he was respected for being honest with it, even after a couple of pints of ale. This night it was not a heroic tale of battle that astonished his listeners; for this night, Robert Laurie assured his audience that the previous winter he had sat in that very pub with his father by his side.

The listeners knew Laurie was being sincere and they also knew that his father had been dead for many a long a year. Robert Laurie now had what he wanted: an attentive audience and one that was willing to keep him supplied with a little more drink, and, perhaps, a little supper. He lived in a cottage close to the Old High Kirk and he reminded his audience that he loved that part of the town. Ach, his audience knew that already. One soul commented that he knew fine that Robert had already secured a plot in the kirkyard for his own burial when the time came. It was a plot very close to his house. The mason in the company knew that too. He had already put a headstone on the plot for Robert.

Robert smiled at the comment. 'Aye, an' did ye no' wonder why the words are tae me an' ma faither, when ye ken weel ma faither lies in the Laigh kirkyaird?'

'John wis as fine a man as ye could meet,' one of the older men remembered.

Robert went on with his tale. He said he could not bear the thought of being separated from his father in death. And yet the desire to be buried in the High kirkyard, close to his home, was also very powerful.

'When I die,' the old soldier went on, 'I will be buried beside ma faither,' and he paused for effect. 'But no' in the Laigh kirkyaird.'

His audience gasped as he then related how one night the previous winter he had gone to the Laigh kirkyard and dug up the remains of his father. On his way home, he had called in at the pub to quench his thirst, while keeping an eye on the sack that contained the last bones of his father.

No one doubted that Robert Laurie had actually done the deed. In later years he often repeated the story and the tale of how a local worthy did a little private body-snatching has now passed into local folklore.

*

'Death's gleg guile' as Burns put it may be something that we shy away from or talk of in hushed tones, but it comes to us all and, like the story of Robert Laurie, various other tales involving death have been passed down through the generations.

Of all the aspects of death, none seems to have evoked more revulsion than suicide. Those who committed suicide were not always treated with respect and were usually even denied a burial in the kirkyard. Early in the nineteenth century, Jenny Whitly hanged herself in Back Street for reasons which do not seem to have been recorded. First her body was stolen away from her house and thrown into a pit near Riccarton. Before long it was recovered and, during the night, was boiled on the town green in a large pot taken from an ironmonger's shop – presumably by someone who wanted it for a skeleton.

It is curious then that the Beansburn area of Kilmarnock is said to have taken its name from a small burn – the Beansburn, which trickles into the Kilmarnock Water near a feature known as Tam's Loup. An old tradition says that it was originally Bienie's Burn, named after a girl of that name who drowned herself in one of its pools.

Suicide is not always a solitary event. Early on 24 October 1844, a couple strolling near the railway bridge at Gatehead were puzzled when they came across a parasol stuck firmly into the ground. On the parasol, there was a hat and a veil. The story that subsequently unfolded caused a sensation throughout Ayrshire, and was to stay in the news for weeks.

As the walkers looked around they were horrified to see two corpses floating in the water of the River Irvine. They were that of a man and a woman, both aged about sixty and tied together with red and white handkerchiefs. The water at this point was not deep and it was clear that they must have taken their own lives. The bodies were recovered from the water and taken to the nearest house. Later in the afternoon they were taken to the church at Kilmaurs.

No one recognised the couple and enquiries were made throughout the area. The investigation revealed that the couple had arrived at Kilmarnock and booked into the Commercial Tavern eight days before. On the evening of 23 October, they paid their bill and said they were going for a walk. That was the last time anyone saw them alive. But still, no one knew who they were, or why they had killed themselves. The only clues lay in a few personal possessions left in a trunk at the Commercial Tavern. From those belongings, it was clear that the couple were, or had been, reasonably well off.

The whole of Ayrshire was buzzing with the mystery. Thousands of people flocked to Kilmaurs, but none of them was able to identify the couple. Reports came in from other towns. The couple had spent time touring Ayrshire and had stayed at various inns, but still no one could identify them. As the story spread, romantic rumours grew. From their personal items, it was surmised that they came from England, but no one knew for sure. The reason for the double suicide could only be guessed at.

Eventually the authorities decided that they had done enough. The couple were buried in the little churchyard at Kilmaurs along with their tormented secret. But that was not quite the end of the story, for efforts to identify them continued. The story was published in several newspapers and such was the interest in the case that even newspapers in far-off England carried the story. Then a solicitor from Birmingham contacted the officials in Kilmarnock. He thought the description fitted people he knew; people who had left Birmingham a couple of months before and had not kept in touch with their home town.

The missing couple's business partner was sent to Kilmarnock. When he arrived, the bodies in the anonymous grave at Kilmaurs were exhumed. The visitor identified the man as Joseph Baker. Part of the mystery had been solved. Soon the rest of the pieces fell into place. The couple, having exhausted all their savings, had decided that they preferred death to a life of poverty.

*

While it might have been acceptable to steal the body of someone who had taken their own life, it certainly was not acceptable to take the body of an honest soul. At the time when those in the medical profession found it difficult to find corpses to study, body-snatching was a common solution. In some places, relatives of the recently buried stood guard over the graves until enough time had passed to render the corpses useless for research. In Fenwick, sentry boxes were constructed to give shelter to those on guard duty. The boxes are still there today.

At one time when an inhabitant of Kilmarnock died, the news was spread by a man with a handbell, known as the Skellat-bell. He announced the death of the individual and details of the burial. The bell was inscribed and dated 1639. It was used until late in the eighteenth century.

Burying the dead can sometimes present a problem, and this was particularly true during the cholera epidemic of 1832. When it reached Kilmarnock, the town was ill-prepared to deal with the crisis and, as we have seen in an earlier chapter, the 250 victims were buried in a mass grave, which is marked by a memorial in the Howard Park.

The dead, of course, can tell tales. When the Laigh Kirk was being rebuilt in 1802, workmen had to take away about two cartloads of human bones from what is presumed to be part of the old burial ground. In later years, land at Bank Street and John Dickie Street also revealed bones during construction projects. Among the bones discovered were the remains of a man believed to have been about seven feet tall.

Of course, the gravestones are intended to be permanent memorials and can often reveal much about a person's life. Some are interesting; some are tragic, such as the case of William Buntin, a Corporal in the Cameronian Regiment. His grave in Fenwick kirkyard tells that at the age of twenty he had been overseas, and was on the point of revisiting his native land and his parents. He reached Ayrshire on 18 November 1825 during a storm. Sadly, before the brig *Greenfield* could reach the safety of the shore, she was wrecked and the young man was drowned.

Printing errors were rare in the nineteenth century but, with the huge volumes of text handled today and fewer checks, they have become all too common. You would hardly expect a stonemason to make a mistake. But, in the grounds of the Laigh Kirk, on the stone in memory of Burns friend, Tam Samson, the town name is spelled as Kilmarnockock.

And finally, as they sometimes say at the tail of news bulletins, here's a tragic tale of death with a mysterious twist. In March 1941, William McCrindle from Kilmarnock was in Clydebank. It was the time of the Clydebank bombing and on the night the Luftwaffe blitzed this important shipbuilding area, the unfortunate Mr McCrindle was seriously injured and lost an arm.

Later, when he was on the mend, he was allowed to travel back to Kilmarnock. But William McCrindle never reached his home town. The ambulance in which he was travelling took a direct hit from an enemy bomber, and Mr McCrindle and all the other occupants were killed. And so McCrindle was laid to rest in the cemetery at Grassyards Road, Kilmarnock. Not long after his funeral, a stray Luftwaffe bomber dropped a load of bombs over Kilmarnock. One of his bombs hit a house in Culzean Crescent, killing four occupants, and others landed in the cemetery. According to the *Kilmarnock Standard*, the explosion 'disturbed' several graves.

Wartime restrictions prohibited detailed reporting, but the reality of the situation was that the explosion caused quite a mess in the cemetery and one of the graves hit by the Luftwaffe was that of poor Mr William McCrindle. God, fate or the Luftwaffe had had their three strikes.

BIBLIOGRAPHY

Books, newspapers and magazines

Adamson A. *Rambles Round Kilmarnock* (Standard Office) 1875

Allen H. *Israfel* (Farrar and Rinehart) 1934

Annals of the Kilmarnock Glenfield Ramblers, various years

Anon *A Famous Kilmarnock Engineer*, 1880

Auckland B. *Postal Markings of Scotland to 1840* (Canning) 1985

Ayr Advertiser, various issues

Ayrshire Railway Preservation Group Newsletters

Barr J. *The Scottish Covenanters* (John Smith) 1946

Boyd W. *Education in Ayrshire Through Seven Centuries* (University of London Press) 1961

Boyle A. *Ayrshire Heritage* (Alloway Publishing) 1990

Brill B. *Mar'se Eddie in the Shire* (unpublished ms)

British Philatelic Bureau *Burns Bicentenary 1996*, 1996

Brotchie A.W. and Grieves R.L. *Kilmarnock's Trams and Buses* (NB Traction) 1984

Brown A. C. *Bodyguard of Lies* (Star Books) 1977

Calder J. *The Wealth of a Nation* (National Museums of Scotland) 1989

Daily Record

Deans B. *Green Cars to Hurlford* (Scottish Tramway Museum Society) nd

Douglas J. *Scottish Banknotes* (Stanley Gibbons) 1975

electricscotland.com

English Mechanic, various issues

Gillespie J.H. *Dundonald* (John Wyllie) 1939

Howieson Revd R.M. *Free St Andrews, Kilmarnock, 1843-1943*, 1943

Hunter J.K. *The Retrospect of an Artist's Life: Memorials of West Country Men and Manners of the Past Half Century* (*Kilmarnock Standard*) 1868

Hutton G. *Mining: Ayrshire's Lost Industry* (Richard Stenlake) 1996

Irving G. *The Devil on Wheels* (Dinwiddie) 1946

James A. *Other Men's Heroes* (Macdonald) 1982

Kilmarnock and District History Group Newsletters

Kilmarnock Chronicle

Kilmarnock Journal

Kilmarnock Standard

Kilmarnock Standard Annual

Kilmarnock Street and Trade Directories, 1833-1957

Kirk R. *Pictorial History of Dundonald* (Alloway Publishing) 1989

Landsborough Revd D. *Contributions to Local History* (Standard Office) 1878

Landsborough M. *Dr Lan* (Presbyterian Church of England) 1957

Love D. *Scottish Kirkyards* (Robert Hale) 1989

Malkin J. *Sir Alexander Fleming: Man of Penicillin* (Alloway Publishing) 1981

Malkin J. *Pictorial History of Kilmarnock* (Alloway Publishing) 1989

Macgregor F. *Famous Scots* (Gordon Wright) 1984

McKay A. *History of Kilmarnock* (Matthew Wilson) 1848

McKay A. and Findlay W. *History of Kilmarnock* (Standard Office) 1909

Mackay J.A. *Burnsiana* (Alloway Publishing) 1988

Mackay J.A. *Kilmarnock* (Alloway Publishing) 1992

MacIntosh J. *Ayrshire Nights' Entertainment* (Dunlop and Drennan) 1894

McMichael G. *Notes on the Way Through Ayrshire* (Hugh Henry) nd

Munro W. *Some Kilmarnock Celebrities* (*Kilmarnock Standard*) 1924

Murdoch J. *A Million to One Against: A Portrait of Andrew Fisher* (Minerva) 1998

North West Writers' Group *Kilmarnock 400 Write*, 1992

Orr Lord J.B. *As I Remember* (MacGibbon and Kerr) 1966

Paterson J. *Autobiographical Reminiscences* (Maurice Ogle) 1871

Pitt B. and Pitt F. *Chronological Atlas of World War Two* (Macmillan) 1989

Ramsay J. *Gleamings of the Gloamin'* (McKie and Drennan) 1876

Robertson W. *Historic Tales and Legends of Ayrshire* (Morrison) 1889

Ross D. *Killie: the Official History* (Harefield) 1994

The Scots Magazine

Smellie T. *Sketches of Old Kilmarnock* (Dunlop and Drennan) 1898

Strawhorn J. *History of Irvine* (John Donald) 1985

Urquhart R. and Close R. eds. *The Hearth Tax for Ayrshire* (Ayrshire Federation of Historical Societies) 1998

Walker J. *Old Kilmarnock* (D. Brown) 1895

Wear R. *Barclay 150* (ILS) 1990

Wood S. *In the Finest Tradition* (Mainstream) 1988

Young A.F. *The Encyclopaedia of Scottish Executions 1750-1963* (Dobby) 2000

Libraries and other institutions

Association of Friends of the Waterloo Committee
Brisbane Planetarium, Brisbane, Australia
British Columbia Archives
Carnegie Library, Ayr
Changhua Christian Hospital, Taiwan
Dick Institute, Kilmarnock
Dumfries Museum
Freealba.com
Guinness UDV Archive, Menstrie
Library of Congress, Washington D.C., USA
The Lord Boyd Orr Memorial and Food Nutrition Library of the United
    Nations Organisation
The Military Museum, Edinburgh Castle
Mitchell Library, Glasgow
The National Army Museum, London
National Museum of Scotland, Edinburgh
Nottingham County Records Office
Nottingham University Library
The Royal Observatory, Edinburgh
The Scottish Record Office
Stanley Gibbons Ltd, London

Personal correspondence

Ann Amor, Bolton
Robert Densmore Brill, Pacifica, California, USA
Hugh C. Forgie, Boynton, Florida, USA
Mark Fraser, Kilmarnock
Irene Gibson, Kilmarnock
James Gracie, East Kilbride
John Hall, Stewarton
Hugh Harper, Kilmarnock
Francisco Haro, Stewarton
David O. Hood, Glasgow
Craig McAvoy, Ayr

Jim McBurnie, South Africa
James McCarroll, Ayr
Dr James A. Mackay, Glasgow
John Malkin, Kilmarnock
Agnes Morton, Glasgow
Mrs J. Rae, Kilmarnock
James Sloan, Kilmarnock
Margaret Hunter Weaver, Pennsylvania, USA
Alexander Wilson, Dunoon
William Withers, Sydney, Australia
Alex Young, Ayr

To all those listed and to those in the libraries and institutions who have helped, I give my sincere thanks.